Richard K. Fenn focuses in this study on the significance of time in modern society, and on the question of why we take it so seriously. He traces contemporary Western attitudes toward time back to the doctrine and myth of purgatory, and makes a provocative case to the effect that, especially for Americans, the sense of the scarcity of time is a sign of social character which is shaped by a "purgatorial complex." He demonstrates the impact of purgatory on Protestant preachers such as Richard Baxter and William Ellery Channing, but also argues that Locke's views of religion, of education, and of the nature of the state can only be understood when placed within the context of a belief in purgatory and the life everlasting. Seriousness about time has become evidence of the good faith of the citizen. Novelists like Robbins, Mailer, Vonnegut, and Brautigan portray a society that oppresses the individual through time constraints. For Dickens America seemed a purgatorial wasteland: a place where time is always of the essence.

Like the authors of the recently published *Heaven: a history* by Colleen McDannell and Bernhard Lang, the author of this stimulating interdisciplinary essay makes apposite connections between theological doctrine and a ubiquitous modern preoccupation. His book will appeal to scholars of American studies, to intellectual historians, and to sociologists of religion alike.

THE PERSISTENCE OF PURGATORY

For John Ordway,
David and Bernice Martin

THE PERSISTENCE
OF PURGATORY

RICHARD K. FENN

Professor of Christianity and Society,
Princeton Theological Seminary

 **CAMBRIDGE**
UNIVERSITY PRESS

Published by the Press Syndicate of the University of Cambridge
The Pitt Building, Trumpington Street, Cambridge CB2 1RP
40 West 20th Street, New York, NY 10011-4211, USA
10 Stamford Road, Oakleigh, Melbourne 3166, Australia

© Cambridge University Press 1995

First published 1995

Printed in Great Britain at the University Press, Cambridge

A catalogue record for this book is available from the British Library

Library of Congress cataloguing in publication data applied for

ISBN 0 521 55039 4 hardback
ISBN 0 521 56855 2 paperback

CE

Contents

Acknowledgments

My debts in composing this book are far too many to be mentioned here. What I have begun to understand concerning the soul, and especially the ties binding the living to the dead, I owe to the psychoanalytic insight of John Ordway. In seeking to understand Anglo-American civilization and spiritual exchanges across the Atlantic one could not have better guides or friends than David and Bernice Martin. Besides making specific suggestions and offering support, they have helped me to understand American society as if it were theirs. I therefore dedicate this book to John Ordway and the Martins.

For introducing me to some of the literature on the subject of time in American society, and for his friendship I wish also to thank James Moorhead; his student, Tim Helfer, was also of real assistance in discussions of William Channing.

I am very grateful to several anonymous readers for the Press who made criticisms and suggestions on earlier versions of this work.

I wish to thank the following publishers for permission to reprint the work of several authors: Alfred A. Knopf, for excerpts from Richard Hofstadter, *The Age of Reform*; Beacon Press, for excerpts from John F. Wilson and Donald L. Drakeman, editors, *Church and State in American History*; International Universities Press, Inc., for excerpts from Jill Montgomery and Anne Greif, *Masochism: The Treatment of Self-Inflicted Suffering*.

Testing claims to grace: the intensification of time

It has become nearly a truism to suggest that Western societies have become inordinately serious about time, but it is not entirely clear why that should be so. The villains of the pieces written on this subject are often the Protestant ethic or the spirit of capitalism: surrogates of the "civilizing process" (Elias 1992). Other writers have noted that millenarian myths also have a way of making at least the mean-time very serious, but so do myths of a future that will outdo the present and the past (Cohn 1970; Boyer 1992). In this essay I will touch on some of the literature on this subject in the course of investigating another possible source for the Western seriousness about time. Here I will be inquiring how the doctrine, myth, and popular belief in purgatory have informed and shaped the Western consciousness of time.

Time in modern societies is often thought to be unduly serious and scarce because of pressures arising from industrialization, from increasing complexity, and from the need to prepare for surprises and threats or to synchronize one's actions with others. Of course, time is more scarce for some than for others; time pressures depend on one's control of one's work or of everyday life, and that control in turn depends on one's place in an organization, in a chain of command, in a hierarchy of social status, or one's other resources. The pressures of time also vary, of course, along with such other factors as one's age and time in life, one's health or frailty, and one's time horizons. No wonder, say some sociologists, that people arrange for "time out" or "time off," and these interludes may provide respites that enable one to return to ordinary time constraints or places from which to rebel against the social construction and control of time. From the point of view of some sociologists, waiting, for instance, is imposed by those with more social power on those with less, e.g. the constraints imposed by prisons, schools, or hospitals on their inmates. We cannot always assume, however, that the experience of time as "waiting" reflects either a lack of synchronization between parts of a society or the weight of institutional demands and pressures.[1] It may come from infancy, as desires for the satisfactions of adulthood are frustrated by the realities of childhood. Fully to understand the significance of waiting, as of other ways in which the meaning and passage of time are intensified and made additionally burdensome on the psyche, it is necessary to turn to the work of historians who have understood the meaning and impact of the doctrine of purgatory.

All societies construct time in the interests of their own continuity and survival and therefore make the observance of certain "times" obligatory on each individual. The problem, however, is not simply with public time, socially constructed time, or even with the invention of the clock. Note that the clock entered Western history along with the notion of purgatory. Indeed, Dante Alighieri is reported to have been delighted and fascinated with the clock (Neustadter 1992:281). The problem we are investigating has to do not only with the scarcity of time or with time-pressures themselves but with seriousness about time itself. Here we will be investigating the meeting ground between individual anxieties about time and the tendency of Western societies to impress individuals with their social obligations by creating a social character that is subservient to requirements for the use of time. In the doctrine of purgatory and its later developments, I will argue, a myth was created that brought together popular anxieties over running out of time with the church's own attempts to control and constrain the individual.

As Karl Rahner (1978:442) has observed, the doctrine of

---

[1] In this paragraph I have drawn on a recent and quite useful review of some of the sociological literature on time: Bergmann 1992.

purgatory concerns a place or a time-interval in the full development of the individual with regard to the core of the person, to the body, and in relation to the world as a whole. The doctrine, he argues, still needs to be perfected, and it should be understood in relation to such Eastern notions as reincarnation. Certainly a society may construe social obligations in terms of time and timeliness, whether or not that society is Christian or Western, industrialized or preindustrialized, and whether or not its calendars and schedules are governed by the cycles of the sun or the rotation of hands on the face of a clock (O'Malley 1992). Nonetheless, I am suggesting that the notion of purgatory, both as doctrine and as folklore, has added a particular intensity to the experience and meaning of time in Western societies. That intensity cannot be accounted for merely by the replacement of the sundial by the clock, or merely by industrialization that has supplanted agrarian ways of life, but by a social character that embodies what I will call a "purgatorial complex."

To imagine that the constraints and domination of time in everyday life are remedial or progressive, to make time of the essence of the individual's growth or rehabilitation, is to confuse the disease with its cure. Western societies have long insisted on efficiency and punctuality as virtues, on measuring personal growth and productivity in time, and on paying one's debt to society by "doing time." Any society that insinuates the pressures of time, not only into work and politics but into the crevices of the private world and into the psyche, stains the soul with what Dante – in describing purgatory – called "the taint of time," which is sin itself. In this book I will argue that American society in particular has become a secular purgatory without hope of redemption from the pressures and illusions, the fictions and the constraints of time. Indeed one's lifetime becomes a theater in which the drama of the soul is played out and its substance or destiny both determined and revealed.

How can a myth like purgatory, whether Dante's version or some other, ever be considered to be part and parcel of the culture of modern societies such as Britain and the United States? Has not Anglo-American culture separated this world from the next, disenchanted the social universe, and relegated magical thinking to entertainment and private neuroses? Not at all. I will inquire here into the possibility that a secularized form of purgatory endures in the West and has so intensified both the meaning and experience of time as to be responsible for some of the ailments of modernity. In doing, so, however, I do not wish to suggest that other Western societies are fundamentally different in this regard. Le Goff (1984:289) makes it clear that purgatory has been enormously popular in the public imagination and "provided a meeting ground where the aspirations of the Christian masses could find their accomodation with the prescriptions of the Church." The doctrine invented a place where popular fears of running out of time, and the widespread experience of the dead in dreams, visions, and apparitions could be rationalized in accordance not only with the church's demand for the satisfaction of its penances but with an increasingly exact scholastic calculation of place and time (Le Goff 1984:243ff.).

As purgatory has become popularized, the consciousness of time has become a continuous – and for some an excruciating – burden. An overburdened awareness of time, once the sign of a sinful consciousness, is now regularly produced by a wide range of social institutions, from therapy to manufacture, from the school to the boardroom. The cure for the disease of sin has become indistinguishable from the disease itself. That is why I will sometimes call it the "purgatorial complex." How so?

First, chronological time came to be embodied in what Wagner (1981:59) would call "a creative swoop of compulsive invention," i.e. in the doctrine of purgatory. While this is not an essay in the history of doctrine, it should be noted that – as a doctrine – purgatory came into being in the year 1274. As a notion about purificatory fires prior to the Last Judgment, however, it has roots in ancient near Eastern apocalypticism. As Le Goff (1984:52ff.) points out, Origen knew the soul to require more time for growth and purification after the death of the individual, and Augustine himself regarded as purificatory the trials of the soul between death and the soul's entrance into paradise. Later in this book I will be arguing that this life becomes purgatorial in a process of secularization through which the other-worldly becomes this-worldly. It is important at the outset, however, to note that the seeds for this development are to be found in Christian theology itself. Here is Le Goff's considered judgment on the this-worldly dimensions of Augustine's thought on life after death long before doctrine made purgatory a specific time and place in the journey of the soul:

Explicitly, it may be true that Augustine situates the time of purgation prior to the Last Judgment, in the period between death and ultimate resurrection; but in the final analysis his deeper instinct is to situate it even earlier than that, in this world rather than the next. Underlying this instinct is the idea that earthly "tribulation" is the primary form of "purgatory." This accounts for Augustine's hesitation as to the true nature of purgatorial fire. If it burns after death there is no reason why it cannot be "real"; but if it burns on this earth, its nature must be essentially "moral" ... (Le Goff 1984:69–70)

The need to give the time of purgatory a specific place only becomes explicit, however, in the twelfth century, when the first use of purgatory as a singular and proper noun rather than as an adjective qualifying "fire" or various "places" comes into textual usage (Le Goff 1984:133ff.). "By the century's end, purgatory would exist as a distinct place" (Le Goff 1984:135). Indeed, the notion that the living could perform services for the dead emerges by the end of the century, when "a liturgical chain was forged binding the dead to the living" (Le Goff 1984:152–153). Those services involved the completion of penance, through which the living pay the penalty for sin that has been repented of and confessed, but for which the sinner did not provide satisfaction prior to his or her death. (These are distinctions, as Le Goff [1984:210ff.] notes, which reflect a corresponding development and sophistication in medieval conceptions of crime, justice, and personal responsibility.) It is still later, in the latter half of the thirteenth century, that the Church propounds the doctrine of purgatory as a place in Innocent IV's official letter to the Greeks (1254) and, later, at the Second Council of Lyons in 1274 (Le Goff 1984:283, 237).

Simultaneously, therefore, in what the anthropologist Roy Wagner (1981) would call a return to conventional forms of social control, purgatory became secularized in prescriptions for spiritual progress and the achievement of selfhood.

> The creation of Purgatory combined a process of spatialization of the universe with an arithmetic logic that governed the relationship between human behavior and the situation of the soul in Purgatory. Before long we find discussions of the proportion between the time spent in sin on earth and the time spent in torment in Purgatory, or again, of time in relation to the suffrages offered to the dead and in relation to the acceleration of their liberation from Purgatory. This bookkeeping was further developed in the thirteenth century, the century of the rise of cartography and the unfettering of calculation. Later, Purgatory time became mixed up with the bewildering question of indulgences ... The Church and the sinners in its charge began keeping double-entry accounts with respect to earthly time and the time of Purgatory. (Le Goff 1984:227–229)

It is important to recognize, moreover, that even the attack of reformers like Luther on the practice of indulgences did not initially threaten the doctrine of purgatory itself. In his Ninety-Five Theses, for instance, Luther was attacking only the excessive Papal traffic in indulgences (Dillenberger and Welch 1954:17). Luther objected to the mis-use of indulgences when their purchase inspired the hope of being saved from the pains of purgatory. As Bainton (1985:40) puts it, "God must kill before he can make alive. This is the pain of purgatory, and one should not seek to be released from it, for in this disturbance salvation begins." While the Pope could release the individual from penances imposed by the Pope, the power of the church could not be used to provide release from the pains of purgatory. Spiritual account-keeping must continue in the next life. There the penitential path is followed only by those willing to do time in this life as well as the next. Conversely, in this life one can purchase time off from purgatory not only for the departed but even for oneself (Cf. Dillenberger and Welch 1954:13).

The intensification of the meaning and experience of time, a sense of being burdened, obsessed, defeated, or constrained by time, is the outward and visible sign of a social character shaped and constrained by the residues of purgatory's effect on the religious imagination and on ecclesiastical doctrine. Those residues leave the modern soul with the experience of time as both fundamental and scarce, as essential for the realization of the self and yet as continually running out, as it were, without the means of grace or hope of glory. More is at issue here than whether one has fulfilled one's obligations to the community or to the creation through the proper use of one's time; it is the life of the soul itself that is at stake.[2] That life, moreover, is on a continuous trajectory linking this life to the next on a single arc of justice, recompense, and renewal:

Death was less and less a frontier. Purgatory became an annex of the earth and extended the time of life and of memory. Suffrages became an increasingly active business. And the revival of the last will and testament also helped to push back the frontier of death, even though Purgatory is not mentioned in these documents until quite late ... (Le Goff 1984:233)

The notion that souls will have time to purify and perfect themselves in the next life keeps open a sense of endless spiritual possibility. Indeed, I will be arguing that purgatory marked the beginning of the modern era's emphasis on the individual as the site of moral responsibility and spiritual possibility. It is not a novel assertion. Le Goff has put it very well:

Purgatory was one of the first signs of the increased importance attached to individual judgment in the final centuries of the Middle Ages. The purgatorial time ascribed by God to each soul at the moment of death was pre-eminently an individual time in the sense that, like a person's time on earth, it varied from individual to individual. What is more, its duration was in part the responsibility of

---

[2] O'Malley (1992) is quite right, it seems to me, to point out that cultural seriousness about time does not depend on whether the society in question is Christian or not, on whether it is pre-industrial or industrialized, or on whether time is measured by the cycles of nature or by more abstract and mechanical formulae. The line between "nature" and "culture" is always drawn by ideology, and no community is without its ideological ways of sanctifying the uses of time. All time, even one's subjective sense of time, is socially constructed, as the phrases "doing time" or "making up for lost time" suggest. He does not attend to the question that I am raising here, however, of how the sanctuary of the self, so to speak, is invaded and governed by time.

the individual. While the suffrages of others mattered after death, what counted initially was each person's individual merits and demerits, virtues and vices, repentances and relapses, confessions and omissions ... If the Renaissance is individualism, then as far as attitudes toward mortality are concerned it begins at the turn of the thirteenth century. If the Middle Ages are community, then the Renaissance remains profoundly medieval, for collective responsibility for the souls in Purgatory did not end, at least not in the Catholic part of Christendom. With respect to purgatorial time and in other ways, the Renaissance was but an episode in an extended Middle Ages ... (Le Goff 1988:77)

With the prospect of future beatitude on one's mind, it is very difficult to waste time, and every moment becomes filled with nearly infinite possibility. Our witnesses will be not only Dante but Catherine of Genoa: not only Catholic saints but Protestant preachers like Richard Baxter in seventeenth-century England and William Ellery Channing in New England in the early part of the nineteenth century. The prospect of joining the saints in the "everlasting rest" has produced centuries of exhortation to remember the future in the present.

Paradoxically the opposite is also the case. That is, in remembering the saints who have entered into their rest, the devout are also remembering their past. The saints, showing the way, got there first. The anticipation of future beatitude not only kept open the seemingly endless prospect of spiritual perfection. The same prospect rekindled affections for those who had indeed gone before. As Le Goff puts it, purgatory was very much an affair of the family and of intimates:

In reality ... responsibility for suffrages fell primarily to the relatives and friends of the deceased. We thus touch upon two of the fundamental structures of medieval society: kinship and community ... (1988:76)

In remembering the prospect of future beatitude, the saints also kept alive the possibility of seeing again those who may still be in the very purifying and refreshing fires of purgatory. Like Beatrice, purgatory was a place where old flames and ancient passions still burned. There, souls still seeking perfection made a claim on the affection and memory of the living. In this essay

I will therefore be asking how purgatory not only made the present subject to the future but also beholden to the past. A present so burdened with obligations was serious indeed.

There is a direct line, I will argue, linking purgatory with the exhortations of preachers from Baxter to Channing and evangelical piety. The preaching of evangelists in the United States has placed the soul before a divine tribunal in a moment of anticipatory judgment that initiates purgatorial suffering and purgation in this life. The tears streaming down the faces of the penitent souls listening to the sermons of Wesley and Whitehead in England and the United States, however, have their origins in the spiritual tears of medieval piety. As McEntire has argued, they are the tears of a spiritual mourning that give evidence of compunction:

In effect, wherever European medieval literature, before and after 1215, contains a penitential moment, the nature of that moment must be examined in the light of the spirituality of compunction ... Dante, too, may have had spiritual mourning in mind when, in *Purgatorio* XXX and XXXI, he repeatedly weeps at the sight of Beatrice ... Dante's tears ... result from the remembrance of past sins. Furthermore, Beatrice herself admits to prayer with tears for him and, before he swoons, indicates that this further penitence is necessary before he will be permitted to pass through the final healing waters of Lethe and forgetfulness into joy-filled blessedness ... (McEntire 1990:162–163)

As I have already noted, Western societies are not the only ones where people remain emotionally attached to the departed. If this were a work on comparative ethnology, we would therefore compare the ways in which various tribes or communities have sought to separate the living from the dead. In funeral rites powerful passions of love and hate are vented. The bodies of the dead are cared for, loved, and venerated, but their bodies are often burned or their skulls cracked. Drums beat, and spears are brandished. The reasons given for such dramatic gestures often mention the needs of the departed for a safe and swift departure, but it is, in retrospect and from the observer's point of view, clearly the living who are the beneficiaries of these rites. The living need to be able to part not only with the dead but with the potent emotional ties, both positive and negative, that bind them to the past. In the West, however, tears of compunction for one's past sins and for the loss of time have been crucial to the relation of the living and the dead. Indeed, the tears of penitence flow into weeping for the sins of others whose souls are saved in this "lacrimal [sic] washing" (McEntire 1990:174).

Unless a community can successfully cut its ties to the dead, new situations will be burdened with the memory and the affections of the past. It will be difficult to enter into new liaisons without rekindling old passions; it will also be difficult to enter new battles without being burdened by the memory of old conflicts. The heart of the lover cannot be free for a new romance unless old affections are consumed in a sacrificial fire. Psyche, according to the myth, is therefore given a funeral, although she remains alive, before she can be lifted on the wings of love to her new dwelling place. Warriors tend to panic when they hear an ancient prophecy that there will be a massacre near the scene of the forthcoming battle. There must be new sacrifices to ensure that the omens have therefore changed for the better and that old scores will not have to be settled in the new battle. Without these sacrifices, every new love repeats the old, and the old passions may well have been incestuous. The burden of guilt is therefore two-fold: guilt over the failure to seize new opportunities and fulfill current passions; and guilt over affections and hatreds.

It does not matter that the living often never do act out their passions. The conscience, we have learned from Freud, instills guilt over acts that one has not committed but has only imagined. The imagination of incest or patricide may not be conscious; it could well surface only in dreams, myths, or literary creations. Nonetheless the burden of such imaginary guilt seems real and can often be intolerable.

Religion has been the primary institution by which societies not only have adjudicated the claims of the living on the dead but have heard the claims of the living to be free from old passions so that they can fulfill the new. The conflict between old and new loves, between former attachments and aspirations for the future, creates a burden for which religion offers a cure that is difficult at best to distinguish from the disease. The burden from which religion relieves the soul seems to return in the form of a demand for purification which extends from this lifetime into the next.

Perhaps the most popular figure who embodies this contradiction in her own spirituality is St. Catherine of Genoa. I mention her not only for her popularity, however, but because she is a figure that unites Catholic with Protestant devotion.[3] As I shall have occasion to mention somewhat later in connection with early American attempts to fortify the soul, Catherine of Genoa gave a legacy to American evangelicalism: the notion of a second conversion, a baptism of the spirit. Along with that legacy, I will argue, she bequeathed her sense that purgatory begins in this life and extends into the next. All of life, even the life after death, is purgatorial. Indeed, the dead suffer or enjoy the same pressures of time on the soul as do the living.

Why, then, is religion both cure and disease? The soul, I will argue, is often captivated by old loves; the individual cannot make spiritual progress until the soul is freed from the spell of affections for those who have departed. It takes a more powerful affection to detach the soul from its old affections and to make them available for new attachments and new loves. Catherine of Genoa believed that God's love indeed can dissolve all earthly attachments, but the cure is a very risky one indeed. That same divine love can also annihilate the soul. I will return to this problem later in our discussion of the legacy of purgatory. Here the point is simply that religion offers a very problematical alternative to old flames; the soul that is seeking purification in the flames of divine love can be destroyed in them.

One way out of this inherent contradiction is to distinguish the true self from the false. The true self is that which can survive even when consumed by God's love; fusion with the

---

[3] In this paragraph, and throughout this discussion of Catherine of Genoa, I am relying entirely on Groeschel 1977.

divine does not extinguish but fills the true self. By this reasoning it is only the false self that perishes in the fires of divine love:
a sort of dross that is smelted away from the pure ore of the true
self. To separate the true from the false self takes time,
however, and there is no guarantee that the process of purgation will be finished during the lifetime of the individual.
That is why Catherine of Genoa extends the process of purification from this life into the next. As Benedict Groeschel puts
it in his introduction to *Catherine of Genoa,*

Catherine sees the life of the deceased individual as a continuation of
this life. Consequently the purgation of the dead is substantively the
same road that the devout striver followed in this life, but with
certain differences that result from passing through the finality of
death . . . she saw the road to victory of Pure Love over the false self as
a long and painful one, often lasting beyond the death of the body . . .
(Groeschel 1977:32)

In this book I will be exploring the myth of purgatory for
insights into the way in which Western societies have thus
balanced the claims of the past on the present and sought to
free the living from the burden and guilt of old hatred and
affection. For instance, Dante remembers Beatrice with the
intensity of the day of their first meeting. Long after her death,
her presence persists as a living memory. Dante therefore
returns to the presence of that old flame with the same enthusiasm as penitents in purgatory return to the fires of purification.
The inability of the living to stop loving the dead creates a taint
on the soul which requires purgation.

During the height of the English Reformation, however,
remembering the saints who had departed was beginning to be
a lost art. Richard Baxter urged his listeners to cultivate the
presence of the saints and never for a moment to forget the
promise of entering into their everlasting rest. *To remember the
future was not only the quintessential act of Christian piety; it defined
modernity.* (I will return to Baxter in Chapter 4).

To enter the future, however, it would be necessary for the
memory to carry as little baggage as possible. For Locke, the
haunting presence of spirits, apparitions, and powerful, often
frightening people and events experienced in childhood could

lead to a lifetime of spiritual timidity and trepidation: hardly a way to remember, let alone to enter, the future. His recommendations for pedagogy were therefore a way of strengthening the soul to part company with those whose presence is burdensome or frightening. Benign early influences, primarily parental, would endure and parental instruction would become so unconscious as to seem natural. Forgetting what one was taught (and perhaps also the beatings that accompanied the earliest lessons) was necessary if one were to enter into the present and future with a sense of one's own freedom and integrity. Remembering, with Locke, becomes a science. In the post-Lockean world, therefore, many of the more enchanted aspects of Western culture have been ignored, suppressed, or altogether discarded. The process of secularization has meant an attack on holy days of remembrance for the dead, the removal of spirits from any active role in modern societies, and the increasing exaltation of God to a place of honor so transcendent that politics, science, education, and even religion itself have been opened to scrutiny, debate, and continuous change without the benefit or hindrance of clergy.

In this book I will argue that the doctrine of purgatory, along with its popular applications and developments, not only initiated this process of secularization but intensified it and expanded its scope to uniquely modern and Western proportions. In that process, I will argue, the drive toward the purification of the self and of one's society turned first on religious institutions and religious culture. Monasteries and guilds, miracles and superstitions, days of obligation and spiritual refreshment, all became subject to social, economic, or political calculation. In such a calculus, furthermore, time itself became subject to extraordinary pressures from a wide range of competitive institutions that, in the long run, were little interested in the soul. It was the extension and expansion of the demand for spiritual purification and growth that secularized Anglo-American societies.

What we call the Enlightenment in economics and politics, in the family and in education, and in science and religion, I will argue, was initially a process for purifying the soul of cherished spiritual attachments in order to ensure the fitness of the soul for the pleasures of heaven. As this world therefore became a secular purgatory, the disciplines of spiritual growth invested the experience and the passage of time with significance for the soul's "eternal welfare" (an expression still in use in the United States well into the nineteenth century). That secularization, I will further argue, has resulted in a tyranny of time in even the most intimate as well as the most public aspects of social life.

On the American side of the Atlantic, in the late twentieth century, remembering has become far less a devotion, art, or science than an institutionalized practice. If Locke introduced (to use Charles Taylor's [1989:159ff.] apt phrase) the "punctual self," modernity has made it obligatory for the individual to remember to vote and pay taxes, to make payments on loans and to send greetings cards, to keep appointments and to meet what are quite appropriately called "deadlines." To put it overly simply, the deadline is the pale shadow of purgatory: the final, diminished, and faint reminder of loves and losses that many have been at considerable pains to forget.

No wonder that modernity is obsessed and burdened with time. Novelists such as Robbins, Mailer, Vonnegut, and Brautigan, have presented us with a thorough and coherent portrait of a society that oppresses the individual through time-constraints (Neustadter 1992). The clock becomes the measure of one's progress through life, a tyrant to whom submission results in sinful alienation from one's own being. To be obsessed with time, with measuring one's accomplishments over time, is a mark of the human consciousness outside of Eden. Now the constant reminders of appointments and deadlines, like the memory of those who have died but remain very much alive in the affections, make individuals forget themselves. Remembering – in the mundane sense – has become an institutionalized practice that can lead to the death, as one used to say, of the soul. Making up for lost time, buying time, and having something to show for one's time, becomes a "disease," a cultural fiction mistaken for reality, a substitute for selfhood, a crippling illusion, and a greedy tyrant.

For instance, Vonnegut's hero Billy Pilgrim makes progress only when he "becomes unstuck in time" and can enter into the past and future (Neustadter 1992:389). The pilgrimage of the soul is complete only when the individual abandons once and for all the illusion and the burden of a time that is socially constructed, imposed by authorities, and mediated through the clock. In modern societies time has become both a measure and a substitute for the life of the soul. "It is said that when Rousseau threw away his watch in order that it could no longer remind him of time, he was full of joy and thanked heaven" (Neustadter 1992:394).

Some of the writers that Neustadter cites object to the tyranny of an objective time which does not respond to the impulses of the mind or of the imagination. They would all settle, however, for a time "in which the endless variety of realities actualized itself in the phases between creation and dissolution" (Neustadter 1992:395). They are hungry for the possibility of inventing themselves and their world without becoming obsessed with the meaning and significance of time. For the rebel, time becomes tyrannous when it functions as the medium for the realization of apparently infinite spiritual possibilities.

In this book I will explore the argument that the invention of purgatory had a profound effect on the development of Western society and on Western social character. To put it formally, this is a sociological investigation into the phenomenology of time. I will be asking how the doctrine of purgatory may have linked "the level of subjective, inner time-consciousness ... [with] the level of social processes that structure the concept of time" ... [with] the level of the comprehensive historical context (Bergmann 1992:124–125). The way individuals experienced their lives, their present as well as the past and the future, in short, their "subjective sense" of time, was intensified by the awareness that the salvation of their own souls, and therefore not only those of the departed, depended on what the living remembered from moment to moment, over time, and throughout a life-time.

This intensification of the inward experience of time, I will suggest, reflected but also reinforced the efforts of individuals and organizations to buy or borrow time, to make up for lost time, to temporize, to initiate the future or terminate the past. Monasteries and guilds, churches and city councils, all engaged in strategies to manipulate and control, to expand and contract, that is, to structure time. These social processes, along with the inner, subjective awareness of time, in turn were reinforced by what became a defining characteristic of Western civilization itself: a deadly seriousness about time. The "taint of time," the sinful consciousness, became entrenched in much of Western civilization, mediated through social institutions, and inscribed, as it were, on the soul.

Time in the West therefore has been serious business for many centuries. Although this discussion begins with the introduction of the doctrine of purgatory, Biblical religion has long made time a proving ground of the spirit and of divine intentions. The end-time was often, if not always, approaching, and occasionally the end was even at hand. It was with the doctrine of purgatory, however, that time took on an added seriousness far beyond that of the apocalyptic. Time in this world became continuous with the after-life, since, in purgatory, clocks tick and the hours and days pass on exactly the same schedule as on earth. When this life is subsumed within heaven, of course, time stands still. It is when the grace of heaven is near at hand, even while the hours and days pass with apparent indifference, that time becomes serious. It is the proximity and possibility of grace, of charisma, that makes for what Durkheim called the sacred: *la vie sérieuse.*

Still, the secularization of purgatory did not occur overnight but only after long years of struggle and after brief periods of intensive reaction, as in the English Reformation and Civil War. To be sure, there are formal similarities between Dante's notion of purgatory (which we take up in the next two chapters) and Richard Baxter's or John Locke's understanding of the need for a disciplined form of suffering and a lifetime of repentance and expectation (which I will take up in Chapter 5). Still, they are spiritual worlds apart. It is to grasp that difference, as well as to track the similarities and legacies of the notion of purgatory, that I undertake this essay. It is just that: an exploration and an inquiry, to see what modernity, with specific reference to Anglo-American culture, owes to the doctrine and practice of purgatory.

With John Locke, only two practices were necessary for salvation. One was to believe that Jesus is the Messiah, the Son of God: no more, and no less. The other is to repent: not just once but many times, not at moments only of spiritual crisis but every day, not only in one's youth but over a lifetime. Penitence thus becomes *the* way of life for the Christian soul. The drama of that soul's salvation, however, is lived out in this world, by the clock, by the hour, the day, the week, the month: year after year. In explaining the meaning of Greek words in the New Testament like *aion*, Locke made it clear that their reference was not to some end-time or to the end of the world but to an era or epoch: a purely secular understanding of time. One lived in one's *aion* as a modern would live in "the times." Christians were not to be open to spiritual infusions from the past and the future; they were to live out their lives in duration, in the protracted mean-time in which penitence and salvation are very much a matter of mundane, everyday life. I mention it here to suggest how different was that understanding of time from what Dante had in mind.

Time for Locke had become sheer duration, with one epoch or constitution succeeding another. There was indeed change in history; Locke called it succession.[4] As one idea replaces another in the mind of the individual, the notion of time dawns. It is that notion that begets the sense that one age can replace another: Christians replacing Jews, who are destined to pass away; a new age of reason replacing an old age in which self-love produced a wicked desire for dominion or a cowering fear.[5]

Memory was therefore problematical. Just as a child must remember not the punishments and humiliations of youth but

---

[4] See Yolton 1993:297–300.

[5] See, for example, John Locke's notes on 1 Corinthians, Chapter II, 6–9; "A Paraphrase and Notes on St. Paul's First Epistle to the Corinthians," in Locke 1963: vol. VIII, pp. 86–89.

the enticements to pleasurable learning and self-determination offered by loving and reasonable parents, so a new age must also forget the bitter lessons of its youth in order to learn both reason and civility. Locke knows that not only bitter memories, but the stories of hobgoblins and spirits told to children while they can yet be filled with suggestion and terror, can take the heart out of a child and weaken the soul.[6] Indeed, Locke knows of trauma, and how the memory can make a fright received in one's youth seem like a clear and present danger.[7] Indeed there is much in the Scriptures that Locke sees as being unfit for youthful learning and is better untaught so that it will not have to be forgotten.[8] A new age requires a new pedagogy and a new citizenship in which the habits of generosity and courage replace specific memories. Growing up is a process of purgation, in which inordinate affections are replaced by reasonable desires. Penitence is, as I have noted, for Locke the work of a life-time. While the child may be caught up in the unthinking succession of giving offense, receiving pardon, and doing penance, the adult has entered the world in which time is stretched into sheer duration. There is succession here: the departure from childhood mimicking the succession from a Catholic to an evangelical epoch in history.

For Locke remembering is a mixed blessing. At the worst it can hobble the spirit with the burden of old injuries to the spirit and outmoded duties, with the memory of spiritual terror or simply of useless trivia, however classical, that pass for education. At the best the act of remembering can operate like a second nature in which the influence of old tutors and friends, parents and siblings is replaced by a high and general regard for the welfare and good opinion of others. Just as the sting of punishment is no longer remembered, except perhaps by the incorrigible, the sting of death and nonentity has been drawn by a sure and certain confidence in one's own being and, of course, in the being of God.

The same ambivalence toward time defines Locke's discussion of *The Reasonableness of Christianity*. On the one hand,

---

[6] John Locke, "Some Thoughts Concerning Education," sec. 138; in Locke 1963: vol. IX, pp. 129ff.

[7] *Ibid.*, pp. 129–131.   [8] *Ibid.*, p. 183.

Christianity, without in any way taking away from what was essential in the law, has made it possible for the truly penitent to receive an indulgence. Locke (1963: vol. VII, p. 112), in *The Reasonableness of Christianity*, calls that indulgence an "allowance" for their sins. The new dispensation is based, of course, on the advent of the messianic king, Jesus Christ. Through a confession of loyalty to this new monarch the believer enters a new dispensation: a new constitution, as it were, in which old faults are expunged, and the new are forgiven in advance. So long, of course, as the believer's faith and loyalty are unswerving, infractions and failures to be perfectly obedient are covered in the new dispensation; it is only a disregard for this covenant, a lax or coldhearted observance, not to mention a callous disobedience, that would forfeit the believer's claim on divine forgiveness under the new king (cf. Locke, 1963: vol. VII, pp. 122–123). The believer thus lives in a state in which the old sentence has been suspended, although the final verdict has not yet been given. There has indeed been a new constitution, a new allowance given; the new succeeds the old, as one idea succeeds another in the mind itself.

It is Locke's intention to keep ideas clear and distinct, rather than to mix them imaginatively together through free association. The result of such an imagination is too often confusion, and sometimes madness. Locke would make it clear that the simplest human being can understand the Gospel. "This is a religion suited to vulgar capacities . . ." (Locke 1963: vol. VII, p. 157).

Those who swear their fealty to the new king will live under a suspended sentence. Because believers therefore live, as it were, on borrowed time, there is no end to the penitence required of them:

Repentance is an hearty sorrow for our past misdeeds, and a sincere resolution and endeavor, to the utmost of our power, to conform all our actions to the law of God. So that *repentance does not consist in one single act of sorrow*, (though that being the first and leading act, gives denomination to the whole) but in "doing works meet for repentance;" in a sincere obedience to the law of Christ, *the remainder of our lives* . . . There are works to follow belonging to repentance, as well as sorrow for what is past.

These two, faith and repentance, i.e. believing Jesus to be the messiah and a good life, are the indispensable conditions of the new covenant, to be performed by all those who would obtain eternal life ... (Locke 1963: vol. VII, p. 105; emphasis added)

For Locke, the soul that lacks a life of perpetual penitence is destined to be little more than a shade, nothing very strong or solid. The average person will know of virtue and her beauty, Locke writes, but abandon her for more immediate rewards. The mundane at heart live without being entranced by or reminded of virtue as "the perfection and excellency of our nature" (Locke 1963: vol. VII, p. 150):

Open their eyes upon the endless, unspeakable joys of another life, and their hearts will find something solid and powerful to move them. The view of heaven and hell will cast a slight upon the short pleasures and pains of this present state, and give attractions and encouragements to virtue which reason and interest, and the care of ourselves, cannot but allow and prefer ... It is not requisite on this occasion ... to enlarge on the frailty of our minds, and weakness of our constitutions; how liable to mistakes, how apt to go astray, and how easily to be turned out of the paths of virtue ... (Locke 1963: vol. VII, pp. 150–151)

Locke's contemporary, the preacher Richard Baxter, could not have said it better. They are together still a lot closer to Dante than to Emerson or Channing, whose stout claims for the soul's capacity to rise to earthly challenges, while not forgetting the hope of heaven, will occupy us in Chapters 5 and 6.

Locke does, however, lack a Beatrice, and in this respect he is removed from Dante. Remember that Locke's view of time is secular in the extreme. The succession of ideas in history leads to new dispensations and epochs, which are no more to be confused with previous epochs than the successive ideas of the mind should be confused with each other. The weight of the past should be lifted, like the accumulation of sins that the believer discards when he enters the dispensation of the messianic king and finds his sentence lifted indefinitely. Contrast Dante's sudden access to feelings from the past on his encounter in purgatory with Beatrice:

Olive-crowned over a white veil, a lady appeared to me, clad under a green mantle in colour of living flame. And my spirit, after so many years since trembling in her presence it had been broken with awe, without further knowledge by my eyes, felt, through hidden power which went out from her, the great strength of the old love . . . [and to Virgil] "Hardly a drop of blood in my body does not shudder: *I know the tokens of the ancient flame*" . . . (Eliot 1929:49; emphasis added)

It is precisely the weight of the past that makes Dante come alive among the departed souls of purgatory, and yet it is precisely those feelings that have to be given up, because they join the living with the dead. Eliot sees in the dialogue that follows "the passionate conflict of the old feelings with the new; the effort and triumph of a new renunciation, greater than renunciation at the grave, because a renunciation of feelings that persist beyond the grave" (Eliot 1929:49–50).

Locke, too, knew the troubling of the soul by the persistent presence of souls long absent; the spirits continued to be disturbing, even in the seventeenth and early eighteenth century. Locke's remedy was a schooling of the memory and a new pedagogy that would insulate the young from spirits, goblins, and the terrors and complexities of a religious past that promised relief but continued to add to the burdens of a soul all too insubstantial in its own right. Dante's remedy is purgatory.

In the quotation above I underlined the phrase "I know the tokens of the ancient flame" because it powerfully suggests the way the past rushes into the present in romantic love. Freud (1961; 1989:21ff.) reminded us that the normal, as well as the neurotic, seeks to repeat previous experiences which are both pleasurable and full of pain. Feelings for the dead produce a romance with death that endangers the living soul and keeps it feeling possessed by a past that it can no longer recover. The soul both dreads and longs for a reunion with a love that has indeed, for the mean-time, been lost. That is a poetic understanding of the troubled soul of the living.

Here our concern is with how this passage opens up the understanding of purgatory from within, as indeed it should, if Eliot is right that Beatrice, and Dante's feelings for her, are crucial to the Divine Comedy *as a whole*. Although Eliot does

not make this explicit suggestion, I would infer from his selec-
tion of passages that love is both the cure for, and also the
disease of, the soul. Dante explains how in his first encounter
with Beatrice he was so entranced that his spirit was "broken
with awe:" a clear expression of the captivated soul that has
become lost to itself in rapture. The spirit can indeed be
broken. As Dante reminds us, his first meeting with Beatrice
had "vanquished" his own "power," so that he "became like
lost, with downcast eyes" (Eliot 1929:53). The self becomes
alienated from its very being, displaced, projected, identified,
or even fused with another, so much so that in the other's
absence, the self, the psyche, is indeed estranged from itself:
simply lost, shadowy, grey, and otherwise insubstantial. The
recovery of the lost presence brings the soul back, as it were, to
its senses. Certainly both Virgil, the soul in "eternal limbo,"
and many of those who greet him on his way through purgatory are mere shades.

On the other hand, love is also the cure and not only the
disease of the lost soul. The onrush of feelings of love can make
souls in purgatory forget how insubstantial they truly are. Here
is Virgil greeting the poet Statitius in Canto XXI of *Purgatory*;
T. S. Eliot translates it this way:

"Brother! Refrain, for you are but a shadow, and a shade is but what
you see." Then the other, rising: "Now can you understand the
quantity of love that warms me toward you, so that I forget our
vanity, and treat the shadows like the solid thing" . . . (Eliot 1929:41)

The act of remembering, then, is a way of reconstituting the
self; old love returns, and in its warmth the soul's own self-
feeling is rekindled. On the other hand, the memory keeps the
soul in thrall to the powerful presence of the other, known even
in her absence, like Beatrice, and long after her death.

What, then, is the cure for such an old flame? Virgil in fact
reminds Dante (Canto XVII) that "Love must be the seed in
you both of every virtue and of every act that merits punishment" (Eliot 1929:46). In words with which Locke would
hardly have disagreed, Virgil finds love at its best when it is
directing the soul "towards the primal goods" and only with

moderation toward secondary rewards: love being at its worst when it confuses the soul by turning "to evil" or "towards the good with more or less solicitude than is right" (Eliot 1929:46). Locke would have been more likely to frame the distinction in other terms, i.e. between short-term pleasures and the rewards that come from a lifetime of discipline and devotion, including the reward of heaven itself.

For Locke, however, it is one's penitence in this lifetime that can purge the soul of lesser loves, whereas for Dante the cure for an old flame is still in the flames of purgatory. Speaking of Canto xxvi, Eliot notes:

In this canto the Lustful are purged in flame, yet we see clearly how the flame of purgatory differs from that of hell. In hell, the torment issues from the very nature of the damned themselves, expresses their essence; they writhe in the torment of their own perpetually perverted nature. In purgatory the torment of flame is deliberately and consciously accepted by the penitent ... (Eliot 1929:39)

It is important to accept Eliot's advice to enter the world of thirteenth-century Catholicism. By suspending our own disbelief, and without needing to adopt Dante's beliefs, we can at least imagine what it would have been like to be so in the thrall of one "old flame" that the pains of a purifying flame should seem curative to the soul and not merely punitive. In the same way it is our task to imagine what it would have been like to be so under the spell of the dead, so much still in love with the departed, that their pain should be virtually unforgettable. Over and over again, the dead call upon the living to remember them: "to be mindful in due time of my pain" (Canto xxvi; Eliot 1929:40).

There is also a special grace being tested in these flames: the gift of repentance. The agonies are self-inflicted, the test of the flame sought after, as a way of proving the soul's capacity for faith and for penitence. The same soul who calls out to Dante to "be mindful in due time of my pain" in Canto xxvi goes on to say, "I see in thought all the past folly. And I see with joy the day for which I hope, before me" (Eliot 1929:40). If time is of the essence of purgatory, it is not only because old affections and future beatitude press in upon the experience of the present. It is also because the soul's claims to grace are indeed being tested. The moment one lays claim to a special grace or charisma, in fact, time begins to run out.

To understand that last assertion it is necessary to move from the poetic language of Dante to the far more prosaic constructions of the sociologist: to discussions of grace in sociological terms, as "charisma." Sociologists writing in the Weberian tradition also have long understood that charisma makes an issue of time. Time begins to run out on the charismatic figure as soon as a claim is made to special graces, to a particular mission, or to supernatural powers. All these need to be tested and proven in real time, as it were. The question is whether the charismatic authority's claims to spiritual endowment will stand the test of time. As it is with religious charisma, so it is with military or other forms of charisma. The next battle, the next sea crossing, may put an end to the authority of the warlord or the merchant, whose claims are only as good as the last performance. There is a theatrical element in charisma that requires dramatic action within a limited time-frame. If charisma is to stand the test of time over a long period, therefore, it must be made customary or reduced to well established procedures. Time becomes calibrated to the measured progress of action from one day to the next, but it is no less serious for being reduced to the motions of the clock rather than of the spirit.

As charisma is dispersed from sacred institutions to the general population, more and more people are exposed to what I will be calling the taint of time. In various of his works David Martin (1978b; 1980) has argued that modernity in the West is shaped by the way charisma has been allowed to run relatively freely outside the confines of sacraments and monasteries and to find channels of its own, even while undermining existing foundations. Sometimes the spirit reaches all the way from the cultural or political center to the periphery; new groups, formerly on the fringes of society, are baptized into civility. It is similar to the process by which Greenwich Mean Time became the time of various villages and regions that formerly enjoyed their own estimates of the hour and the minute.

In some cases the spirit becomes encapsulated in regions that are relatively isolated or in groups that are unable to improve their social chances above those, say, of the lower middle class (Martin 1990). Even in these cases, however, the Protestant attempt to disperse charisma to the laity injects an element of freedom and personal responsibility, of choice and mobility. It is easier for charisma to disperse from the center to the periphery when popular religion faces no elite groups with a monopoly on certain graces (Martin 1978a). It is more difficult for charisma to disperse to the periphery when religious establishment and elitism continue to enjoy a purchase on grace. The more widely charisma is dispersed, the more individuals like Catherine of Genoa will be able to claim the special grace of a second conversion. Indeed, perhaps a third of adult Americans say that they have been "born again." I would expect them to bring a particular seriousness about time as each day brings a fresh test of their charisma. As charisma is dispersed among the laity, they seek to purify their own souls in the midst of mundane and of practical activities. Elections become more democratic, education becomes more utilitarian, and both faith and science become more experimental.

Our discussion of the secularization of purgatory will take us from seventeenth-century England across the Atlantic to nineteenth-century American society. We will find in Richard Baxter exhortations to spiritual purification in this life that echo the trials of purgatory, and even for John Locke time takes on the burden of spiritual proof for the inquiring and developing soul. Their notions of spiritual progress were enjoined on a variety of religious communities in American society from the New England center to the mid-Western periphery. I will focus, for instance, on the work of William Ellery Channing to demonstrate one channel through which the work of purifying the spirit through personal growth, education, and civic responsibility entered the American mainstream. On the other hand, the preaching and organizing of Thomas Campbell brought a Lockean seriousness about time, penitence, and spiritual perfection to the frontier. At both the center and the periphery, souls were put on trial and individuals placed on spiritual probation. On this form of spiritual progress no one had a monopoly, although many laid claim to special graces.

If time became increasingly serious as more people on both sides of the Atlantic laid claim to charisma, why did time also become increasingly in short supply? Contact with eternity is supposed to suspend time. Indeed, John Sommerville (1992) points out that this was precisely what annoyed a succession of English monarchs about the peasantry, who seemed to be taking a great deal of time out of productive activities for their devotions and revels. Their fleeting immersion in eternity during the mass was echoed by their observance of holy days on which they could do no labor. As holy days were increasingly co-opted for utilitarian purposes, the clergy were instructed to lay the consciences of the laity to rest on this matter. In the same way James I urged the laity to relax their Sabbatarian scruples long enough to allow the younger men to enjoy their sports on a Sunday afternoon. The monarchy sought to inculcate not only industry but refreshment in the population: to keep them reasonably content as well as productive.

As the nation became somewhat more differentiated from the state, and the church from society, the disposition of time was increasingly contested. I have mentioned the contest of the monarchy and the church with the people for their use of time on holy days. On the issue of playing on the Sabbath the lines were drawn again, with some of the dissenting clergy and the laity insisting on time out even from such "recreations" as football. The laxity and luxury of the center were opposed by a social periphery bent on controlling their days and hours. So it was with the question of tithes, which consisted not only of money but also of time itself. As Sommerville (1992:100) points out, some scholars were arguing as early as 1618 that the case for tithes rested on the common law and not on divine law, and thus the collection and allocation of tithes could depend on utilitarian considerations. In the church's reaction:

apologists in the 1640s were still trying to answer the utilitarian argument – that one only needed to make tithes rates answer the needs of the clergy. Sir Henry Spelman aggressively argued the claim of tithe to the subject's time and land as well as produce, using arguments from natural law and from the mystical qualities of the number ten ... (Sommerville 1992:101)

Even the primitive separations between church and society, nation and state that can be observed in England early in the seventeenth century set in motion a contest for the time of the laity.

It becomes more difficult to discern the religious sources of conflict over time when a society develops literally tens, perhaps hundreds, of thousands of corporations and organizations, agencies and commissions, volunteer groups and informal associations. The control of time is the focus of a wide range of conflicts between employers and employees. Demands for family time, for personal time, for unspecified time off, or for "flexi-time" all suggest that time has become an increasingly scarce resource for which individuals compete with their employers. As we will discover later in this discussion, scholars disagree on whether Americans really have less time at their discretionary disposal than they did twenty or more years ago. Nonetheless, parents are increasingly frustrated by their inability to get corporations to make allowances for the needs of their families, while more employers are asserting that their employees will not gain credit on the job for time spent in serving their communities. The competition for the individual's time, however, extends to churches and voluntary agencies, civic groups and friendship circles, as the social order becomes increasingly diverse and complex. Thus the differentiation of modern societies increases the competition for the time of the individual and intensifies the awareness and experience of time as being in increasingly short supply.

It is far easier to see the religious sources of spiritual conflict when the bells of the monastery and of the city are chiming in concert: the one ringing out the hours of devotion, the other marking the times of work and civic obligation. As Sommerville has noted, however, the times of the early seventeenth century, at least in England, were more clearly out of joint. Church and society competed for the tithes of the individual's time, and the nation and the monarchy were at odds over how to define obligations of the Sabbath and other holy days. Were these times at the disposal of the community or were they to serve the purposes of spiritual obligation? Objective and existential times, so to speak, are always in potential tension. In modernity the two have begun not only to vary more independently of one another but to interact with more or less intensity. The purgatorial aspects of time are the more difficult to discern as the interaction between existential and objective, private and public times becomes more complicated.

As the anthropologist Roy Wagner puts it:

Time ... is in this sense our most important product. We make time (and not only when we are "dating"). Like space, time could never be perceived without the distinctions we impose on it. But we have fortified ourselves with a welter of temporal systems and distinctions that would make a Mayan priest dizzy. *We* create the year, academic and fiscal, and the day, whether holiday or workday, in terms of the events and situations that make them significant and worthwhile, and we do so by *predicting* them and then seeing how the events and situations impinge on our expectations ... Our realization that our preparations and predictions have failed to some degree ("it's later than you think") amounts to an experience of "the passage of time." (Wagner 1981:73–74)

Of course, there is far more to the individual's sense of the "passage of time" than this gap between projections and experience. It is a truism that any society's construction of time will be to some extent out of joint with the individual's experience of the passage of time. Individuals tend to run out of time faster than do social systems, but there are other, more inaccessible sources of an individual's sense of time than the merely existential. To understand how a society's "objective" construction of time reflects or shapes the individual's experience of time as purgatorial requires the assistance of some notions about human nature.

Wagner is right, of course, to consider time to be a "projection." One imagines oneself in some state, e.g. as successful or beloved, or with Bunyan's pilgrim entering a celestial city. In this imaginary act one creates time and starts the meter of one's soul, as it were, running. Once started, that meter can make time seem fast or slow, inevitable or arbitrary. Everything depends on what one takes as given, essential, innate; the rest is chancy or predictable, evasive or recalcitrant. In that sense everyone is like a scientist living life in terms of expectations and by observing how life does – or does not – live up to those expectations.

There are other "projections," however, that are not so simple as mere expectations or predictions. The individual projects the self out over time, into projects, into conversations with those who have gone before, into spiritual transactions with the departed and with ancestors. Indeed, some of these projections are acted out not only in fantasy or prayer but in funeral processions and pilgrimages.

Religion has been the institution which has been most responsible for filling in the gaps between "objective" and "subjective" time. With the process of secularization, however, the gap between socially constructed, "objective" time and the individual's subjective experience of time has widened considerably. The fate of purgatory is a case, a prime case, in point.

My interest is primarily with what has become of the soul in the course of the secularization of time from the thirteenth century, when the doctrine of purgatory was introduced, to the late twentieth. Of course such a project as this cannot begin to satisfy so broad an interest, but I intend to take some spiritual soundings, as it were, at strategic points along the way. We will listen first of all to Dante, and then to Baxter and Locke, to Channing, Emerson, and Campbell, in order to assess at least their discourse about the soul. As the notion of purgatory became transformed into a spiritual state of continuing growth and struggle in this life and the next, individuals still engaged in spiritual transactions with heaven even in this life. The social construction of time allowed for considerable ambiguity, however, about the nature of the everlasting rest and about how to prepare for it. Some preachers exhorted souls to convert, while others urged a lifetime of self-purification. Slowly exhortations to spiritual growth began to displace injunctions to purify the soul. As the self has become increasingly responsible for the fate of the soul, individuals enjoyed increasing degrees of spiritual freedom in arriving at their spiritual destinations. Yet even preachers like Channing spoke well of purgatory, and Mormons undertook to get the living to be baptized for the souls of the dead in latter-day indulgences.

While I will be exploring the proposition that the modern self was constructed in the process of secularizing the doctrine of purgatory, to trace the secularization of that doctrine in every century is far beyond the scope of my own scholarship, let alone of such a work as this. Here I intend only to rely on a few representative figures and texts. It will appear from a close reading of some of these texts that the modern self emerged as Westerners began to lose their sense of being in spiritual conversation with unseen spirits and with departed souls. What was being secularized was the social construction of time. As time was heightened and intensified by thoughts of purgatory and a continuing life for the soul after death, individuals came to be acutely aware of their own responsibility for spiritual progress and for the state of their own souls in this life and the next. In the course of assuming that responsibility, individuals became both detached from their immediate experience and yet responsible for it. Thus developed what Charles Taylor has called the "reflexivity" of the modern self. This "reflexive" selfhood was first developed in spiritual conversation that linked the souls of the living with those of the dead in a communion of the saints: a conversation that persisted not only through the English Reformation but well into the "new world."

In the process of secularization, the immediacy of the encounter with invisible spirits yielded to a more distant awareness that what one does with one's soul in this life is merely a prelude to – rather than a participation in – a heavenly conversation. The traces of purgatory, however, were still to be found even in such post-Reformation figures as Baxter and Locke on one side of the Atlantic, and in Channing and Emerson on the other side. In the transatlantic crossing, the conversation with invisible presences, and even with the departed saints, intensified the demand for spiritual growth.

Individuals are put on trial or probation as the soul grows from strength to strength. The awareness of spiritual presences becomes more muted and indirect as the believer undertakes more enduring and extended spiritual journeys. The time of the soul's purgation is thus extended over a lifetime and beyond.

Among sociologists who have studied religion, few have been more concerned about the soul and its fate than Max Weber. In his studies of asceticism and mysticism, for instance, he has suggested that, at least in the West, religion is both a cure for the individual's uncertainty about the state of his or her soul and yet also a source of chronic self-doubt about the salvation of the soul.

For Weber a classic case in point is the mystic. Even contemplative mystics must prepare "a place for god upon the earth, i.e. in their souls" (1964:175). However, the quiet possession of their souls in tranquility and peace cannot last indefinitely for Western mystics. Some feel compelled to introduce others to their own state of grace and become mystagogues. Other mystics seek to create communities filled with the love with which their god has imbued their souls, while others require the world as a foil for their humility. Without such a foil they might relapse into a satisfied contemplation which would in effect nullify the spiritual gift they have received (Weber 1964:174ff.). For the mystic, activity in the world is a stimulus to – or a by-product of – the soul's beatitude but never a necessary condition, as it is for the ascetic, of certainty and certification of the state of the soul. Indeed, the conflict between ascetic and mystical tendencies helps to keep believers in continuous doubt about the state of their souls. Once secularized, such spiritual uncertainty keeps the modern individual subject to a discipline of self-testing and to a lifetime of probation.

The need for such testing goes back, Weber argued, to charisma itself. The recipient of grace is always unsure of his or her gift; indeed, it is in the nature of a gift that the owner can not possess it with the confidence of something that has been achieved or acquired. To turn a gift into such a possession, however, is theologically speaking a sin. The charismatic leader, then, needs continual testing to gain reassurance that the gift is genuine. Thus charisma is proved in battle or in commerce, in the market-place or the sanctuary itself.

Not only does the charismatic leader require testing to remove doubts about his or her gift; so do the leader's clientele or followers. While charismatic leaders require loyalty and subject their followers to discipline, the followers also subject their leaders to continual testing. The New Testament is full of the tests administered to Jesus by his followers and audiences: tests of skill in debating with the pharisees, of power over demons, or of knowledge of the Scriptures. It is interesting to note that Jesus not only refused to take such tests but, in the temptation narratives, refused to put God to the test when urged by the devil to cast himself from a high place. It may well be that Jesus attempted to circumvent the circular process of social interaction between charismatic leaders and their followers. That would have been one way of keeping the soul from being overwhelmed by the pressure of time.

Charisma is one instance of what Weber has called enchantment: the relation of the individual to a person, place, or object as though the latter contained an extraordinary, supernatural quality or power. As the medieval world became increasingly disenchanted, and as churches and monasteries lost their monopoly on the sacred, charisma took root in other centers of power, notably in the state, the professions and, more recently, in large-scale corporations. Eventually charisma was driven from major institutions to the periphery of social life, where it survived in small, informal groups or sectarian organizations.

Precisely such an argument has been made by a wide range of sociologists. Most recently Lynn Chancer (1992) has pointed out that secular relationships between employers and employees reflect many residues of the Protestant ethic. Primary among these is what she terms the sadomasochistic relationship between those with relatively greater power in such organizations and those with less. Unsure of their own authority and power, those with higher status in an organization seek challenges in the form of limited displays of independence and criticism from their subordinates: limited within a reliable framework of loyalty to superiors and submission to their authority. Similarly, she notes, capitalists seek new technologies and wider markets for repeated tests of their entrepreneurial skills and wisdom in investment: the boundaries having been eroded that otherwise would have set reliable limits on acquisition and growth.

In this system many are called, but relatively few are chosen: a rule that obtains not only in the competition among employees for favor and advancement but among corporations themselves:

> In other words, the capitalist is no more able to relax vigilance and rest than could the Weberian Protestant pursuing salvation ... Rather than give up the game, the capitalist can only try some new strategy, reach deeper and deeper into new forms of technology, new methods of control, all aimed at procuring a limitless power that can never be won and a recognition from others that can never be bestowed ... What the capitalist, like the sadist, is unable to grasp is that the process in which he or she is engaged may itself point toward destruction, physical and psychological; in the capitalist's obsession with an unattainable goal, he or she is compelled to destroy not only the other and/or the environment but himself or herself as well ... (Chancer 1992:109)

In this process bureaucrats and capitalists require more expressive yet disciplined performances from their employees; the contribution of the worker must come from the heart and often from the soul as well as from the body (Chancer 1992:104). A form of expressive asceticism is required of those who work in service organizations so that interactions will go smoothly and produce satisfaction, just as in a liturgy. These heightened requirements for personal commitment and self-control, along with diminished control over the conditions in which they work, give modern employees additional reasons for anguish and self-doubt. The ascetic tendency to take far more responsibility for the world than is realistic in the light of one's actual control produces the contemporary equivalent of dedicated workers; for "dedicated" Chancer suggests that we substitute the term "masochistic." The diffusion of charisma has thus produced a modern world in which processes of enchantment continue unrecognized and unabated. Even though some sociologists and psychologists have called attention to the danger of a subliminal form of the sacred in secularized societies, few would argue that religion continues to have adequate powers to contain or control the sacred.

Of course, studies of secularization tend to stand or fall on their definition of religion. Here I would define religion simply as that which adjudicates the social and spiritual tension between those who are present and those who are absent. Religion not only gives access to that which is not present. It also provides and sustains the awareness of a presence that is known primarily in its absence. The prime case in point, of course, is access to a deity such as Yahweh.

There is a paradox in such a definition of religion, and it can easily escape the notice of those who use it. Take for example John Sommerville's (1992) excellent book *The Secularization of Early Modern England,* in which he defines religion as "that which gives access to supernatural powers or to the presence of such powers" (1992:7). One might think that access to powers renders the individual or group who gains such access more powerful. Certainly access to the powers-that-be in modern capitols is presumed to carry with it the benefit of increased status, influence, or power. Not so, however, with religion. As Sommerville goes on to point out, access to heavenly powers can – and authentically does – give the individual "feelings of remoteness, 'otherness,' and dependence [which] derive from an awareness of a wholly alien power" (1992:7). Of course, one cannot have access to a power that is wholly alien; access itself reduces a power from being wholly alien to being at least partly accessible. There is in religion, then, a peculiar combination of experiences; what is beyond, distant, absent is felt as a present; what is clearly present is experienced in terms of its absence or transcendence.

When one has access to a divine presence without the slightest hint, as it were, of absence or distance, time becomes merged with eternity. At least such was the claim of the pharaoh and of every king with a claim to immortality

(Sommerville 1992:4). When the presence of the supernatural or the divine is felt more keenly in its absence, time begins to enter into the calculations of religion and into religious experience. Periods of concentrated presence, e.g during the conduct of religious rituals, are experienced as relatively "full" or timeless, whereas periods in which the absence of the divine is felt far more keenly than its presence are relatively "empty"; then time drags. As rituals become more closely associated with everyday life in politics, work, education, and the family, time becomes intensified; one might use the word "sacralized" to convey the awareness of activity sub *specie aeternitatis*. When activities are carried out under the auspices of religion but without strong ritualization, those activities remain serious, and the actors involved are exhorted to be conscientious, but the presence of the divine is felt more keenly in its absence than in its presence. When the presence of invisible powers is experienced in the absence of outward and visible signs of their activity, of course, their presence is felt as uncanny. There is a continuum of religious experience, then, that runs from the presumably total immersion of time in eternity, through the sacred, the serious, the uncanny, and, finally, the empty. Each of these forms of religious experience is associated with a distinctive, if not wholly unique, awareness of time.

I will suggest that the popular belief in the doctrine of purgatory intensified the meaning and experience of time by mixing asceticism with mysticism: a mixture that produced a hopeless dilemma for the soul. On the one hand, believers were urged to appreciate and enjoy a spiritual endowment that fitted them for heaven; they were also instructed to purify their souls so that they would be better prepared for a conversation with heaven not only in this life but in the next. The endowment of a soul received from and destined for heaven, once accepted in conversion, required continual maintenance and supervision: a continuous purification through spiritual trials. In addition to this asceticism, however, *believers remained in spiritual communion with ancestors and saints who had gone before. Thus the believers' time, and often their inner experiences, were not entirely their own. The creative tension between mystical and ascetic ways of apprehending the soul's existence in time placed the soul on endless trial.*

In pursuing this inquiry I will draw on anthropological insight into the social construction of the soul. The young have "weak souls," as Wagner (1981) reminds us, and they can easily become enthralled or captivated by the world, their elders, and by loves that lie outside the range of the permissible or the possible. In every generation, then, souls are in danger of becoming captivated and enthralled, enervated and drained, until the soul itself is empty. As Dante put it, "all sense of self was ravished out of me" by the sight of the penitential spirit in adoring prayer (Dante 1955:126; Canto VIII, line 15).

That weakness is why souls must appropriate to themselves the powers that they see in the world around them; culture becomes a sort of talisman that one wears to appropriate and yet ward off the potency of its symbols. Undergraduates wear sweaters with institutional emblems, very much as soldiers wear uniforms; those who seek to take the mystery and authority out of a society's symbols in order to gain breathing space, as it were, for their innermost selves tend to disfigure idols or burn flags. To wear the regalia of office or to sport the feathers of the elders in a performance that is only quasi-serious and at least half in mockery is the defence of the young soul against the power of the elders: the defence of "invention" against "culture." It is a story as old as Icarus, arrayed in the feathers of his father's office, but imbued with a disregard for the elder's instruction and authority. To rebel against time it is necessary to mock the pretensions of culture, just as it is the pressure of expectations on everyday life that sets time in motion. As the story of Icarus suggests, however, such rebellion can be tragic and very short-lived indeed.

There are other ways to lose one's soul besides becoming fascinated by new-found powers (Icarus) or by remaining captivated by the demands of one's culture (Daedalus).[9] Many of the characters in Dante's purgatory are weighed down by the burden of their sins. Some have engaged in conquest or

---

[9] I have discussed the meaning of this myth in some detail in Fenn 1991.

exercised brutal power in office; others have sought to eclipse the talents of rival artists, while still others have used the status of their own families to stifle the claims of others to recognition. Time is running out on these souls, who are still trapped in purgatory, because they are all weighed down by the debt that they owe to those at whose expense they have either lived or died. Thus their burdens, like heavy rock, are the result of the pressure of the culture on the hard reality of human nature, greed, or pride.

As a result of these pressures, a social character has emerged which is overtly narcissistic and covertly masochistic. However, its seeds were to be found in Dante's poetic vision of purgatory:

> Even thus, for their and our good speed, arose
> Prayer from those souls beneath their burden curled
> And going, as in dreams one sometimes goes,
>
> Where the First Cornice its slow length unfurled,
> Painfully round, diversely laden thus,
> Purging away the tarnish of the world,
> (Dante 1955:151; *Purgatory*, Canto xi, lines 25–30)

In these portraits of burdened souls we see what Wagner (1981:74) meant by referring to Westerners as people who "'do' an embattled Culture, harassed and motivated by time." Dante's souls in purgatory are crushed by the weight of psychic obligation to the social order. As Wagner reminds us, when individuals take too seriously the burden of social obligation into their innermost selves they become neurotic, sickened by the internal voice of reproof and censure. Time for the living indeed becomes of the essence, and it becomes essential, a matter of desperate spiritual struggle, for them to "redeem the time" in this life by even a last-minute act of humility and charity or through prayers for souls who have departed into purgatory (Dante 1955:157 [note by Sayers on *Purgatory*, Canto xi, line 127]).

In addition to being weighed down by "culture," souls in purgatory have the additional burden of not having repented in time – that is, before their deaths. To the burden of having been tardy in reaching spiritual maturity is added the weight of the recognition that death makes any spiritual effort "too little and too late." Caught in the double-bind between inventing themselves and still maintaining a connection with their community, these souls were not playful or creative enough in their life-times; that is, they did not engage in the play of ritual or invent themselves anew as contrite sinners seeking to give satisfaction for their sins.

The need for such interpersonal creativity and spiritual self-invention is particularly acute in a society not only burdened with ecclesiastical and civic administration but also with possibilities for emulation, envy, acquisition, achievement, and conquest at the expense of others. Wagner puts it this way:

We live our lives by ordering and rationalizing, and re-create our conventional controls in creative swoops of compulsive invention; tribal and religious peoples live by invention in this sense (which makes them so provocative and interesting to us), and revitalize their differentiating controls from time to time in bursts of hysterical conventionalizing ... (1981:59)

The doctrine of purgatory was just such a "burst" of invention: hysterical, perhaps, in its insistence on transcending the limits of time and space, and conventional also in its insistence that the new order cast a shadow over and displace the old.

In the long run, one is left only with the residues of a secularized purgatory in the temporizing strategies of modernity. These strategies are serious, since they are informed by the unconscious with the burden of making up for lost time; they are conventional, in the sense that the time-constraints adopted by modern individuals are also imposed by the institutions in which they live and work. The irony is that social institutions forged in an attempt to intensify, relieve, and satisfy a sense of sin have resulted in a chronic, low-grade consciousness of sin that lacks the name or the remedies of the initially religious invention.

CHAPTER I

Silent anguish: distinguishing the cure for soul-loss from the disease

In his excellent study of primitive magic, De Martino argues that a fragile sense of one's own "controlling presence" under-lies the threat of losing one's soul. "The theme of the possible loss and eventual regaining of the personal presence" is at the root of all magic, and particularly of shamanism (De Martino 1988:73). In fact, some shamans' strategies resemble various children's games; a shaman might prove his or her powers by sending souls on journeys or by imagining themselves throwing out objects, only to discover and retrieve them as if by magic (De Martino 1988:47, 60). In the same way, children are often willing – at least in their imagination – to despatch their parents on one-way trips to oblivion. Freud noticed one young boy, for instance, playing with a yo-yo and came to the conclu-sion that the boy was imagining himself in control of his father's disappearance and re-appearance; the boy in fact dismissed his father "to the front," where he might well be eliminated once and for all. In his imagination, the boy was the one who controlled his father's presence or absence, and, in so doing, his own.

Religion, as I have suggested, is the social institution which adjudicates the tension between the presence and absence of the self and of others. Conversely, religion, like the boy in Freud's story and the shaman, can dispose of others so that their presence can then be recovered. In the same way religion adjudicates the passages of the soul. Just as some lose their souls by falling under the powerful attraction or influence of a person or place, so a shaman may demonstrate his or her powers by discovering lost souls or by retrieving what was hidden from view in a soul, i.e. its secrets (De Martino 1988:47, 53). In recovering the lost object or soul, the shaman demonstrates what De Martino calls the "controlling presence," which is the only cure for a soul whose own presence seems fragile and all too likely to be controlled, whether by passions or by objects of one's own fascination. If magical thinking is the cause of the person's feeling that the soul is endangered, so magical practice is its cure.

There is little doubt that such strategies for the recovery and restoration of lost souls have profoundly shaped Western culture and institutions. In his study of Greek religion and myth, for instance, Walter Burkert (1983) describes a number of cults and mysteries, most of which follow the pattern of shamanic cures for the loss of soul described by De Martino. In each there is a period of searching and wandering. Often the initiates are left alone, blindfolded, anxious, uncertain of their place in the world, captivated, and in danger of losing their souls. The secret of the soul is revealed, perhaps symbolized by a grain of wheat, after the initiate has engaged in the "work" of the ritual through symbolic gestures like crushing the grain and preparing from its residues a spiritually curative potion. Darkness turns into light as the priests or priestesses unveil chambers of fire: the vision of which further purifies the soul and prepares it to enter into the paradise of the blessed. Souls are returned from their sojourn in Hades, and in their return the initiates find guarantees that their own souls have been rescued from bondage. As Burkert puts it:

The collective ritual which, in the history and tradition of man, has become associated with the soul is able to pull that soul into its rhythm so that many actually experience what is expected of them, and the remainder feel ashamed in their isolation ... (1983:287)

What Burkert does not say, however, is equally important: that the rescue of the soul from one captivity through magical rites leads to a new bondage. The souls of the initiate are enthralled by their new vision, perhaps of a goddess's daughter returned from Hades. It seems on the surface that the initiate can now be released from the duty of performing these rites; as

Heracles is reputed to have claimed, "Lock up Eleusis and the sacred fire ... [for] I have seen Kore" (Burkert 1983:286). Nonetheless, as Burkert himself points out, the initiates had to return annually to renew the vision and repeat the yearly sacrifice. The shamanic cure for the soul is difficult to distinguish from the disease of soul-loss.

At the very least, I am arguing, the danger of losing one's soul and the need for magical cures have created cultural purgatories, of which the mystery cults of Greece were clearly an early example. Whether these rites were indeed some of the sources for the later Christian doctrine of purgatory is a question I will leave to the experts. I would suggest, however, that Le Goff (1984:23) prematurely dismisses the influence of these mysteries on Christian doctrine as at best indirect.

The point is simply that, for those who live in the world of magic, the soul is always in jeopardy. Even the cures of the soul create new forms of possession, of thrall or of addiction. Therefore to redeem the soul from the influence of unseen presences and to prevent the soul's captivation has been the task of salvation religions, and Christianity is no exception. The paradox is that religion has tried to beat magic at its own game: to fight magical fire with spiritual fire.

If magic makes the soul a slave to unseen presences, it has been necessary for religion to provide a counter-magic, a superior potency that will break the spell cast over the soul by powerful people and places, spirits and things, especially when these influences operate *in absentia*. To find what C. S. Lewis calls a "deeper magic" that will redeem the soul from its bondage to such forces has been particularly the task of the soul in places of purification such as purgatory. There the soul must pass tests of the spirit and endure trials, but since its fate is still in the hands of invisible presences like angels and demons, these forces must be offset by other presences invoked *in absentia* by the prayers of the faithful or by the divine spirit. Thus purgatory and other times of trial resemble the disease, which is the individual's dependence on outside powers, but purgatorial times of trial also present the cure: redemption from bondage to such external forces.

Religion also helps individuals to recover their own sense of presence, their own being-in-the-world, when their presence is threatened by outside forces or by internal disturbances. "Presence" or "absence of mind" are modern residues of the fear of soul-loss, but contemporary usage can hardly recover primitive terror at the prospect of having one's innermost being taken away by some external presence. To offset that terror requires what De Martino (1988:70) calls a "drama that helped create the world of magic." On the one hand, individuals feel captivated by other people or things, spirits or places, and so lose confidence in their own presence in the world. Their own presence is controlled by another, which becomes the enemy and must be contained or harnessed to the powers of the individual's own soul. Through what psychoanalysts have been calling processes of identification, fusion, and internalization, the individual steals or borrows the powers of the external object, and that object becomes a self-object: an internalized presence, whether that be of a meteor or an ancestor, a plant, an animal, or a witch-doctor.

The world of magic, De Martino argues, lives within the drama of danger and redemption. On the one hand the soul must feel the danger of being entranced, captivated, possessed, or enslaved; on the other, the soul must feel the need "to be free to function . . . [and] the need to redeem itself" (1988:70). This is the tension between mysticism and asceticism: a tension that is preserved in the notion of a purgatory: a place of considerable torment for the soul. For instance, De Martino notes that "a typical and easily-recognizable type of anguish is produced" (1988:70). However, although the anguish may be quite ordinary, it is easily lost to the view of those who see only the religious forms of communion or community, the social bonds cemented by religion, and not the attempt of the soul to redeem itself by substituting these bonds for a worse sort of bondage. The dramas are also lost to the view of those who examine only the surfaces of social interaction, the play of appearances, and the façades of the self engaged in the games, the strategies, and the routines of everyday life.

The magical drama of the soul seeking redemption from its

bondage can also be found in the world of work and politics. Le Goff (1984) documents the struggle between artisans, especially in the textile industries, and their employers for control over the time of the working day. The workers understandably demanded time for themselves as well as for their work: time for personal pursuits or for other remunerative work, and they also needed more time on the job to make up for income lost to inflation. On the other hand, the employers sought to regulate the time at which the workers would come to work and leave, as well as the time for meals, in order to rationalize production and enhance productivity. The capitalist struggle for the control of time thus had begun in earnest well before the Reformation. The struggle for the control of time, however, was symptomatic of conflict between workers and employers, citizens and magistrates, for control over the right to be present or absent.

In this conflict one can see how time becomes of the essence of the soul's liberation from debts of various kinds: from financial debts, of course, but also from bondage to authorities among the bourgeoisie and in the church itself. Le Goff (1984:50–51) speaks of a popular Dominican preacher, Domenico Calva, who indeed made time of the essence of the individual's spiritual salvation. Not a moment of time was to be wasted:

Beginning with traditional considerations of idleness and using a merchant's vocabulary (wasted time was for him the lost talent of the Gospel – time was already money), he developed a whole spirituality of the calculated use of time ... (Le Goff 1984:51)

As Le Goff (1984) demonstrated in his later work on the subject, the church in the thirteenth century succeeded in making time of the essence; every moment on earth could save one time in purgatory, where time, still of the essence of the soul's salvation, dragged on as if for an eternity, although it eventually came to an end. Furthermore, individuals in this life could save time in purgatory not only for themselves but for the departed, who were imagined to be pleading their cases to a jury of the living, on whose intercessions they were relying for a shortened stay in purgatory. Not only time, therefore, but the payment of debts of all kinds in this life became essential for salvation. Those who owed others money or who had not fulfilled their other social obligations were going to have to do time in purgatory; thus not only usury but all forms of indebtedness were grist to the mill of salvation, and only those who had paid their debts could be considered sufficiently refined to be fit for the communion of the saints in paradise. Those who were experienced as present, even though they were absent, were assumed to have unfinished spiritual business for which they needed the additional time offered by purgatory.

Clearly the spirit of Catholicism was crucial for the development of the ethic of capitalism. As Le Goff points out, the Catholic humanist soon began to introduce

his business organization into everyday life and regulated his conduct according to a schedule, a significant secularization of the monastic manner of regulating the use of time ... (1984:51)

Of course, the ethic of capitalism needed support from other sources than the spirit of Catholicism: from science, from city administrations, and from the state itself. Such support was soon forthcoming. As for science, time in the fourteenth century became nominal rather than real, conceptual rather than natural, continuous rather than discontinuous, calculable rather than mysterious, predictable rather than eventful. The clock replaced the church bell and the bells that had summoned workers to their tasks (Le Goff 1984:50).

Thus the new tyranny of time served the interests of those who wished to control presence and absence in the fourteenth-century city and the state. Aldermen who themselves had placed bells in the city to signal the times for work or for the market found themselves being summoned to meetings by other bells placed in the appropriate towers by magistrates, who charged the aldermen for tardiness just as monks had been punished for being late to mass (Le Goff 1984:48). In 1370 Charles V in Paris ordered the bells of the city to conform to the clock at the palace, and "The new time thus became the time of the state" (Le Goff 1984:50). The point is simply that time had become of the essence of political, civic, and commercial life in the fourteenth century: the bell summoning the living to pay their debts and fulfill their obligations. Only a century earlier time had become of the essence to enable the living to pay the debts of the dead and to obtain their own redemption from social and spiritual bondage.

As purgatory became domesticated in everyday life, the drama of the soul's danger and redemption was being played out at work and at home, in the city and in the market place, in the provinces and in the capitol cities. The danger was that the worker would become enslaved to schedules set by the bourgeoisie, who may have worked a half-day themselves but who insisted that the workers put in a day whose length would be determined by market forces and by productivity rather than by the motions of the sun or the demands of family life and personal interests. Redemption would come in the form of paying off one's debts, both financial and social, spiritual and emotional, so that one could then have time at one's own disposal. Control over one's time became the hallmark of those who had arrived.

It would be important to know the personal anguish felt by those who knew that they were running out of time, in every sense of the word. What did it mean to live in purgatory in this life as well as in the next? One would assume that the purgatorial intensification of time was painful. For instance, in his advice on prayer, the author of *The Cloud of Unknowing* makes it clear that one should pray in the full knowledge that time is running out on the soul and that time is therefore of the essence of one's salvation. Death may come before one has finished one's prayers. Confession is not enough, and neither is contrition, although together they are essential for the amendment of one's life. Salvation, however, depends on satisfying all one's debts and making up for one's previous sins; one must make up for lost time, as it were, and buy time for the full satisfaction of one's sins. If in the course of praying as though one might not live to say "Amen," however, the prayer itself will suffice for the satisfaction of one's sins:

I think what is going to help you most when you start your prayer . . . is to make quite sure that you are certain that you will die by the time it is ended, that you will finish before your prayer does! . . . if you do die before you reach the end having done what you could, then God will accept it as full payment for all your neglect from the time your life began up to that very moment ... (Wolters 1980:223–226)

Certainly by contemplating one's own nothingness, one's "nothing" and one's "nowhere" (as we have seen in a passage quoted from *The Cloud of Unknowing* in the previous chapter), one's past sins will come flooding into one's consciousness. If one does not die, therefore, but continues to live in this purgatorial consciousness, time becomes intensified as a medium in which one's soul can be purged and its peace achieved. If, however, one's soul is required even in the act of such contemplation, it is as though the partial payment of the soul were to be taken as fully satisfying its mortal debts.

Purgatory was a collective belief-system, as important to the people who embraced it as it was to the institutions, like the monasteries and the churches, that used it for the regulation of duty and obligation. In participating in this drama of redemption, the European was engaged in a "primitive" drama of salvation, like "the Shaman's psychic voyage to heaven or hell" (De Martino 1988:86). In that voyage the shaman enters caves, encounters spirits and demons, struggles with his or her spiritual enemies, and risks losing his or her soul forever, and may return in ghostly fashion to the community, only to recover it in time (De Martino 1988:94). Many of the same elements of dramatic spiritual journey can be found in the poetic or ecclesiastical accounts of purgatory. Indeed, purgatory was a collective spiritual drama, infused with magical thinking, in which the soul was endangered and eventually redeemed.

Hell is quite simply the place where one has run out of time: time for repentance or contrition, time to acquire merit and to undo the past. In purgatory, however, there is still time in which to redeem the soul: to pay its debts to the living, to make up for lost time on earth, and to pass the tests that separate the soul from its true, eternal essence. Those still in this life can buy time not only for those in purgatory but for themselves, not only by penitent action and humility but by praying for themselves as well as for those whom they have loved. All souls are in danger of purgatory if not hell. The emphasis on time is paramount: the number of years of prayers in this life having a calculable effect on the actual time the soul must remain in purgatory.

To be able to buy time or to make up for lost time, however, is to have hope. That is precisely Le Goff's point. Sins which had previously put the soul in certain danger of damnation could now be redeemed through prayer and action; for instance, monks who committed sins of lust and apostasy now had hope, where there had been none in the past (Le Goff 1984:305). Even more indicative of the new urban world were the prospects of occupational groups "whose work involved spilling blood, handling money, or trading in unclean commodities" (1984:305). These now had some hope after death, if only their relatives and friends were willing to pray and make sacrifices for them. Time was now on the side of new occupational groups in the urban middle class: groups whose work or way of life had previously put them outside the pale. The self was beginning to be able to be constructed and negotiated, even while the fate of the soul was being made contingent on timely prayer and sacrifice.

Le Goff (1984:291) notes, for instance, that the thirteenth century marked the beginning of narrative and of a tendency to psychologizing. The emergence of the individual as a social unit and of the self as a center of independent moral activity is also clearly one of the themes or achievements of purgatory. Note, moreover, that when individuals separate themselves out from their families and communities, withdrawing some of the social and emotional credit that they had previously invested in such institutions, there is a new psychological and a moral debt to be paid. If the urban context was conducive to a new sense of personhood, purgatory was also an ideal way for persons to pay what they owed for their first steps toward individuality and selfhood. It is therefore not surprising to find that these autonomous individuals took to writing wills, to make sure that their debts would be paid after their death, and thus that their souls would be speeded out of purgatory into paradise (Le Goff 1984:326–328). Redemption was contingent on the efforts of both the living and the dead.

Some occupational groups, previously despised, no longer left matters to chance or to the good will of their friends and relatives. The surgeons and barbers, who treated corpses and were accordingly of very low social status indeed, owing to their impurity, found it convenient to become a confraternity in close association with the Dominicans (Le Goff 1984:327–328). Through this relationship they were promised a number of benefits in the next life, such as an accelerated passage through purgatory for those members of the Confraternity chosen to have masses said for them, and in this life they enjoyed a status somewhat enhanced by relating their work to the means of salvation. By endowing the masses to be said for their deceased members, the surgeons and barbers could be said to be working out their salvation – in this life – in somewhat less fear and trembling. At least they had the rudiments of a calling and a purchase on an improved status in this life and the next.

More is involved here, clearly, than the success of new status groups in pressing their claims for recognition on the church and its system of awarding social credit. A new sense of time and its possibilities is opening up for both the saved and those who have previously been outside the system of social credit. Even usurers, according to Le Goff, are being saved by the living from the pains of purgatory, and they are being saved, furthermore, by their spouses, and not by the usual patriarchal and aristocratic sources of social credit in this life and the next (Le Goff 1984:304–305). There are new claims being entered here for those who had previously been unable to earn or receive social credit, and as Le Goff points out, the advent of usurers and their spouses into the system of purgatorial payments helps to lay the foundations of monogamous marriage and capitalism. Le Goff therefore speaks of the advent of new hope and discerns the seeds of modernity in the complex urban world of the thirteenth century: new options and possibilities, new opportunities and dangers, new relationships both within the society and with those previously considered outsiders, are opening out.

For a system built on notions of purity, of course, such a

period poses very real dangers. If usurers and those who handle blood or "unclean commodities" are any example, the urban world of the thirteenth century was bringing together those who represented both the virtues of the city and those who represented the sources of its potential undoing. Under these conditions it is not unusual for a society to dramatize itself as an area freed from the contradictions of decay and death, of sexuality and license, of individuality and the intrusion of outsiders. It may well be that the popularity of the doctrine of purgatory came from this desire to sacralize the world and to purify it from contamination. Death, if it were not already the enemy of the soul, would have to be invented. In the case of purgatory, however, the new order was already partly secularized. The lives of the dead inhabited the same time-frame as the living.

As in the societies generally considered "primitive," however, the medieval city – indeed the whole community was caught up in the periodic drama of the soul. It is a collective drama in which shamans risk losing their own for the sake of the community:

The magic-man's risk and redemption is not strictly a personal drama. It is the community as a whole, or one of several of its members, who through the figure head of the magic-man and through the drama in which he plays, become aware of the adventure and the loss and recovery of the "being-here." This relationship is particularly evident in shamanic magic ... (De Martino 1988:87)

The impure are an anomaly in any society, and at worst a threat to the survival of the community. For urban blacks in the United States, Korean merchants or money lenders represent as palpable a threat to the survival of the black community as did newcomers in the thirteenth-century cities of the west: threats, and yet also new possibilities for investment and expansion, goods and relationships. As for usury, simply consider that the urban poor often pay interest rates from 40 to 50 percent on loans, as well as high prices and rates for a wide range of good and services. In the medieval city, however, debt was compounded by the demand for purification and the salvation of the soul in corporate dramas of redemption.

Merely the lack of social credit suffered by particular groups, and the high level of financial debt or high interest rates that they must correspondingly pay, would not by themselves account for the surprising invention of an ideological system that compounded punishment and hope. It is in purgatory, after all, that – according to Dante – one hears "how God wills the debt be paid" (*Purgatory*, Canto x, lines 107–111; quoted in Le Goff 1984:352).

Purgatory not only reinforced certain values, like moderation, by offering more moderate punishment and renewed hope for the future (Le Goff 1984:306–309). It also offered a way out of a debt crisis that could well have immobilized Western society at a critical moment in its development. Some debts were clearly financial; and the obligation of survivors to the departed was primarily to pay back money and property that the dead still owed the living. Other debts were to the soul and had to be paid in time, on time, and over time.

In view of the disastrous plagues of the fourteenth century, it may also be that what has come to be known as "survivor" guilt and anxiety may well have afflicted the survivors. Certainly Le Goff speaks frequently of the bonds of solidarity not only among friends and relatives but among other citizens of the urban communities: bonds that brought with them increasing levels of responsibility to the living and to the dead. It is entirely possible that such debts underlay the widespread experience of seeing ghosts and the souls of the departed, all of whom had unfinished business and wanted the living to pay for the debts of the dead. It may well be that the debt of the living to the dead was becoming heavy and unconscionable and that the living needed a way of paying such debt in order to take advantage of the opportunities offered by the present. The presence of those who are really absent can be a very heavy burden indeed, and it is the living who therefore need the indulgence and refreshment.

In a world in which solidarity is increasing, it is especially difficult for individuals to separate themselves, to become free from social obligations, and to live a life in which they are relatively free of obligation to the living and to the dead. Le

Goff (see, e.g., 1984:326) describes the thirteenth century as a time in which boundaries were being crossed, not only between the living and the dead, but between the monastic and the lay communities, through the use of stories concerning the souls in purgatory, and through disseminating monastic practices of devotion, penance, masses, and pilgrimage for the relief of their suffering. It is as if these rites and the myth of purgatory formed a massive bond of spiritual obligation that unified a world that longed for – and was scared by – the freedom of any soul from social bondage.

Only the soul that has been purged of its sins can be free from obligation and yet remain a trusted member of the human community. Le Goff notes that Dante is free from his spiritual guide only when he has passed through purgatory and is on the verge of Paradise. With a purified will, Dante would hence-forth "be in error not to heed / whatever your own impulse prompts you to: / lord of yourself I crown and mitre you" (*Purgatory*, quoted in Le Goff 1984:335).

It is very difficult, from the perspective of an American toward the end of the twentieth century, not to see in this verse the birth of the free-standing, autonomous, and purified indi-vidual. Such an individual would be free-standing in the sense of having emerged from the embrace and confinement of the family and the household, as well as from such other sources of obligation as the guild or the church. Autonomy would consist in being self-regulating: not a law unto oneself but having overcome the tension between the self and the conscience. As for being purified, the new individual no longer has to fear the passions that can tear apart and dissolve the soul. They have become subsumed within a passionate self capable of suffering, enduring, and standing upright: no longer bent over under the weight of memory and time, passion, and remorse. In the Christian dispensation the new individual has become a his-torical possibility. To live "on the verge of paradise" is to be "lord of yourself." It would be a mistake for lords not to heed their own impulses. But to know which impulses and sensations are truly one's own requires the education of the soul through reason, as John Locke saw it: a point to which we shall return in our discussion of the shape of purgatory after the Reformation.

No one has made this point with more clarity and spiritual force than Catherine of Genoa. Indeed, if modernity begins with the doctrine of purgatory, it takes shape in the form of this saint of the Catholic Reformation. Aristocratic, philanthropic, humble in her devotion to the poor, and skilled in the administration of a hospital for their benefit, she is reported by her confessor and by her disciple to have insisted on the need of the soul to become lord of its own impulses. It was the impulse toward fusion with God, the instinct for beatitude, that was the most powerful and, if resisted, the most dangerous to the soul. Rather than wait for purgatory to begin the removal of every barrier to the fulfillment of this spiritual imperative, the soul in this life must begin and continue the process of self-purification. Time is of the essence for this process, and the sooner the soul begins the suffering that comes with purgation, the sooner will its suffering in purgatory be over.

Time, sheer duration, is therefore the medium through which the soul moves in its passage to God. If the medieval soul went on pilgrimages through space, the modern soul therefore takes up its trajectory through time:

> Those in purgatory simply suffer.
> Since they are without fault, for suffering cancelled it,
>   their suffering is finite
> and, as we have said before, is diminished by time,
> (Groeschel 1977:74–75)

Souls in purgatory are "without fault," she has argued, because they can no longer sin. Indeed, they do not know why they are being punished in purgatory, since that knowledge disappears after the moment of death, when they are briefly made aware of their fate and the reasons for it. Not even their punishment strikes the soul in purgatory as a form of suffering, since that soul is already in harmony with God's will. Nonetheless, the soul still suffers because its instinct for beatitude is held back. No longer sinning, the soul still is covered with the residues of sin, and it is this covering or stain which needs to be burned away by the fires of divine love before the soul can fully enter into the joy of the saints in heaven.

God's love, then, is both the cure for the sin that stains the human soul, but it is also the reason for the soul's discomfort. Catherine argues that the love of God indeed slowly cures the soul of its impediments, its barriers, and its resistance to the divine presence. The key term is "slowly"; purgation takes time, but in time the suffering of the soul in purgatory will indeed end. On the other hand, "this harmony with God's will also brings about a very great suffering" (Groeschel 1977:72).

Note the paradox: divine love being both the solvent for sin and separation, and yet also the source of intensified yearning for restoration to perfect unity with God. As purification increases, so does the suffering that comes from a heightened awareness of the smallest degree of separation. To resolve that contradiction takes time; indeed, time becomes serious precisely because it bears the weight not only of the residues of sin but the hope for total salvation.

CHAPTER 2

Purgatory as a way of life: time as the essence of the soul

If we examine Dante's purgatory we will see why time was to be made the essence not only of the sacred but of the secular in Western societies. For Dante purgatory is the place where souls linger in a time between their latest and their final departure; in this ghostly interim, time is always running out. The moon is waning; hours are passing; and souls are waiting through the succession of days and nights, months and years, either for their release or for Judgment Day: whichever comes first. In the meantime they clearly reenact their life-times on an other-worldly landscape. To be sure, Dante often envisaged purgatory as though he were in a dream. Indeed he explicitly describes some of the most heavily burdened characters in purgatory as "going, as in dreams one sometimes goes ..." (Dante 1955:151; *Purgatory*, Canto xi, lline 27. (Similarly, John Bunyan described *Pilgrim's Progress* through the lens of a dream.)

Yet there is already something this-worldly about purgatory. As Sayers reminds us,

"... it is only in purgatory, which is situated *in time*, that Dante sleeps at all; not in Hell or Heaven, which are *eternal* states." (Dante 1955:140; *Purgatory*, Canto ix, line 10)

Thus Dante places purgatory *in secular time* (Dante 1955:140). As Sayers reminds us, the church dwells in time, whether in this life or the next. Indeed, for Dante, time was of the essence of purgatory; his imaginary characters were doing time and serving an indefinite sentence for crimes of the heart, the mind, and the imagination as well as of word and deed.

The boundary between this world and the next, between the living and the dead, is as vague in purgatory as is the boundary between dream-states and waking consciousness. It is precisely the vagueness of the boundary between dreams, fantasies, and normal consciousness that creates certain trance-states even in everyday life: many times a day, perhaps, and in virtually any social context. Various forms of possession or soul-loss, in which the soul is indeed at least temporarily displaced, are relatively widespread even in "modern" societies, where they are conducive to hysterical, neurotic, or masochistic aspects of social character. Indeed, it is not unusual for "normal" individuals to be caught up in the same dream-states as Dante's figures in purgatory: caught between despair that they will never see again those from whom they have parted and dread of a final departure filled with the pains of death.

The spiritual self-discipline that emerged from the doctrinal innovation of purgatory intensified the Western experience of time in ways that were instrumental and perhaps necessary to the development of modernity itself. Making the most of one's time, having something to show for one's time, seizing the moment, and also making up for lost time and temporizing with the constraints placed on one by social institutions: all these secular strategies, I will suggest, are prefigured in the vision of purgatory and in the translation of that vision into prescriptions and recipes for self-discipline and self-improvement. If the purgatorial vision yielded a form of discipline that offered renewed subjection to the tyranny of time, the irony is due not only to the interests of entrepreneurs and of capital, or to ideological domination by particular institutions like the church and the monastery, but to the tendency of the unconscious to infuse everyday life with the dream-state. No wonder individuals tend to repeat the past and to confuse magical solutions with more effective ways of cutting the ties between the living and the dead, or between the present and the past.

Not only is there some irony in this development but also, perhaps, some tragedy. Sin, for Dante, was the "taint of time" on the soul, and it was the task of purgatory to expunge that taint. In the intensification of the meaning and experience of time that emerged from the doctrinal innovation of purgatory, however, the "taint of time" was driven more deeply into individual consciousness. Instead of an innovation that could succeed in freeing the soul from the burdens of the past and from dread of the future, purgatory was the beginning of a discipline that made time of the essence of a wide range of social institutions capable of putting the individual on probation and subjecting the self to successive privations and testing over a life-time.

In more formal sociological terms, the doctrine of purgatory represented a stage in the development of Western society in which "biographical" and "social" time were very closely entwined with each other. It was also a stage, however, in which individuals were beginning to enjoy a few degrees of freedom in paying off their "debts to society" and whatever financial obligations or penances were left unpaid at the moment of their death. Thus the timing of the doctrine of purgatory suggests that, in addition to "timetables" for the payment of debt, "schedules" were beginning to appear by which individuals could enjoy some discretion in satisfying their debts; they might even take their time in doing so.[1] Societies thus reconstruct themselves by re-inventing their own sense of time, and in the case of purgatory the invention was fateful for the development of modern societies and for a particular type of social character that intensifies the experience of time.

Take a moment to imagine even one major difference, however, between the context in which the doctrine of purgatory was first introduced and contemporary American society. Granted that by the late thirteenth century monastery bells were governing only some of the time-rhythms of the city; clocks were being introduced that increasingly regulated the rhythms of work and of civic life. Grant also that the rhythms of the body and of the soul resist all such regulation by social

---

[1] For a discussion of these and similar terms, see Bergmann 1992:103ff. In the preceding paragraph I am relying on his interpretation of this aspect of what has become a fairly sizable and complex literature.

time; they have their own circadian patterns and less frequent or regular seasons: aging, dark nights, significant moments, and times of renewal that escape every attempt to regulate them. Nonetheless, the "plurality of times" is far more complex in American society than it ever was in the medieval city. There are vastly more appointments to be kept and opportunities for missing them. The rhythms of one aspect of life seldom conform to the rhythms of others, so that pregnancies and productivity at work are no more likely to be synchronized than are depressions of the spirit and of the economy. Thus in American society there are many more opportunities for individuals to have the experience that their most personal or subjective 'times' are out of joint with the obligations and appointments, rhythms and requirements of the social world. There are many more occasions for the "taint of time" to spread over the soul. For it is still expected that individuals will seize opportunities, rise to occasions, and have something to show for their time. For some it is still expected that they live their lives as if they could be called to account whether for their expenditure of every day or for their use of an entire lifetime.

There is in Western civilization, and particularly (although not peculiarly) in the American context, an intensification of time that leaves indelible marks on social character. In part that is due to the convergence of Catholicism with Protestantism in this country; both religious communities share equally in what has been thought of as the "Protestant" ethic, with its intensification of time and seriousness about the future. (I will return to this point in the Epilogue.) In part, the marks of a "purgatorial complex" reflect the burdens on the soul of a people torn by separation from their countries or communities of origin and confronted with both an intractable environment and a public order that was often chaotic and brutal.

It would take a more extensive book than this one to determine how widespread is a "purgatorial" social character that is burdened, even obsessed, with time. Various commentators, of course, have suggested that Americans have undertaken to increase their burdens or that social masochism is becoming increasingly widespread in the United States during the 1980s and 1990s (cf. Trilling 1963; Cooper 1988). Only a careful and comprehensive examination of character in a wide range of contexts and communities could begin to give the answer, of course, and such a study cannot even be attempted here. There is some evidence that evangelical and fundamentalist Christians, especially in their private schools, place children under intense, even excruciating time pressures (Rose 1988). Time in these contexts is filled with moral obligation and spiritual significance.[2] The sense of sin, I would argue, would therefore vary according to the nature of "social time" in each context.

The development of a social character burdened by time, however, is prefigured in the notion of purgatory itself. In Dante's vision of purgatory, the dead are in the same time-zone as the living. They share the same burden of time, of everyday life, of being quotidian and therefore captive to the tyranny of time. Indeed, they are serving their time. Just as the dead still occupy the same time-zone as the living, the living share the same burden of time as the departed and suffer a similar burden of real debts or of imaginary obligations stemming from the unconscious. Both the living and the dead are doing time, serving their time, in punishment for sins not only of commission but of the imagination and the unconscious mind.

SIN AS THE "TAINT OF TIME"

The hallmark of that sinful state is what Dante calls "time's deep stain" (Dante 1961:121; Canto XI, line 35). Some souls have been precipitate in their pursuit of fame and glory: impatient, fast-forwarding to their future glory or to their destruction. Others have been tardy in their life-time, slow to respond to others' needs and delaying their own payment for their sins until it was too late. Having kept others waiting in their life-time, they in turn are punished by being kept waiting

---

[2] Some have argued, furthermore, that women and African-Americans are not subject to the same purgatorial time-constraints in the formation of social character (for African-Americans see the discussion in McGrath and Kelley 1992:405ff.; for women, see Forman, ed. 1989).

for their salvation. If they have been presumptuous in pushing others out of their way on earth, then in purgatory they are pushed aside and burdened with time indefinitely. A soul burdened with time is in a state of sin. Purgatory is a place where precedent, what has gone before, still dominates the present in such a way that every moment exhibits in part a repetition of the past in the form of penance.

According to Dorothy Sayers, ante-purgatory is filled with those who missed crucial opportunities to avail themselves of the "means of Grace" in their own life-times. Their penance fits their crime; now they must wait even to enter into the gates of purgatory, where they can begin to be purified from their sins (Dante 1955:63; Sayers, "Introduction" to *Purgatory*). Note the symmetry, then, between the imagined offense and its appropriate sentence; being too late and missing opportunities in this life means being kept waiting in the next. There is an implicit law at work here: a spiritual eye for a spiritual eye, as it were. Freud spoke of it as the *lex talionis* and located it in the unconscious. It is at the root of the "purgatorial complex" and the resulting masochistic social character burdened with a sinful, however secularized, consciousness.

If the stain of time in the soul is sin, then it is delay in acting on impulses of love that first stains the soul. Virgil's constant advice to Dante on their way through purgatory is never to delay: never to fail to seize the day. "Remember, this day will not dawn again" (Dante 1961:133; *Purgatory*, Canto xii, line 84). Between the impulse to love and the fulfillment of desire there enters a fatal delay: a pause that allows desire to remain unfulfilled. Granted that what Dante had in mind was the feast of divine love, of agape, attendance at which should never be delayed; it was nevertheless delay itself that produced the fatal stain of time on the soul.

Furthermore, Dante would have agreed with Freud that it is frustrated desire that turns into envy and eventually into the fit punishment for envy: tedious duty and the heavy burden of the soul in purgatory (cf. Dante 1961:167; Ciardi's note on Canto xv, line 51). In purgatory one pays for possibilities that were not grasped, and salvation comes from making the most of the

possibilities for true repentance and amendment of life in the
time remaining.

Indeed, it is those who have delayed in responding to "sweet
invitations to the feast of love" (Dante 1967:140; Canto XIII,
line 27) who are now in purgatory. Having kept others
waiting, it is they who are now delayed in their spiritual
progress. To sin is thus to forfeit the opportunities to give and
receive love. The punishment for this crime is to be kept in
constant remorse for having wasted time and forfeited these
possibilities. The only hope for the repentant sinner in purgatory is to be so purified of time's stain that one can allow
memory to flow through one without remorse, "that memory's
stream may flow without a stain in joys to come" (Dante
1961:942, Canto XIII, lines 89–90).[3]

It is the same relief, of putting the past truly behind one in
the forgetful waters of Lethe, that allows the future to begin
and, in particular, gains one's entry into a state of grace.
Without that purification, there can indeed be no relief from
the stain of time and thus no future. By the fourteenth century
purgatory had become a way of life; it was now incumbent on
all souls to acquire a new fate, a new *moira* or *daimon*, in the time
remaining, regardless of whether one is living or dead.

As a cultural invention, then, the doctrine of purgatory
made of everyday life a scene in which spiritual battles were to
be fought minute by minute, day by day. Indeed, as Le Goff
notes, the command never to waste a moment of time was well
established by the end of the fourteenth century. The force of
this cultural injunction to *carpe diem* derives from orienting
libidinal energies toward this-worldly activities on behalf of
spiritual goals. Desire – frustrated and delayed in its full
satisfaction – became a bottomless well of inspiration for the
purgatorial soul. In part, the injunction to *carpe diem* gets its

---

[3] Ciardi notes: "At the top of Purgatory, the finally purified souls are washed in Lethe,
and it removes from them the very memory of sin. *Thus Dante is uttering a wish for the
more rapid advancement of these souls*, a sentiment all of them would take in good part"
(Dante 1961:146; emphasis added). Dante himself, then, exhibits the demand of the
conscience never to waste time, to make the most of every moment; it is not only
Virgil's instructions or the voices of the souls in Purgatory that carry this message.
Dante's compunctions about time are his own.

force from the memory of old loves and passions, and in part, of course, from the anticipation of beatitude. Finally, the force of the injunction to *carpe diem* comes from the claim to a share in divine grace, i.e. of charisma.

The "sweet invitations to the feast of love" which Dante had in mind come, of course, from heaven itself, and the feast is intended to be far more chaste than libidinal. However, it is delay in responding to more earthly promptings of love and desire that turns these very promptings into something more strenuous and forbidding, for example into cultural commands never to waste time. Under the conditions of repression, of course, these promptings seem to come from unseen sources, just as in purgatory the souls seeking their own purification heed the promptings of unseen (and, I would add, unconscious) messengers to make the most of their time so that the day of their salvation can be hastened.[4]

Remember that the world of the unconscious is one in which the punishment fits the crime. The law of the unconscious is, as Freud reminded us, the *lex talionis*. It is only fitting, therefore, that the proud should suffer in purgatory and do penance in a fashion that fits their (real or imaginary) crimes. For instance, Omberto Aldobrandesco suffers in purgatory because in this life he failed to pay the penance for his "haughty ways." Having subjugated others it is only fitting that he should therefore bear such a weight of stone that he can scarcely raise his head (Dante 1961:122; Canto XI, lines 49ff.). It is precisely repressed love or anger that fuels the punitive conscience, the superego. That is the so-called higher self, that towers like a mountain above the self and weighs heavily upon it, often to the point of crushing what Dante so often calls "the laden soul."

This higher self, like the Mount of Purgatory, does indeed weigh the self down with the burden of time. That is because every new beginning, every apparent forward step, involves a repetition of the anxiety of separation experienced at one's birth.[5] Thus even the spiritual progress of souls in purgatory,

---

[4] It is not clear what, if anything, souls can do to speed up their progress in Purgatory.
[5] In this discussion I am following John Forrester's recent treatment of the repetition compulsion; see Forrester 1992.

according to Dante, is marked by a repetition of past errors and a return of repressed desires; certainly Dante's own progress is marked by a repetition of the states of mind that marked his life on earth and to which he will return unless his journey through the imagination cures him of the compulsion to repeat the past.

It is this compulsion to repeat the past in order to repeal it which stains the soul with time and constitutes sin. The past repeats itself in acts of the conscience that seek to "whip" or "rein" in (to use Dante's imagery), to stimulate and to check, initially unsatisfied desires. The Mount of Purgatory is indeed the repetition of past desires and fears in a new situation that withholds its promise so long as the compulsion to repeat remains alive. That is why time reigns in purgatory as well as on earth, and why it stains the soul (cf. Forrester 1992:290).

The compulsion to repeat is like the yearning of the pilgrim to return home, each new departure being helped but also hindered by the last:

> Now – in the hour that melts with homesick yearning
> The hearts of seafarers who've had to say
> Farewell to those they love, that very morning –
>
> Hour when the new-made pilgrim on his way
> Feels a sweet pang go through him, if he hears
> Far chimes that seem to knell the dying day –
>
> Did I suspend the office of my ears,
> And turn to watch a spirit rising there,
> And beckoning with his hand for listeners.
>   (Dante 1955:126, *Purgatory*, Canto VIII, lines 1–9)

For this "pilgrim," as for Bunyan's, time is of the essence of the soul. A sad departure leaves him with an unfinished farewell; his homesick yearning therefore calls for more words to be spoken, but it is now too late. The despair of never returning is quickly transmuted, however, into a fatal anticipation: a "sweet pang" that comes from hearing bells in the distance. In the sound of these bells the pilgrim hears the announcement of a death: a final departure that consummates the farewell that has been uttered by the lips but not by the soul.

Note the unmistakable sounds of seduction and torment. On

the one hand, the pilgrim longs to return home to the archaic matrix of the soul in which time never runs out. On the other hand, however, succumbing to the yearning for that matrix immediately starts the pilgrim soul feeling the shortness and scarcity of time; it is time that is running out and placing the soul in fear of being late for its appointment: fear of being unable to make its eternal connection.

As the rhythms of monastic life became institutionalized in the city, they were supplemented by other times of obligation. As I will shortly demonstrate, the author of *The Cloud of Unknowing* introduced his flock to the significance of the purgatorial "hour": a moment that seems endless, since it captures the heart and fastens the soul, as it were, between two departures, both painful. In that "hour" time is of the essence of the soul, and words typically fail.

One can hear the same anguished and intense experience of time in the Protestant form of purgatory popularized by Bunyan, a way of life in which time is always of the essence. Bunyan's pilgrim is always hurrying toward a luminous goal, despairing over time that has been lost, seeking in despair to make up for lost time, temporizing (with nearly fatal consequences), and only occasionally seizing the moment. Compare the soul in purgatory, "the new-made pilgrim on his way," with the perpetually time-obsessed pilgrim of John Bunyan:

"How far," thought Christian, "have I gone in vain! Such was the lot of the Jews for their sin; they were sent back by the way of the Red Sea; and I am made to tred those steps with grief which I might have trod with joy, had it not been for this sleep. How far might I have been on my way by this time. I am made to tread those steps thrice which I need not to have trod but once; yea now too I am like to be lost in the night, for the day is nigh well spent. O that I had not slept!" (Bunyan [1884]; 1939:30–31)[6]

Neither Freud nor Dante counsels that one fulfill every desire or act on every impulse, loving or otherwise. Civilization will – it must – have its discontents. There is in the soul an immortal

---

[6] All references to *Pilgrim's Progress* are from Bunyan [1884]; 1939, a modernized version edited by Mary Godolphin in 1884 and published in Philadelphia in 1939.

struggle, and it is human fate, if not human destiny, to be punished for the impulses that one has not fulfilled. These turn on the self and in the name of a higher law condemn the self to carry a mounting burden of guilt. Thus desire is the "whip," and in the name of humility or love it lashes one on to acts of compassion and self-sacrifice; love delayed then turns into a "rein" that holds the sinner back with reminders of the punishment that falls to the proud or hard of heart. In this tension between desire and prohibition, time enters into – and stains – the soul with grief over actions delayed and opportunities forfeited. Indeed, the "central sin" of purgatory is acedia, the failure to act on the impulse of love or at least to respond to the needs of the world: failure to live in the world on its own terms and for its own sake.

Here, then, is the paradox. On the one hand, the vision of purgatory appears to carry within itself the seeds of modernity. The future is open, the past remains to be settled and effaced, and salvation depends on seizing the day, making the most of its possibilities, and entering the future with a clean slate. This bold stance toward both the past and the future is a peculiarly, if not uniquely modern impulse, and it has been carried particularly, of course, by the bourgeoisie. One does not ask for the impossible and the unprecedented but only for time to make the most of the opportunities that the world has to offer without constraint by the past or fear of the future.

On the other hand, however, the same vision of purgatory also carries within itself the seeds of a new tyranny: the tyranny of time. There is no escape from the past until and unless every old debt is paid, every score settled, every real and imaginary act of pride is compensated for by years of penance and self-mortification under weights commensurate with the burdens one has imposed on others; the past weighs heavily on the soul that is seeking to make the most of the time remaining.

The result is a modernity that has turned time into a new source of obligation and hegemony: time being the resource that one must never waste, the metronome that regulates one's activities, and the fate that carries one to one's death. Modern societies indeed have synchronized activities to the point that time exerts an exquisite pressure on all who are regulated by their interdependence with others rather than by the flow of tides and seasons or by biorhythms and the stars. As more of social life is mediated and controlled by institutions and corporations, their calendars, schedules, and time imperatives constrain the fate or daimon of everyone who is seeking to be approved, credentialed, tested, promoted, probated, tenured, appointed, ordained, adjudicated, or elected, to name only a few of the processes of purgation that modern societies have developed. Thus modern societies become secular purgatories.

Of course, in a book as brief as this, there is no way even to suggest all the links between medieval and modern conceptions of self and society. Some of the linkages developed over a long period of time: in the experience of marginal peoples or of slaves, on whose lives time is running out; in apocalyptic religious culture that slowly developed more attenuated versions of the end of time; under strong pressures for coordinating social life according to terms set by monks, councils, ministries, or the machinery of government and industry. All these can produce an intensification of the experience of time that, when taken into social character, turns time into an insupportable tyranny. Under these conditions, individuals, groups, and communities inevitably seek to make up for lost time, to buy time, and to temporize in any way that indeed they can.

No doubt the doctrine of purgatory intensified the demands of the community on the individual: demands for sacrifice and renunciation, for hard work and endurance, for unflagging zeal and compassion. These also are the demands of modernity. Even in the twentieth century political scientists have flailed the "amoral familism" of the households of Italy for failing to support a civic culture, just as Dante's vision warned of the corrupt and self-serving households that tore the fabric of the city states of the fourteenth century (Banfield 1967). Indeed the poem, *Purgatorio*, is itself a warning to the inhabitants of warring and corrupt city-states that their time is also running out. Some will be slaughtered by the envious; others, however good they may have been compared with their enemies, will die without issue or spiritual legacy, and their houses will thus come to an end. The beginnings of a succession-crisis can be found in the lines of prophetic warning, as well as the prophetic denunciation of the brutal wars among city-states in Tuscany (Dante 1961:159–160; notes by Ciardi Canto xiv, lines 103ff.). Thus the poem is a dramatization of its own vision of purgatory, that time is of the essence, and only those who repent themselves in time and who complete a timely penance can avoid damnation, however long their period of purification in purgatory must be. As I have noted, these demands may well have been mediated by Dominican monks in Italy who counseled against wasting a moment of time; they certainly were conveyed by priests like the anonymous author of *The Cloud of Unknowing* who counseled his flock to turn their lives into a purgatorial form of penance and purification from the weight of past sins.

For some, these demands from the community offered welcome opportunities for entrepreneurs and for status groups anxious to increase their standing. Le Goff, in fact, shows that marginal status-groups like the barbers or surgeons in medieval cities sought to enhance their social standing by affiliation with the monasteries, in return for which they undertook to pay off the debts of the departed members of their occupations. Thus the intensification of the demands of the city for new forms of commitment and citizenship also intensified the meaning and significance of one's own moral commitments over one's lifetime. Part of that intensification required the payment of debts in time, the seizing of new opportunities as they came along, and the obligations of the living to satisfy the debts of the departed.

To enter modernity, however, requires not only renunciation but a way of overcoming the compulsion to repeat. As I have noted, purgatory, translated into this-worldly efforts over a lifetime, intensifies the tendency of each new departure to rekindle the memory of previous separations and disappointments. Thus the purgatorial intensification of time and of moral obligation reinforces the compulsion to repeat, even though it purportedly demands that one finish old business before undertaking the new. The purgatorial cure, then, is part and parcel of the old disease of souls tainted by time. It is therefore not surprising that the brave new world, for which the pains of purgatory were intended to be a preparation, turns out to have its own forms of tyranny, in which time becomes, in its own right, something of a tyrant itself.

In *The Cloud of Unknowing* this intensification of time turns the daily life of the spiritual pilgrim into a this-worldly purgatory:

When a man is experiencing in his spirit this nothing in its nowhere, he will find that his outlook undergoes the most surprising changes. As the soul begins to look at it, he finds that all his past sins, spiritual and physical, which he has committed from the day he was born are secretly and somberly depicted on it. They meet his gaze at every turn, until at last after much hard work, many heartfelt sighs and many bitter tears he has virtually washed them all away ...

For he that perseveres does at times feel comfort and have some hope of perfection, for he begins to feel, and indeed to see, that many of his past sins are by grace in process of being rubbed away. Though he still has to suffer, he now believes his suffering will one day come to an end, for it is all the time getting less and less. *So he now begins to call it not "hell" but "purgatory"* ... (Wolters 1980:143–144; *The Cloud of Unknowing*, Sec. 69; emphasis added)

The soul that is not thus purified will die. Indeed, the death of the soul is the inevitable result of a spiritual life that fails to intensify the moment in meditation both on the sinfulness of the individual and on the glory of God. As I will show in Chapter 3, this sense that the use of time is a matter of life or death for the soul persists into modernity long after the doctrine of purgatory is ignored.

The transformation of purgatory into a this-worldly spiritual state, by the author of *The Cloud of Unknowing*, foreshadows post-Reformation treatments of the soul. Richard Baxter, for instance, places the believer midway between heaven and hell in this life. In order to ensure one's passage into the former rather than the latter, Baxter instructs the believer, it is necessary to pray with an intensity that allows not even for a moment's interruption:

But if the ravenous fouls of wandering thoughts do devour the meditations intended for heaven, I will not say flatly, it signifies thy death; but this I will say, that so far as these intrude, they will be the death of that service; and if thou ordinarily admit them, that they devour the life and the joy of thy thoughts; and if thou continue in such a way of duty to the end, it signifies the death of thy soul as well as of thy service ... (Baxter 1909:395–396; emphasis added)

No wonder that for Baxter time was the litmus test of the state of the soul. Some believers, he noted, keep postponing the time for their meditations on the pretext that they do not have enough time, so busy are they with their duties on behalf of others. Others "will trifle away the time in delays, and promise this day and the next, but still keep off from the doing of the business" (Baxter 1909:390–391). For these individuals he recommends that they never take "no" for an answer from their own heart but that they should "use violence with it; bring it to the service, willing, or not willing" (Baxter 1909:392).

Whereas the author of *The Cloud of Unknowing* urged his or her flock to meditate as if they might die before their prayer were done, Baxter urges his audience to live in that same fashion:

What a mercy is it to be driven from the world to God, when the love of the world is the greatest danger of the soul! Be ready to die and you are ready for anything. Ask your hearts seriously, what is it that I shall need at a dying hour? And let it speedily be got ready and not be to seek in the time of your extremity ... (Baxter 1868:33)

So the end becomes the present. For Baxter, not to keep the end always in sight was a recipe for the death of the soul. The life of the soul could only be ensured by a lively apprehension not only of one's last days but of the end for which the creature had been given life and later redeemed in Christ. The "mean-time" was always part and parcel of the end-times, just as surely as, for those who had been living in hope at least of purgatory if not of heaven, the clocks in purgatory kept the same time as the clocks on earth.

There are other reasons why modernity should turn out to intensify and deepen the very "taint of time," i.e. sin, from which it was supposed to provide purgatorial redemption and release. The souls in purgatory, after all, were temporizing; that is, they were protracting their moral debts until the last ounce of suffering and purification should have been paid. In this way they could not only delay the time of their ascent into heaven but also protract the period in which others, the living, could be called on to pay the debts of the departed. It is not surprising, therefore, that the living, subject as they were to purgatorial self-discipline and to the "whip" and "rein" of moral exhortation and reproof from ecclesiastical, monastic, and civic offices, should also seek to defend themselves by temporizing. Those souls in purgatory who sought to return to the past may have been seeking to make up for lost time, to buy time, or to postpone judgment on their lives until they could withstand a rigorous accounting.

So it is with the temporizing strategies of quite normal and ordinary individuals in modern societies, who resist the intensification of demands on their time and seek to buy time for themselves. Think for the moment of academics who try to "buy" time back from their institutions through grants, or of "release time" in the public schools, or of the myriad strategies for getting "time out" or "time off" that typify the hapless individual caught up in the relentless demands of a complex society for the synchronization of individuals according to the rhythms of corporate schedules. Through the pursuit of happiness and in the requirements of civic duty, modern societies have intensified the meaning, significance, value, and scarcity of time. Dante's "whip" and "rein" have been transformed into injunctions not only to gain satisfaction at the feast of love but also to control one's own impulses in a civic ethos of enlightened self-restraint.

Underlying what appear to be rational strategies for temporizing, I would argue, are magical notions about one's ability to intensify or manipulate time. Further, the survival of magical thinking may be due in part to some confusions in the fourteenth century about the role of reason. Both the author of *The Cloud of Unknowing* and Dante blur the distinction between the relation of reason to the imagination, of dreams to external reality, of the past to the present, and of the living to the dead.

Despite Dante's frequent praise for reason and free will, regardless of his claims to have emerged from dream-like states of mind, there is still a slight tendency on his part to obscure the difference between his imagination and reality:

> When finally my soul could see and feel
> 　things which were true outside it, I understood
> 　my not-false errors had been dreams, though real
> 　　　　　　(Dante 1961:165; Canto xv lines 115–117)

His dreams, Dante insists, are "real," and his "errors" certainly "not-false," though nonetheless errors. Clearly imagination is necessary both for entering purgatory and for leaving it.

An imaginative, even a trance-like state of mind also makes its contribution to the sense that one has been wasting time or running out of it. Indeed, there is some reality to the sense of having wasted time, since one becomes arrested in one's development so long as one remains wedded to one's fantasies and entranced by one's premature sense of having arrived at the full possession of one's soul. The soul thus arrested in its development

> ... tastes small pleasures first. To these it clings,
> 　deceived, and seeks no others, unless someone
> 　curb it, or guide its love to higher things,
> 　　　　　　(Dante 1961:173; Canto xvi, lines 91–93)

It is both too much and too little imagination which marks souls in purgatory.

With reason, however, souls can move on when they make up their minds – and their wills – to do so (Dante 1961:148; Ciardi, note on line 103). As we shall see in our discussion of John Locke's essay on education, reason can be an aid to the soul, if only by keeping it from being dominated by the imagination. It is the imagination – dissociated from reason and unenlightened by grace – which haunts the soul with images and hallucinations: false intelligence, as it were, from the past as well as from the present. If imagination is the work of the unconscious, which deceives the believer into confusing the spiritual with the material, the past with the present, then reason enlightened by grace can lift the soul above this miasma, straighten the stooped body, and place the soul in its proper company among the angels: all of these images being those of Dante's work on purgatory.[7] Although reason can enable the soul to sustain its purgatorial endeavors, of course it requires grace to complete them.

The role of reason is to prevent an obsessive alternation between Dante's "whip" and "rein": between the impulse to satisfy the yearnings of the soul and the prohibitions and restraints that a society must inevitably impose on them. The "reality-principle" thus comes to represent a compromise, and social life itself becomes a "compromise-formation": a symptom, in Freudian terminology. For the author of *The Cloud of Unknowing*, the believer – short of a state of grace – lives within the tension of dread over the consciousness of death and the hope inspired by the promise of forgiveness and by the gift of the love of God. Impelled by this tension, as it were, the believer "may safely climb the high peak of perfection": a clear reference, I would argue, to the purgatorial mount.[8] Within this tension one can become obsessive about time, since "the dread of dying" leaves the believer with an intense awareness of "the shortness of time," as contrasted with the abundance of time enjoyed by those who "times without number in the course of a single hour" offer their lives and hopes to God.[9]

There is something both strenuous and modern in this form of self-discipline. Contrast with these purgatorial exertions the way in which souls may be redeemed in "traditional", as compared with "modern," societies; in the former, according to Roy Wagner, the soul is always in danger of being lost and requires being found because it is essentially passive and inert:

Whereas error and excess are expectable tendencies of an individual self, to be "corrected" by discipline and education, the soul, as a comparatively "passive" quality of discernment, can only be "lost." And when the soul is lost, the only recourse is to *restore* it, to "find" it, rather in the way that a perspective or insight is "found," and not to constrain or educate it . . . (Wagner 1981:98)

---

[7] The stooped posture of the sin-burdened soul and the presence of angels are also taken up in sections 61 and 62 of *The Cloud of Unknowing*.

[8] See "The Epistle of Prayer," in Wolters 1980:224ff.   [9] *Ibid.*, pp. 228–229.

However, it still takes time to develop or acquire a soul in modern societies: a long process of growth, training, development, and education; that is why the soul is more likely to be more neurotic than hysterical, since the crisis of its self-possession never arrives. In traditional societies, the soul must indeed be found, when it is lost; hence the possibility of hysteria. In modern societies the purgatorial development of the soul has no clear beginning in rites of penance and no clear end in spiritual exaltation; hence the possibility of neurosis. In a traditional society that confronts the young with the powers and authorities of their elders in critical rites of transition to adulthood, however, hysteria and the potential loss of the soul to these representations are entirely possible. Time runs out on the soul much faster in traditional than in modern societies: hence Wagner's distinction between hysteria and neurosis:

Growing up" or "becoming adult" in this way is a cure or control of hysteria, of one's own deficiencies in the invention of self and world, in the way that our "personality development" (which is individual) is a cure or control of neurosis. "Growing up" may be helped along by confession (the differentiation of self from sin), by more guidance, or by the special magic of moral myths that "compel" and crystallize the innate morality of the listener, but it is useless and pointless unless the individual has already learned invention, the thing it constrains, in the mild hysteria of childhood ... (1981:99)

Thus modernity, I would argue, fails to enable the possession of the soul whether through cultural invention, through the mysteries, in rites of initiation, and with the honors accorded both the living and the dead. Instead, modernity offers only process and development in and through time: a process and a development in which the soul may never be recognized while the self is being acquired. In that process, time is made scarce by organizational pressures and intensified by the secular residues of a purgatorial culture. Those residues leave on the psyche the "taint of time": a neurotic and diffuse consciousness of sin without religious expression or ecclesiastical remedy, made chronic rather than relieved by the combined efforts of a pedagogy that relies on reason and the imagination.

CHAPTER 3

The modern self emerges: Baxter, Locke, and the prospect of heaven

The sense of yearning for God that is a this-worldly form of purgatory is not confined either to mystics or to Catholicism. Indeed, the line of descent, if that is the proper word, runs in the seventeenth century preeminently through the preaching and writing of Richard Baxter. Baxter, like Catherine of Genoa, also knew that the prospect of eternal bliss should be the only preoccupation of Christians, and that such a prospect could not only lift the spirits but intensify a sense of yearning to overcome the time and space that still separate the soul from God. It is worth listening to Baxter's (1909:350ff.) directions to Christians regarding their eternal life.[1] It is a life in which the soul is destined either for bliss or misery, in separation from the body, while both await the general resurrection of the dead at which they receive their final sentencing. First, Christians are to persuade themselves that they understand and believe in the notion of heaven and an eternal rest for the faithful. They should seek confirmation not only from the Scriptures, but from their own needs and from whatever other information they may have about the implications of what Baxter calls a "case" for believing that there is "a rest remaining for the people of God":

Proceed then to consider of the duties which do appear to be such from the doctrine in hand, which is commonly called a use of instruction, as also the reprehension of the contrary vices.

---

[1] It would be unfortunate to write off Baxter only as a figure in seventeenth-century England. We have it from one of his more devoted editors, the Reverend Alexander B. Grosart (1868:18–19), that not only was Baxter translated into several European languages, but he was also widely read in the United States. Grosart cites Cotton

Then proceed to question and try thyself, how thou hast valued this glory of the saints; how thou hast loved it; and how thou hast laid out thyself to obtain it. This is called, a use of examination. Here thou mayest also make use of discovering signs, drawn from the nature, properties, effects, adjuncts, &c.

So far as this trial hath discovered thy neglect, and other sins against this rest, proceed to the reprehension and censuring of thyself. Chide thy heart for its omissions and commissions, and do it sharply till it feel the smart. As Peter preached reproof to his hearers till they were pricked to the heart and cried out, and as a father or master will chide the child till it begin to cry and be sensible of the fault; so do thou in chiding thy own heart. This is called a use of reproof. Here also it will be very necessary that thou bring forth all the aggravating circumstances of the sin, that thy heart may feel it in its weight and bitterness; and if thy heart do evade or deny the sin, convince it by producing the several discoveries . . .

So, *as it respects thy duty for the future*, consider how thou mayest improve this comfortable doctrine, which must be by strong and effectual persuasion with thy heart. First, by way of dehortation from the fore-mentioned sins. Secondly, by way of exhortation to the several duties. And these are either internal, or external. First, therefore, admonish thy heart of its own inward neglects and trespasses in thy practice against this blessed state of rest. Set home these several admonitions to the quick. *Take thy heart as to the brink of the bottomless pit, force it to look in, threaten thyself with the threatenings of the Word; tell it of the torments that it draweth upon itself; tell it what joys it is madly rejecting; force it to promise thee to do so no more, and that not with a cold and heartless promise, but earnestly with most solemn asseverations and engagements.* The next is, to drive on thy soul to those positive duties, which are required of thee in relation to this rest; and to rejoice in the expectation of it . . . (Baxter 1909:352; emphasis added)

Thus the future is now a time of continuing probation; the trial is not over, but is extended into an indefinite future. It is a future defined, in fact, by a promise to continue the process of putting oneself on trial to see whether one has lived in accordance with one's profession of faith in an eternal rest. Dante's whip is used to "drive on" the soul to its duties, just as his rein is employed to pull the soul back from its sins, which otherwise will lead it to the very edge of the bottomless pit. The future,

Mather in this context as knowing of an Indian chief who graced his own death with a copy of Baxter's "Call to the Unconverted."

indeed every moment of every day in the future, is devoted to this continuing trial of the soul poised midway between the torments of the pit and the blessings of heaven and eternal rest.

That trial is lived out from day to day in all of one's relationships but primarily through work. Yet, as John Sommerville (1992) has reminded us, for Richard Baxter work was less of a calling than a possible obstacle to the soul's contemplation of its heavenly reward. Work can indeed be a tiresome preoccupation that distracts the spirit from its destiny; Baxter therefore not only exhorted his hearers to cheerful diligence in God's service while at work but also warned them against becoming immersed in the mundane and bored with God:

Thus he approves of diligence in work, but only so long as one is concentrating on one's attitude. One needs to think about the worker constantly; to think about the work is worldliness. This comes out more clearly when Baxter suggests that one should choose a calling which will not engage the mind, so that one can concentrate on spiritual matters. So by the end of this classic statement of the work ethic he has not progressed beyond his initial comment, which was to "Be very watchful redeemers of your time, and make conscience of every hour and minute." In effect, work is measured not by the powers exercised or the service rendered or the thing produced, but by the diligence shown in the time God has given," (Sommerville 1992:80–81; quoting Richard Baxter, *A Christian Directory*, in Baxter 1854:115, 377)

On the one hand, Christians should avoid becoming so immersed in the means of their existence that they forget their true end, which is to enjoy the rest and reward of the saints in heaven. On the other hand, they should look upon every minute much as the writer of *The Cloud of Unknowing* urged on his or her flock, that is, as a test of the soul's fidelity in the service of God. The mystic's indifference to work is here combined with the ascetic's striving to pass the test of time. One works in spiritual *absentia*, although one lives with intense spiritual concentration.

In the long run, the mystic's indifference to work was rewarded by the society's indifference to religious culture and institutions. On the other hand, the world had become an arena in which the soul could prove itself, and religious faith accordingly made serious business of everyday life. Speaking of the sixteenth century, Sommerville notes, "One did everything religiously, meaning piously, with due regard for the unseen forces that could aid you or trip you up" (Sommerville 1992:187). I would simply add that it was this constant awareness of the presence of unseen forces that made time itself so loaded with significance and fraught with consequence. In the seventeenth century thinkers like Richard Baxter and John Locke continued to speak of the presence of spirits known by their absence and, conversely, of absences felt to be present: a point to which I will shortly return. The present no longer was a vestibule of purgatory, but existence could be said to be purgatorial.

In the seventeenth century, then, and specifically during the English Revolution and its aftermath, a fundamental shift took place in the relation of religion to society. Up to this point, and especially in the work of Richard Baxter, I will argue, we can witness a gradual secularization of the doctrine of purgatory. This life becomes the spiritual arena in which the soul is to be purified and thus made fit not only for heaven but for self-mastery. In its struggle for purity the soul is aided by acts of remembrance. Baxter thus exhorts the faithful not only to remember the unseen yet effective spiritual presence of the saints, but also to remember their own eventual and everlasting rest. The prospect of the latter would sustain them in their struggle to become lords of themselves and in the task of self-purification.

With Locke, however, the forces of purification have turned on religion itself. Religion was to be purified of its excess baggage and relieved of the heavy weight of unnecessary and unreasonable myths and doctrines, practices and punishments. Indeed, as Sommerville puts it, "Protestants believed that the essential features of their religion could not only survive the separation from other aspects of culture but would be purified by the process" (1992:179).

Let us now return to Richard Baxter's insistence on the purgatorial aspects of this life and of the next. Not only was he serious about the meaning and significance of time among the living; he was sure that the dead, just as much as the living, also were subject to the passage of time. Among those whose opinions on this matter he was eager to refute was one Lushington, who had insisted that the dead exist in a deep (and apparently dreamless) sleep and so remain untroubled until the day of Resurrection. Finding neither joy nor sorrow in such a sleep, Baxter could hardly compare it to eternal life; on the contrary, he believed that eternal life brought with it many joys, prior to the day of Resurrection itself. In that eternal life, however, time nonetheless continues to pass: "Doubtless there is time also to the dead, though in respect of their bodies they perceive it not" (*The Saints' Everlasting Rest*; Baxter 1909:186). As time passes, furthermore, the saints will come to the mount of God where they will encounter "the spirits of just men made perfect" (Baxter 1909:185; quoting Heb. xii. 23). In the meantime, the saints await the resurrection of their bodies. Presumably they also must continue in the work of sanctification, since their works follow them beyond the grave (Baxter 1909:184); eventually they, too, are made perfect and come at last to "mount Zion, the city of the living God" (Baxter 1909:185; quoting Heb. xii. 22). In any event, the topography of eternal life is clearly that of purgatory, beyond the bounds of which the outlines of eternity become obscure to Baxter (1909:183), and questions of spiritual place yield to affirmations about the time peculiar to the soul.

As purgatory becomes this-worldly, however, it is the living rather than the dead who have to struggle for eternal joy. Rather than be swayed by moods or depressed by unrealistic expectations of bliss while they are still on earth, Christians are to engage in a process of spiritual testing to determine whether their joys and satisfactions are really from God and can therefore be trusted, or whether they are ephemeral. The constant soul will continually discard mundane pleasures for heavenly joys that will be able to stand the test of time:

But this is the misery of man's nature; though every man naturally abhorreth sorrow, and loves the most merry and joyful life, yet few do love the way to joy, or will endure the pains by which it is to be obtained ... (Baxter 1909:257)

The process of proving, testing, probing, and purging is now the task of the living, so that when they enter into the rest of the saints, they may have the joys that God gives the saints who have indeed persevered.

How is one to decide whether one's joys are from God or from some more mundane source? How does one know which joys one should trust and which ones to discard? Baxter's answer, like Locke's, is "reason":

> If I find a great deal of comfort in my heart, and know not how it came thither, nor upon what rational ground it was raised, nor what considerations do feed and continue it, I should be ready to question how I know whether this be from God ... so I think a Christian's joy should be a grounded rational joy, and not to rejoice and know not why. (Baxter 1909:256)

The same advice applies to sorrows as it does to joys. If many believers see God's "dealings" with them as "grievous," it is because they have lost sight of the end. Had they kept the end in view, they would have known that God was "threshing," "winnowing," and "grinding" them to make them fit to serve at his heavenly table (Baxter 1909:278). Much of Baxter's advice boils down to exhortations to keep the end in view: the end being the believer's exaltation to heaven. No suffering is therefore too great if it leads to a glory commensurate with the saints' reward in heaven. In the meantime, believers must "fall to the work" and undertake "the trouble of duty" (Baxter 1909:274). It is a daily discipline of meditation and contemplation, of study and prayer, through which the soul learns to discard all that does not belong to itself. Through the purification that comes from having one's spiritual chaff blown away, what will be left is the life of the soul that has come to its senses.

It would therefore be a mistake to read Baxter only for his asceticism. In many passages, as we have seen, there are clear traces of what Weber called the mystic's indifference to the mundane. Granted that only a long-term investment of spiritual energy is likely to produce the heavenly reward that Baxter holds out to his hearers. Nonetheless, there are many passages in which he speaks of the foretaste of heavenly joy as though it would melt in the believer's mouth. Monetary gains are also like a mere down payment or "earnest" of our heavenly reward (Baxter 1909:316). As for economic activity, it is sweet only if graced with conversation about heaven with someone whose own conversation is with heaven:

> If thou travel with this man on the way, he will be directing and quickening thee in thy journey to heaven; if thou be buying or selling or trading with him in the world, he will be counseling thee to lay out for the inestimable treasure ... (Baxter 1909:283)

Nonetheless, a worm of doubt eats away at the core of spiritual self-satisfaction. If in purgatory souls wait until they have been purified of inner fears and faithlessness, it is precisely because such doubts about one's state of grace require renunciation or self-mortification. Only after a spiritual struggle and arduous self-improvement can those doubts be replaced by spiritual confidence and joy. Purgatory is thus the symptom of the disease of self-doubt as well as its purported cure.

In the same way, I would argue, Baxter's prescriptions for the soul are similarly both cure and disease. As Baxter reminds his hearers,

> We may confess heaven to be the best condition, though we despair of enjoying it ... but we can never delightfully rejoice in it till we are somewhat persuaded of our title to it ... (1909:305)

Fully to be persuaded of our entitlements, however, we must work as hard as if our life, our eternal life, depended on our exertions. Those who are not fully engaged each day in the contemplation of their heavenly reward may lose that reward to which they would otherwise have been entitled had they not forfeited it by premature spiritual overconfidence or slackness in the soul. It does not take a psychoanalyst to discern here a "Catch-22": a dilemma from which there is no exit. Certainty of heaven is necessary if one is to have joy at the prospect, but only doubt can drive the soul hard enough to get there.

It is the combination of mystical and ascetic strivings that adds up to this vicious circle. On the one hand, the mystic is capable of seeing through the fog and the mist of everyday life to what lies beyond. That vision fills the mystic's soul with foretastes of peace as well as with the foreknowledge of a heavenly rest and reward. Those foretastes of heaven make this life lose some of its savor and enable the mystic to keep at a safe spiritual distance from its temptations and insults. On the other hand, the ascetic Christian values every temptation not simply because it points to a higher satisfaction in heaven, but because it offers a test of the believer's capacity to endure even the sufferings of Christ, which were a necessary prelude to the Resurrection. In temptation and in suffering the ascetic Christian therefore finds grist for the spiritual mills which winnow the soul, purifying it of its chaff and leaving only the solid core.[2] For the individual's soul to be thus purified is quite literally to be restored to one's true self.

That is indeed the core problem: to enable the soul to be sure of its own being. The sense of a heavenly entitlement, while being offered here as a form of spiritual reassurance, thus requires continuous and rigorous testing lest the individual lose that confidence and settle for something less than a heavenly reward. Souls that do so are like empty tombs from which the life is departed. On the other hand, the ascetic must take the challenges and opportunities of this world with utmost seriousness, since they provide the indispensable means of testing the soul's fortitude and direction. The entitlements claimed by the mystic lead only to a precarious confidence; the soul's certainty must therefore be achieved through spiritual combat with the spirit's own tendency to sadness and despair.

Why, then, does the spiritual cure, which is to find in everyday life a foretaste of heaven, intensify the disease of spiritual uncertainty? The answer comes in Baxter's insistence on reenchanting the world of everyday life. The business of raising a family, of spending and saving, of investing and profiting, of learning new knowledge and discarding old truths, cannot be entered into on its own terms. There is more to such activity than meets the secular eye. To the eye of the

---

[2] It is interesting to note that mystery religions' "secret" was simply a bit of grain: a purely mundane object that to the unbeliever contained no mystery at all, but to the believer signified the soul contained in its earthly husk; cf. Burkert 1983.

believer, this world is reenchanted by the heavenly vision. It is as if an imprint of that vision were left on the believer's retina and becomes superimposed on the scenes of everyday life. These scenes in turn point beyond themselves to a heavenly rest and an eternal kingdom; they can never be what Dickens called the "eternal foreground": a view of the world that never sees beyond the immediate horizon. *If the Puritans thus disenchanted the spiritual world of the medieval church, divines like Baxter reenchanted this world with the residues of heaven.*

In the Reformation the West gained its own distinctive approach to time. On the one hand, God is known only when the divine presence can be acknowledged in and through its absence. There is a "desacralizing" thrust to Christianity, and particularly to Protestantism, that insists on the knowledge of God in and through an awareness of God's absence. As Charles Taylor reminds us, the peculiar asceticism of the Puritan called for the individual to be "dead" to the world or at least to use it without loving it. The reason was that only this sort of disenchantment could turn work, consumption, or marital affection into a conduit for the individual's love of God. Thus if one's heart is properly "set" on God, it cannot be set on the things of this world. God was to be known *in absentia*.

However, along with the desacralizing of love and work came the sacralization of everyday life. If certain forms of time and space had become disenchanted, so that one could no longer so easily honour God on certain days or in particular places, everyday life itself had become enchanted or hallowed:

The crucial potentiality here was that of conceiving the hallowing of life not as something which takes place only at the limits, as it were, but as a change which can penetrate the full extent of mundane life. Perhaps the first important realization of this potentiality in the broader tradition was in Rabbinic Judaism, at the very beginning of the present era, in the Pharasaic idea of a way of living the law which thoroughly permeated the details of everyday life. But the Protestant Reformation brought about an extension of this form of spirituality which was unprecedented in Christendom ... (Taylor 1989:221)

Thus in every activity of everyday life one was to see an opportunity to know God even in the absence of the deity. This meant that one could love one's spouse all the more as a way of receiving and responding to the love of God manifested in the creation. Through work one could continue that creation, preserve it, and even add to its blessings, only so long as one was aware that in its workings one could discern the purposes of God and in its design perceive the divine mind. By going back to the basics of everyday life and taking a disciplined approach to experience and work, one could also take a properly detached and experimental scientific approach to the workings of nature and the universe (Taylor 1989:230ff.). In such a world one could discern the presence of a God worshiped *in absentia*.

The experience of time under these conditions is very likely to be "serious." That is, everyday life is itself to be lived as though in the sight of – and for the sake of – a God who is distantly affectionate and easily horrified. The distance provides a reminder of God's absence even in a world in which God is reputed to be present. Conversely, the affection of God for the creation, both in its making and in its preservation, calls for an awareness of God even as one goes about continuing and remaking the world in activities so mundane as to seem beneath the interest or dignity of an exalted God. If God is easily horrified, it is because there is so little order and discipline in a world left to its own devices. God is horrified at a society that is disorderly, at classes that are self-indulgent or undisciplined, and individuals who are intemperate (Taylor 1989:229). As the Anglican Book of Common Prayer used to put it, "inordinate desires" and "sinful affections" could only ensue from those who, unmindful of the presence of God in the creation, were led entirely by the "devices and desires" of their own hearts. It is no wonder, then, that Christians were exhorted to be conscientious and disciplined, frugal and productive, not only in the minutiae of everyday life but down to every minute of every hour. Time had become serious business indeed.

On the one hand, individuals are to cultivate a sense of the absence of God in times and places where they used to be on more familiar terms with the deity. On the other hand, they are never to forget the presence of God even *in absentia* throughout all the nooks and crannies of creation and indeed at every moment of the day. Such a theological recipe could only issue in a certain amount of spiritual torment. Tempted to enjoy the freedom of the creature and especially of the Christian according to the terms of the new ethic, one would be liable to censure for having neglected the requirements of the old ethic or for failing to give proper honor and glory to God. Unduly absorbed in worship in order to give the deity proper recognition, however, one might find oneself censured for having neglected one's duties in the world.

Certainly such a theological climate would make it difficult for individuals to be sure of themselves. To submit to such directives individuals would have to be willing to become increasingly scrupulous in their self-understanding and critical of any inner tendency to love the world for its own sake or, worse yet, for their own ends. They would also have to be rigorous in examining themselves to see whether they had been sufficiently disciplined in their work and study, not for their own advancement, but for the advancement of the sort of piety and learning that would give honor to God.

Out of the tension between spiritual presence and absence has emerged what Charles Taylor (1989) has called a "radically reflexive" self. It is profoundly disengaged not only from the authority of the past but from immediate experience. Like Freud's ego, it keeps an eye on what is coming from the superego and the id, from received authority and from powerful impulse. This self also resembles Max Weber's portrait of the ascetic Protestant who could be relied upon to pay his debts on time, and whose life-time was a sphere of responsible moral development and action.

More than David Riesman's study of the inner-directed American, Taylor's "radically reflexive" self is characterized by a problematical relation to time. In his discussion of Locke, for instance, Taylor (1989:159–184) refers to the development of what he calls "the punctual self." It is a self charged with the responsibility for its own making and remaking; "rather than following the telos of nature, we become constructors of our own character" (Taylor 1989:197).

For Taylor, the origins of this self are to be found in Augustine, whose commitment to inwardness, and to taking responsibility for the self underlie the moral seriousness of the modern project of self-construction. In modernity, however, there was a radical disengagement of the self from its social and natural surroundings. There was no model either in the cosmos or in nature to which the self could adhere. The world was disenchanted, in the sense of offering no clues to our selfhood. For Taylor the radical point of departure from the enchanted universes of the past is to be found in Descartes.

However, in this work I have suggested rather that the modern self began to emerge in the medieval notion of purgatory. There the task of making the most of one's time in order to remake the self achieved not only official but popular support on a previously unprecedented scale. To be sure, the modern self could fully develop only if a radical disengagement took place between the self and the world. Had individuals not acquired, thanks to the Reformation and Descartes, a world of their own, they would not have been able to pursue the task of self-reformation; their lives would have been at best reproductions or instances of models and forms to be found elsewhere, if not in nature, then in the cosmos or the mind of God.

I am arguing, however, that the impulse to self-reformation already appears in the widespread belief in purgatory. There the individual quite literally has time in which to reform the self, albeit still within the confines of a world in which the individual can only be Lord of itself who properly acknowledges and adores the Lord of the universe. Nonetheless, the impulse to self-reformation takes on a very broad social base, outside the monastery, in the piety and sacrifices of a wide range of individuals and groups bent on improving their chances for moral and social credit in this life and the next.

As I have noted, the medieval social universe was thus "coeval," in the sense that the living and the dead were present to one another even in everyday experience. Even as late as 1600, notes John Sommerville, the social universe was partly spiritual, partly material; there was an interpenetration of presences, so that things were personal or spiritual, and spirits could take on quite individual or material form. Indeed,

Sommerville (1992:153–157) points out that a belief in spirits was relatively widespread not only among the less educated but among the higher intellectual classes. Not only the ecclesiastical defenders of the soul but also Cambridge philosophers attempted "to prove the existence of a spirit world by the evidence of apparitions and witches" (Sommerville 1992:153). Not only were alchemists still seeking ways to purify the soul, as if purgatory and better living could be achieved through chemistry (cf. Sommerville 1992:153); even such notable scientists as William Harvey and John Ray maintained the notion that spirits were present within and under the outward and visible forms of the human body (Sommerville 1992:156). It is therefore no wonder that Locke himself was still very much within the thought-world that understood and embraced notions of a purgatory of the soul in this life and not only in the next. As Sommerville puts it:

Locke's secularity has often been exaggerated. It has been shown that his view of economic relations explicitly involves God, as first maker and possessor. And he did not think that society could be bound together without considering obligations to the creator, as well as to one's fellows. Scholars were embarrassed by Locke's statements on the political untrustworthiness of atheists, until they recognized that this was consistent with the rest of his views ... his proposals on toleration would have excluded David Hume, for example ... (Sommerville 1992:151)

It is one thing to deny the existence of the supernatural. It is quite another to argue that the mind should find relief from the fear of the presence of spirits and apparitions. In Locke's generation many still believed in the need for blessings and curses, charms and a variety of magic, since "Minds, spirits, appearances, objects, all mingled with one another in ways that some well-educated contemporaries termed 'superstitious'" (Sommerville 1992:78; quoting Cook 1986:31ff.). The remedies of the educated may have been more "rational," but they were still antidotes. Reason may well have been a reaction-formation, in the formal, psychoanalytic sense of the term, to a wide range of spiritual excesses and distortions of the soul.

Certainly Locke's appeals to reasonableness are based in

part on the need to forget goblins and ghosts, superstitions and other religious burdens on the soul. Locke wanted to train the memory so that it would have relatively few obligations, burdens, and terrors. His essay on education urged parents to avoid imposing tasks on children unsuitable for their age or constitution. It was unnecessary to memorize trivia in school or long passages of Greek and Latin; heroes were made of stronger impulse and more spontaneous affection than was compatible with schoolboy recitations. Parents were instructed to avoid beating their children wherever possible, to use reasoning in the course of administering corporal punishment, and to delegate such tasks to servants so that children would not become averse to their own parents' presence and ideas. The memory of pain is long, although the good it does is short-lived. In the same way childhood traumas can persist into adulthood, with the result that many adults still are unnecessarily cautious, watchful, and timorous. The memory can burden or crush the soul, and the act of remembering is therefore critical for what may be jettisoned from the self as well as for what is retained.

Remembering is therefore not only a cause of the discontents that come with civilization; under the auspices of reason memory can become the cure. Locke insisted that the mind creates a succession of ideas: a succession in which one idea leads to or follows another. In this succession there is the possibility not only for madness but for progress. The unnecessary or unrealistic association of ideas with each other is responsible, Locke argues, not only for imagination but for a sort of madness, in which individuals not only invent their worlds but seek to impose them on others. There is much that would be better ignored or even forgotten, at least in the formative years of childhood, and in adulthood much that is better left to the discretion of the adult rather than made obligatory.

Locke's tendency to focus on the succession of ideas, to let outmoded or secondary concerns go while taking on the new, informs his long essay on *The Reasonableness of Christianity* and his exegesis of certain epistles. A lengthy discussion is out of the question here, but it is important to note the selective and liberating intention in Locke's approach to Scripture:

Thus we see our Saviour not only confirmed the moral law, and, clearing it from the corrupt glosses of the Scribes and Pharisees, showed the strictness as well as obligation of its injunctions; but moreover, upon occasion, requires the obedience of his disciples to several of the commands he afresh lays upon them; with the enforcement of unspeakable rewards and punishments in another world, according to their obedience or disobedience. There is not, I think, any of the duties of morality, which he has not, somewhere or other, by himself and his apostles, inculcated over and over again to his followers in express terms. And is it for nothing that he is so instant with them to bring forth fruit? Does he, their King, command, and is it an indifferent thing? Or will their happiness or misery not at all depend on it, whether they obey or no? They were required to believe him to be the Messiah; which faith is of grace promised to be reckoned to them, for the completing of their righteousness, wherein it was defective: but righteousness, or obedience to the law of God, was their great business, which if they could have attained by their own performances, there would have been no need of this gracious allowance, in reward of their faith; but eternal life, after the resurrection, had been their due by a former covenant, even that of works; the rule whereof was never abolished, though the rigor was abated. The duties enjoined in it were duties still. Their obligations had never ceased, nor a wilful neglect of them was ever dispensed with. But their past transgressions were pardoned, to those who received Jesus, the promised Messiah, for their kin; and their future slips covered, if, renouncing their former iniquities, they entered into his kingdom, and continued his subjects with a steady resolution and endeavor to obey his laws. This righteousness, therefore, a complete obedience and freedom from sin, are still sincerely to be endeavored after. And it is nowhere promised, that those who persist in a wilful disobedience to his laws, shall be received into the eternal bliss of his kingdom, how much soever they believe in him ... (Locke 1963: vol. VII, pp. 122–123)

The structure of purgatory remains intact in this passage; its location has shifted clearly to this world. All the old burdens of the law remain intact; only the "glosses of the Scribes and Pharisees" have been removed. The joys of heaven still await the faithful, and for the transgressors there remain still the pains of hell. Instead of indulgences for those who died before their penances were complete, however, we have "this gracious allowance," the forgiveness of sins and release from the burdens of *past* debt and obligation. One thing alone is required as a pre-

requisite for receiving the new dispensation, that is, the confession of faith.

Indeed, for the better part of his essay on *The Reasonableness
of Christianity*, Locke made it clear that the point of entry into
the new dispensation was the confession of faith that Jesus
alone is the Messiah (Son of God, Anointed One, etc.). As we
shall see, in the early nineteenth century the admirers of Locke
took this reasonable form of Christianity into the American
wilderness; there individuals were all too burdened by obligations that they could not sustain, and there they also faced
overwhelming spiritual challenges. The people of the frontier
required a very potent Friend indeed. With such a Friend,
however, the newly converted also undertook the second half of
the Lockean bargain; the graceful allowance of the new dispensation initiated them into a lifetime of continuing penitence
from which death alone would provide a final release.

As Locke made clear to one of his detractors, nowhere did
he consider this confession of faith a magic charm or a substitute for every other Christian belief or practice. It was,
however, a *sine qua non*. Without it there would be no release
from the perpetual burden of sin, penance, failure, and the
need for punishment or purgation. With it, the Christian who
remained steadfast could hope to continue in the favor of the
king whose overlordship he had embraced and whose protection from the consequences of sin he had thus received.

Of course there are various levels at which one can read this
text. The most obvious is as a relic of the feudal social contract,
in which vassals receive protection from their lord in return for
confessions of loyalty and fealty. In the more immediate
context it is well to remember that Locke himself was part of
that same order still; he, too, could have received pardon from
a Stuart king in return for a confession of faith and loyalty,
although he reserved his confession until the advent of a new
king who would provide a new dispensation and exemptions
for his subjects without sacrificing the moral code or lessening
its sanctions.

The point here, however, is not the ideological function of
such a passage or Locke's "elective affinity," as Weber might

put it, for such a feudal viewpoint. It is that Locke himself is demonstrating precisely what he is discussing. That is, Locke is bringing forward an old code under the aegis of a new dispensation. The old code is clearly purgatorial: pains and penalties that must be incurred for the soul who is to avoid hell and yet hold on to the hope of heaven. The new dispensation, however, is this-worldly. It is a new constitution, in which reason establishes the order and sets the limits of Christian as well as secular obligation.[3]

Locke does not hesitate to interpret the entire New Testament in terms of a this-worldly purgatory. Those who deny Christ rather than themselves will lose their souls (Locke 1963: vol. VII, pp. 116–117). The fate of the soul continues to hang in the balance in every moment, and every moment in turn is a test of the individual's willingness to confess Jesus as the Messiah. Thus the young man who is told to sell all that he has to the poor and to follow Jesus is being given a test of loyalty to Jesus as the Messiah; the stakes are still eternal life in the new dispensation, but the test is in this world (Locke 1963: vol. VII, p. 120).

The asceticism of self-denial is still, even for Locke, a practice that exhibits and shapes the soul, just as asceticism tests and determines the soul's progress toward a future state of blessedness. Nonetheless, although the soul gained a new friend in Jesus, the soul also was befriended in the new, Lockean dispensation by reason itself. It is reasonable to reduce as many beliefs and practices as possible to facts. Reason also allows the believer to reduce the weight of uncertainty concerning the fate of the soul by an act of remembering the terms of the new Christian order: its confession of Messianic faith. Through reason the believer is able to distinguish between ideas that

---

[3] There is no doubt that Locke is seeking to clear the Christian memory of encumbrances and to focus the act of faith in terms that are clear, simple, and consistent. His detractor, Mr. Edwards, complained that Locke had ignored a number of doctrines, articles of faith, and creedal affirmations (e.g. original sin, Atonement, the Trinity, etc.), to which Locke replied that he had intended to speak of "... those doctrines of faith ... which are only such as are required to be actually believed to make a man Christian" ("A Vindication of the Reasonableness of Christianity, &c"; Locke 1963: vol. VII, pp. 168–169).

came before and those that came after: to recognize the succession of ideas and therefore to allow one idea to succeed – to supersede – another. Otherwise the religious imagination, like the imagination itself, can become overburdened and confused with the welter of ideas, facts, injunctions, and obligations. In explaining why he did not discuss the epistles in more detail in his essay on *The Reasonableness of Christianity*, Locke explains that "the necessary articles of faith are, in the epistles, promiscuously delivered with other truths, and, therefore, they cannot be distinguished but by some other mark, than being barely found in the epistles" (Locke 1963: vol. VII, pp. 168–169).

Thus the social order itself became infused with a spiritual significance as the proving ground of the soul. Not merely Protestants but Catholics felt obligated to support their civic claims with spiritual *bona fides*. Sommerville notes, for instance, that

James II was England's first born-again king; he sounded the new note in his self-reproach, seeing the Revolution as God's act 'to "scourge him, and humble him ... in order to save his soul ..."' (1992:166; quoting J. R. Jones, *The Revolution of 1688 in England* [New York, 1972], 76)

What Sommerville (1992:166) goes on to call "God's character-building project" extended not only to the king but to the people. If the king were the exemplary soul in the process of being scourged for the sake of better things, the average individual was representative of God's intent to purify a people soul by soul, individual by individual. What was happening at the confessional center, in James II's public reference to his spiritual scourging, was mirrored even in the early English novel's depiction of "humble lives" at the periphery (Sommerville 1992:166).

There is a spiritual symmetry here, which we will meet once again when we discuss some aspects of the legacy of Locke on American soil. There we will find William Ellery Channing pronouncing from his New England pulpit on the need for continual self-purification on the way to a heavenly reward while exhorting those on the periphery to mind their self-culture. The exemplary soul at the center found its mirror in the representative individual, even if that individual were from the poorest of the Boston poor or struggling for spiritual survival on the American frontier.

This process of mirroring the soul's scourging and purification on its way toward better things does not happen, as it were, by magic. The alchemy is accomplished through what sociologists sometimes call "mediating institutions." It would be a mistake, for instance, to underestimate the influence of preaching in creating at least the facsimile of a coeval society in which individuals of previous generations are present among the living in a lively spiritual communion (cf. Sommerville 1992:167). More important, I would argue, were organizations such as the Society for the Propagation of the Gospel in Foreign Parts or the Society for Promoting Christian Knowledge. Sommerville notes that there were approximately twenty similar societies in London alone by the beginning of the eighteenth century. Their mission was to reform the manners of the people: to purify them from the various practices that can assault and afflict the soul. They therefore concentrated not only on gambling and drunkenness but also on profanity, blasphemy, and the observation of the Sabbath. In this they had the full, if private support of the monarchy, as well as the cooperation of Christian congregations. The exemplary and the representative met each other on a field of common spiritual struggle. The faith they professed was reasonable enough by Lockean standards, and the virtues they demanded were no more than what one would expect from the resulting commitment to a lifetime of obedience.

This pattern was to shape the polity of the newly federated American states. There the state was to be hospitable to religion without either inhibiting or establishing it. In return the citizens were to take their part in learning sobriety, becoming literate, and paying their taxes. The mediating institutions went by different names, such as the American Temperance Union or the American Sunday School Union, but there was no doubt that the center and the periphery were to be joined in the same combat against the forces of spiritual wickedness. The connection with England was still quite visible in the new American states during the first half of the nineteenth century. Indeed, as I have already suggested, Locke influenced the pursuit of spiritual purity under the auspices of a reasonable Christianity both in the cultural center of the American states and in the frontier states of Ohio, Kentucky, and Tennessee.

Purgatory was part of the very enchanted universe from which modernity is supposed to have emerged. The dead were still part of the moral and spiritual universe of the living; indeed the living could engage in spiritual transactions on behalf of the dead to the great advantage of the departed. Not only sacramental ties linked the living to the dead; both inhabited the same time-zone, as it were. Clocks were running in both this world and the next, and the days of the week unfolded in precisely the same order. The dead were thus a real presence among the living, just as the living were still able to act instrumentally on behalf of the dead.

Is it paradoxical that the task of remaking the self, as a moral project over one's lifetime, thus took hold in so enchanted a social universe? On the contrary, I have suggested that it is the presence of unseen and yet significant others that makes the task of self-construction so urgent. Indeed, sociologists have long argued that the presence of a "generalized other" was conducive to the moral development of the self in Western society: an other that was more than the sum total of an individual's actual encounters with other persons in a complex society. Their presences, whether mediated by education or entertainment, by politicians or religious leaders, impinged on the individual in a variety of contexts. The self was made and remade in a continuing process of social interaction with invisible others. Whether in defending the self against these presences, adapting to them, or identifying with them and thus depriving them of their "otherness," the modern self has had ample reason to feel uneasy in the presence of these invisible others. Indeed, it has been in their absence that the American self has seemed to be empty and deflated.

CHAPTER 4

Locke, reason, and the soul

That duties have multiplied in modernity seems to be out of the question. Scholars since Weber have agreed that the development of bureaucracies in the military, in government, in education, and in the private sphere have exacted a toll on the individual. As Taylor puts it:

The tremendous strength of Locke's punctual self through the Enlightenment and beyond comes also from the central place of the disengaged, disciplinary stance to the self in our culture . . [i.e. from] the rise of disciplinary practices over a wide range in this period in the military, hospitals, and schools as well as the related practices of bureaucratic control and organization . . . (1989:173)

In other words, the social fabric was already filled with various command structures that required the development of an ascetic social character that would take responsibility for its acts. In the interest of increasing productivity and rationalizing agricultural labor, for instance, Queen Elizabeth issued a decree in 1559 that made it obligatory to work on saints' days. The queen makes it clear that her concern is with conscientious labor and sought to relieve the consciences of those who would have felt it impious to work on days that had previously been holy. Indeed she instructed the clergy to reprove people if, for reasons of conscience, they should still seek to keep those days holy by avoiding labor (Sommerville 1992:78). The monarch could therefore exercise control over labor discipline even in her absence: her presence being felt not only by intermediaries such as the clergy but by her control of time and the calendar itself. The movements of conscience would henceforth reflect her presence, even in her absence, as individuals were ordered to transfer their conscientiousness about holy days to their diligence in work. Time was still the arena in which social forces contended for domination of the soul.

Modern structures, like the trains, do indeed run on time, and thus they require a self that takes time seriously. These command structures must operate, in fact, when the authorities are not looking. One must therefore work to please God rather than to curry favor. Thus Baxter went on to drive home the point about presences who are effective even in their absence by demanding that individuals be conscientious with regard to their attitudes toward work at all times; as Sommerville points out,

> work is measured not by the powers exercised or the service rendered or the thing produced, but by the diligence shown in the time God has given ... (1992:80–81)

I will turn later in this study to the emergence of clocks and watches as emblems of the responsible self in American society during the nineteenth century, but clearly time was central to the structures of Western society long before.

As Taylor notes, "Locke's person is the moral agent who takes responsibility for his acts *in the light of future retribution* (Taylor 1989:173; emphasis added). That retribution would not come from earthly masters alone. Granted that officers and law-makers would catch up with and punish offenders; the latter should rightly anticipate such an outcome and thus take responsibility for controlling their own "animal spirits."

In the end, Locke believed, individuals must face their eternal rewards and punishments in the life that comes after death. There the soul meets its true reward or its eternal punishment at the hands of a very just God indeed. In his essay on Locke, Yolton thus concludes that "the backdrop for Locke's discussion of punishment in the state of nature is this eschatological doctrine" (Yolton 1993:196). That is precisely the point. The responsible self lives in a present that is already in the shadow of the future. The ascetic social character takes self-discipline to heart and can reasonably anticipate the consequence of wrong-doing: disciplinary proceedings from his or her superiors in any of the command structures that have developed in Western society. The "radically reflexive" self, however, is quite opposed to taking orders from any custom or authority without first weighing those commands in the balance of the individual's own judgment.

Left to his or her own devices and desires, the individual has to take into account only the impending judgment of God. That judgment, eschatological though it is, casts its shadow from the future to the present and weighs more or less heavily on the Lockean soul. For all that Locke seeks to dispense with traditional concepts and innate ideas so that the self can make up its own mind in its own time, still the soul, to which Locke also continues to refer, has to anticipate in the present the future judgment of God. It is as if, having cut its ties with the past, the new "punctual self" has to keep a fateful appointment in the future before a divine tribunal.

To read Locke on the self without discussing Locke on the soul or on spirits is therefore like performing a lobotomy on the modern mind. Locke continued to believe in "finite spirits or spiritual beings other than humans"; why not extend the "chain of being" from the visible and the living to the invisible and the beyond (Yolton 1993:274)? He even believed that invisible spirits could give humans their ideas and shape their perceptions. Indeed, it seemed perfectly logical to Locke that there were spirits or beings higher than he in the scale of knowledge and perfection: intermediary somewhere between the divine and the human, like "the spirit of just men made perfect" (*Essay on Human Understanding*, 4.17.14, quoted in Yolton 1993:275). These spirits could and did operate wherever they wanted to; wherever they operated, there they were, so to speak, in person. Indeed, they could be in several places at one and at the same time:

Locke says that "finite Spirits do operate at several times in several places", so they must be able to change, as well as be located at, specific places (2.23.19). He includes humans in this remark: "For my Soul being a real Being, as well as my Body, is certainly as capable of changing distance with any other Body, or Being, as Body itself; and so is capable of motion" (Yolton 1993:275, quoting Locke's *Essay on Human Understanding*)

The secularization of the notion of purgatory clearly has left the mental universe of Locke inhabited with a number of spirits and beings whose presence among the living could still impinge on their thoughts and perceptions. I doubt that he was alone. As we have already noted, well into the sixteenth century workers in various guilds had continued to pray for the souls of deceased members, or else they arranged for monasteries or recipients of their charities to perform that service for them (Sommerville 1992:77). The intermingling of the spirits of the dead with those of the living through the agency of intercessory prayer could hardly have seemed strange to Locke, therefore, who was steeped within an Anglican tradition however much he had earlier been influenced by Presbyterians and Independents.

The individual's own experience, therefore, might in fact be the result of suggestions emanating from another spirit. For instance, Locke

also suggests that spirits "may excite ... *Ideas* in me, and lay them in such order before my mind, that I may perceive their Connexion" (4.19.10) ... (Yolton 1993:275, quoting Locke's *Essay on Human Understanding*)

If Locke believed that he could be having the thoughts and memories (*Ideas*) of someone other than himself, I would argue, that alone would be a sufficient spur to the radical sort of reflection on experience that Locke required of himself and recommended to others. Otherwise one might not know whether one's experience, perceptions and thoughts are truly one's own or are, instead, quite alien. The antidote to being the recipient of alien ideas is, of course, to alienate oneself from one's own immediate experience. One then becomes the alien in a position to examine one's own experiences and thoughts as if they could just as well have been those of another.

The enemy of the self here is a sort of possession or enchantment. Locke is indeed acting as an agent of the process that Weber has so aptly termed the "disenchantment" of the West. His "radical reflexivity" was, I would argue, a determined attempt to distance himself from experience that may have been inspired by invisible others, "spirits" or souls who could move beyond the ordinary limitations of time and space. Taylor suggests that a sort of disenchantment is indeed in progress, but he does not go on to explore its spiritual dimensions:

The point of the whole operation is to gain a kind of control. Instead of being swept along to error by the ordinary bent of our experience, we stand back from it, withdraw from it, reconstrue it objectively, and then learn to draw defensible conclusions from it. To wrest control from "our appetites and our preceptors," we have to practice a kind of radical reflexivity. We fix experience in order to deprive it of its power, a source of bewitchment and error ... (Taylor 1989:163; quoting Descartes's *Discours de la méthode*)

For Locke, simply having an idea of other finite spirits was enough to warrant a claim for their existence (Yolton 1993:190). Such powerful presences require a controlling presence of one's own.

Now there is a rather dismal paradox here. The measures that Locke prescribes for exercising control over what may be alien sources of perception and experience are intended to reassure the self of its own being and to give it control over what it takes to be knowledge. The more that the "radically reflexive" self puts its experience to the test of reflection, however, the more difficult it is to gain the required certainty of one's own being. This is what Taylor implies by "radical reflexivity": "The turn to oneself is now also and inescapably a turn to oneself in the first-person perspective – a turn to the self as a self" (1989:176). There is no external ground for the self that disengages itself from its own experience; "The punctual agent seems to be nothing else but a 'self,' an 'I'" (Taylor 1989:175). That is what it means to be made in the image of the God whose name is "I am": no more, and no less.

For Locke, spirits could still be in more than one place at the same time, and indeed be in several different time-zones at once, so to speak. So could the self transcend the apparent boundaries of time and space. The self, "as far as the same consciousness can extend to actions past and to come," is the same self (Locke, *Essay on Human Understanding* 2.27.10: quoted in Taylor 1989:172). The self can indeed repeat in the present what it was thinking or perceiving in the past. Memory therefore guarantees to the self a knowledge of its own being. The same warrant applies to claims that the self makes for its presence in the future, inasmuch as it can contemplate a future present. Self-consciousness in the present is thus a sign of the continuity of the self both in the past and the future.

This modern self emerges directly from what I have been calling the secularization of purgatory. For Locke, the goal of education is a purification of the self from pride, laziness, and a desire for mastery over others.[1] In his view, it is no longer only the hope of heaven and the fear of hell but education itself that will transform the affections that "arise only from the lower parts of the soul" into self-mastery and useful pursuits rather than to crude pleasures or the domination of others (Tarcov 1989:90). *Whereas Dante used the image of the "whip" and of "rein" to describe the incentives to spiritual progress in purgatory by which the penitent would eventually becomes lords of themselves, Locke uses the image of "the Spur and Reins" to describe the various forms of reward and punishment conducive to developing individuals who, no longer seeking mastery over others, are masters of themselves.*

It seems clear that, for Locke, the hope of heaven is merely a religious analogue to children's awe and reverence for their parents, just as a fear of hell is the religious analogue to the child's dread of receiving a beating. These early motivations to virtue must soon yield a concern for the good opinion of others: the love of Reputation and its rewards (Tarcov 1989:96). These rewards, of course, are supposed to be side-effects or indirect consequences of others' esteem, and they should be conducive to industry rather than to pride. Only thus will the individual arise who can be master of himself or herself: one whose reason alone is sufficient as a guide to political discourse and civility. As the self is purged from vicious motives, bad habits, self-serving motives, and a fear of punishment, an adult will emerge who is concerned with maintaining the good opinion of others and the love of his family.

---

[1] In this and the following paragraph I am heavily indebted to the discussion by Tarcov (1989:87–107).

Like Baxter, who was concerned that individuals should not forget their true reward in heaven, the saints' everlasting rest, Locke is concerned lest reason forget future pleasures and pains and be caught up in a short-sighted calculus of merely present rewards and punishments. Just as Baxter was concerned with keeping up the believer's enthusiasm for heavenly rewards, Locke wishes to maintain the individual's Spirit: "a sort of confidence or expectation that one can fulfill one's desires, though not an imperious demand that others shall fulfill them" (Tarcov 1989:98). The best way to sustain the individual's "Spirit," furthermore, was to follow the dictates of Reason. That is because Reason itself is the best guide to the place where true rewards and satisfactions are to be found. It is "the Light God has given him," and in following the light of "reason" individuals will be led to discovering what really constitutes virtue, duty, and satisfaction (Tarcov 1989:106; quoting Locke, *Some Thoughts Concerning Education*, sec. 61). Even though the concept of reward and punishment, virtue and satisfaction has been generalized to include the results of pedagogy and public opinion, Locke still directs Reason to heavenly "Hopes of Acceptation and Reward" (Tarcov 1989:106; quoting Locke, *Some Thoughts Concerning Education*, sec. 61).[2]

For Locke, "Reason" was therefore a spiritual guide, a sort of Virgil who could set one's foot on the path that goes from the lower reaches of the soul to the higher levels from which the soul can best perceive its true satisfactions. Thus guided by Reason, the individual may indeed desire a future consisting of "the spiritual pleasures and pains promised by Christian revelation," but the individual may also be oriented toward other more worldly satisfactions (Tarcov 1989:98–99). Only

---

[2] Tarcov argues at various places that Locke was seeking for other supports for virtue than Christian hope alone could provide, perhaps because Locke was not an ascetic or dominated by a religious imagination. On the other hand, as Tarcov duly notes, Locke distinguishes between reputation and true principle: a distinction that adults rather than children are likely to make in the light of a mature reason. In a discussion that seems rather to twist and turn at this point, Tarcov nonetheless acknowledges that, for Locke, "reason finds the obligation or morality to lie in the prospect of divine reward and punishment" (1989:106).

thus will the individual guided by Reason avoid "luxury, pride, and covetousness" (Tarcov 1989:99).

Not only is it therefore unreasonable to waste time. Time itself becomes a yardstick of the soul. For Locke, as I have noted, the individual who cannot substitute distant rewards for present satisfactions is in danger of yielding to the affections in the lower reaches of the soul. It is not only the future, however, but the past that is crucial for the health of the soul. The early fears and joys of childhood, the beatings and the affectionate rewards for good behavior, are forgotten but not gone. They have become part of the fabric of the soul that is in adulthood hungry not for sweets but for the good esteem of others who may be quite unknown: the "generalized other" to which American social psychology more recently has ascribed good behavior. Those who, like Tocqueville and his followers, think of American individualism as decaying into a sort of mass conformity, have been mistaken. It is conformity which is the natural result of an emphasis on individual liberty framed by concern for the good opinion of others:

the operation of the desire for esteem also necessarily entails the additional action of the spur of "Pleasure in what they have begun by their own desire ..." For to act from a concern for reputation is, according to Locke, to act freely and from something within ... even if the particular objects that bring reputation have been carefully selected by others. In this way the reliance on esteem and the reliance on liberty are complementary parts of one and the same policy ... (Tarcov 1989:116; quoting Locke, *Some Thoughts Concerning Education*, sec. 76)

Note that the policy of raising children is part and parcel of a policy for raising up a citizenry that can be counted on to do the right thing even when no one is watching. These citizens will be convinced that they are acting from their own inner spiritual impulses when in fact they are acting out the long forgotten requirements of parents and other influential adults who once made it clear to them that love and approval are won by good behavior. This is the same Locke whose instructions on liberty influenced the writers of the Declaration of Independence and the framers of the American Constitution.

If therefore freedom of religion, for instance, were desirable, it would be only in part because it was demanded by the people. The same freedom could also turn the people's desire for recognition and esteem into civility. To "turn" the child was indeed one of Locke's major emphases, and it was a strategy that required mixing punishment or its threat with medicinal doses of affection and the promise of reward. In the end, Locke was sure, the adult would forget the childhood origins of the impulse to please and think of it as an expression of his or her own spiritual freedom.

What begins in childhood and becomes habitual is therefore a continuing aid to later reason and reflection. Long before the individual can claim reason as a guide to virtue, to distant rewards, and to the true satisfactions only to be found in heaven, habit is at work in the soul. The soul thus based on proper habit can indeed stand the test of time. As Tarcov interprets Locke on this point, "through habit children can be cured *forever* of their faults" (1989:108; emphasis in original). What is purgatory if not an eternal purification of human failings?

Locke goes well beyond habit in curing the youthful soul of pride and despondency; his virtues are inculcated through a careful calculus of pain and suffering administered by parents who are composed and rational, and who administer explanations along with their beatings in order to convince the child that the process is meant to be curative and not merely punitive. The overtones of the penitential order are still audible in Locke's insistence that such beatings are not only to make the child "pliant" but also "penitent" (Tarcov 1989:151; quoting Locke's *Some Thoughts Concerning Education*, sec. 112).

What is at stake is not merely pedagogical, however, but existential. Through punishment something more than civility is learned; it is a sense of one's own very being. That sense, moreover, is bound up with the "knowledge of the goodness of God" (Tarcov 1989:151). Through carefully guided experience, correction, punishment, pain, and suffering the child comes to an awareness of its own being in relation to itself, to others, and to God. The path is not a simple one leading through pain and pleasure; it is the suffering of the spirit alone that can cure the soul of self-love in the form not only of pride and anger but also of softness, querulousness, timidity, and a tendency to complain (Tarcov 1989:152–153). The overtones of purgatory are clear in Locke, despite his emphasis on the secular virtues and on a careful calculation of the proper doses and administration of pleasure and pain to the child and the future citizen.

Mehta (1992) is quite right in finding in Locke an attempt to come to terms with the irrational, arbitrary, and uncontrollable aspects of the self. Certainly the imagination was threatening to get out of control, and diaries of the seventeenth century reflect an enormous range of imagined experience as well as a desire to get the self within bounds. Mehta (1992:12) notes with approval the comment that Locke is contending with emotions like uneasiness and sadness. As I have noted, Locke's discussion of spirits suggests that his universe was not wholly disenchanted; he was especially concerned with the effect of the supernatural and of apparitions on young souls. Fear, terror, a loss of courage, and chronic anxiety are the clear signs that the soul is in danger of being lost. If Locke was seeking to secularize the sufferings of purgatory by turning them into a curative pedagogy, it was no doubt partly because the world of spirits continued to take the heart out of people.

It is easier to dismantle the doctrine of purgatory than it is to get rid of the dead. The dead have a way of continuing to dwell among the living. Most communities and tribes have rituals and other practices by which they entertain the dead briefly at stated times of the year, all the more thoroughly to despatch them to more suitable accommodations for the rest of the year. It is crucial to be able to summon the dead in times of crisis, but it is equally crucial, of course, to make sure that their appearances are never uncalled for. A community habituated to making prayers for the souls of the dead, as was England right up to the beginning of the seventeenth century, might understandably still be host to a variety of spirits for decades, perhaps centuries, after the doctrinal issue had been settled and the formal practices of praying for the souls of the dead had been drastically reduced. I would therefore expect to find various traces of Locke's Christian faith in his writing. Mehta, on the other hand, finds it quite remarkable. Whereas Bentham later gives no hint of a Christian legacy in his secular calculus of pleasure and pain,

Locke must acknowledge the true principle of virtue even while he points to its similitude with a crass reputational calculus. It is as though the Christian in Locke is obligated to flag his own apostasy by simultaneously pointing to his former and present self . . . (Mehta 1992:146)

Fully to appreciate the latent Christian influences on Locke's writing, however, it is necessary to keep in mind some of the typical prayers, i.e. "collects," that Locke would have heard, especially in his adulthood, in virtually any Anglican parish. Take, for example, the following:

O Almighty God, who alone canst order the unruly wills and affections of sinful men; Grant unto thy people, that they may love the thing which thou commandest, and desire that which thou dost promise; that so, among the sundry and manifold changes of the world, our hearts may surely there be fixed where true joys are to be found; through Jesus Christ our Lord, Amen. (The Collect for the Fourth Sunday After Easter, Book of Common Prayer, in Shepherd 1950:174)

This wording, which dates back to 1662, reflects more than the growing interest, which we have already noted, in civility and, above all, in public order. The prior wording had spoken only of a singleness of heart: "O God, who dost make the minds of faithful men to be of one will" (Shepherd 1950:175). True, Locke told parents "If . . . you . . . make them [the children] in love with the pleasure of being well thought on, you may turn them as you please, and they will be in love with all the ways of virtue" (Locke, *Some Thoughts Concerning Education*; Axtell, ed. 1968; quoted in Mehta 1992:145). But the problem for Locke, as Mehta reminds us, is with the heart, the imagination, the mind fevered with restless desire and fears of strange presences in the self that can hardly be named, let alone controlled:

with an underdeveloped individuality without internal moorings, habits, or direction – almost possessed by natural capacities that are not fully fathomed or controlled. Such a person is in need of distinction, of a mold that will supply individuality ... (Mehta 1992:126–127)

These same anxieties, about the emergence of the unruly and unformed soul, can be found much later on the other side of the Atlantic: in Channing's warnings about the need for self-culture, in Dickens's sad appraisal of the lost or disrupted American soul, and in Emerson's injunctions toward manliness and virtue, courage and vigor, self-knowledge and self-trust. Many Americans may well have lost their moorings when they crossed the Atlantic or the endless prairie.

There seems to be no doubt that what Locke had in mind was a secular pedagogy that would be the functional equivalent of purgatory and would smooth the path of the individual to heaven. It is not simply, as Mehta puts it, that Locke was interested in "the construction of human nature or, at any rate, of something that could not readily be distinguished from human nature" (1992:132). Locke is secularizing the spiritual discipline of the Anglican church and turning parents into a surrogate for the slow workings of providence in shaping the human heart. The purpose of spiritual discipline is not only to shape the soul but to cure and, if need be, save it. As one collect puts it:

We humbly beseech thee that, as by thy special grace preventing us thou dost put into our minds good desires, so by thy continual help we may bring the same to good effect ... (*The Book of Common Prayer*, Collect for Easter Day)

The wording is an antidote to Pelagian tendencies, since it gives humans no credit for either having good desires or acting on them to good effect; providence both prepares the way and brings motives to fruition. An earlier conclusion to the collect, however, had petitioned for redemption from "the death of the soul" (Shepherd 1950:163). It is the underlying threat of soul-loss, I am suggesting, which was the perennial enemy of the Christian; paradoxically, in the wake of the Reformation, soul-loss was still very much the threat faced by Locke and his contemporaries. For them the soul was desperately in need not only of control and discipline, but of a limit to the imagination.

Spiritual growth would thus develop a reservoir of desires that could be transmuted over time into good intentions. Rather than petitioning a heavenly father for good desires, however, Locke in *Some Thoughts Concerning Education* (Axtell, ed. 1968; quoted in Mehta 1992:145) urges parents to produce in their children "a love of credit, and an apprehension of shame and disgrace ..." In this way children will receive "the true principle, which will constantly work, and incline them to the right."

An emphasis on the soul, its life and death, its very existence, had been subsumed into a concern for doing the right thing. Locke therefore employed not only a Machiavellian but an Anglican policy of shaping the desires of the citizen according to the interests of the state. The shift is visible in small changes in the collects made for the 1662 version of *The Book of Common Prayer*. For instance, an earlier prayer had petitioned:

Grant to us, Lord, we beseech thee, the spirit to think and do always such things as are right, that we *who cannot [even] exist* without thee, may by thee be enabled to live according to thy will; through Jesus Christ our Lord.

The 1662 version substitutes the words "who cannot do any thing that is good ..." for the italicized phrase about the petitioner's very existence (Shepherd, 1950:200). Clearly the editors of the 1662 book, like Locke himself, were profoundly concerned with shaping the will and the heart, with imprinting the soul with public standards and with a spiritual readiness to comply with the authoritarian, patriarchal family (Mehta 1992:142).

Imagine therefore a spectrum along which the policy of shaping the soul ranges from the most subtle pedagogical inducements to the "harshest methods" of the state (Tarcov 1989:122). At the latter extreme is the state's ability to impose physical punishment on the offender; at the former end is the parent's constant reminder of the connection between good behavior, parental affection, and other less direct rewards. Where this liberal pedagogy fails, parents – like the state – are obligated to use even extremely severe physical punishment, but the final recourse of the parent of the most recalcitrant and impenitent child is prayer (Tarcov 1989:122).

Beyond the imposition of severe physical penalties, therefore, the final solution is providential. Of course, even politics can fail to redeem the most criminal natures. To further a spiritual and civil pedagogy, to inculcate the right habits, to assist reason in its development, and to ensure a high regard for others' esteem, it is therefore necessary to change not only education but society itself (cf. Tarcov 1989:112). We are on the verge at this point of a theory of social order which is itself to cure the soul *forever*, as it were, so that its entrance to heaven will be ensured.

Critical to this political pedagogy is the separation of good from evil both in the child's self-perception and in the adult's perceptions of the state. There is a form of psychological splitting at work in Locke's advice to parents. He suggests that parents use other children or adults as examples of what is bad, in order to soften the child's resistance to seeing himself or herself in a negative light (Tarcov 1989:120–121). In the same way the state may punish various offenders as a deterrent to others who might be tempted to disobedience. Parents are urged not only to give their child rewards and affection but also to delegate the task of corporal punishment to the servants or others, so that the child will be even more dependent than ever on the parents' good opinion and unlikely to resent the parents' authority.

Similarly, the state should also be divided between a legislative (familial) and an executive (punitive) branch so that the grateful citizen's negative emotions toward the law should be directed not at its givers but only at its executors. The state thus personifies the domestic relations of parents and servants, with the citizenry in the role and status of children. It is indeed a bit of Machiavellian advice to the liberal princes of freedom and self-determination (Tarcov 1989:121).

We should make no mistake about the intentions behind such a liberal pedagogy or politics. It is to bend the soul into the shape of civility. The primary instrument of this policy is shame; even when the punishment is corporal rather than spiritual, the purpose is to inculcate a shameful sense of having been thought deserving of such punishment (Tarcov 1989:117). The target of the whip or the cane is not the body but the soul. Punishment and praise must pass the same test as the soul: the test of time. That is why it is the child's future conduct rather than the parents' anger over prior offenses that must govern their pedagogy and choice of punishment (Tarcov 1989:119). That is also why Locke prefers the skillful use of positive and negative examples: that is, because nothing penetrates so deeply or lasts so long (Tarcov 1989:121). The use of the promise of affection, the deterrence of punishment, and the emphasis on example produce a pervasive and deeply rooted sense of shame and a profound uncertainty about the state of the individual's own soul.

If "the Christian promise of eternal life and bliss and the threat of damnation" were the earliest whips or spurs provoking the soul to virtue, modernity is defined by its emphasis on shame. The fear of losing the good opinion of others is the proper rein, "the only true Restraint" (Tarcov 1989:104; quoting Locke, *Some Thoughts Concerning Education*, sec. 60). The responsible citizen, then, is free only to the extent that shame permits. The religious imagination, the sense of possibility, and the hope of transformation both for the self and the social order are governed by a reason which is indistinguishable from common sense and the limits set by the prevailing public opinion. Of the recent commentators on Locke, Mehta says it best, perhaps:

the freedom, the rationality, and the equality Locke celebrates and on which he bases liberal politics is not the natural freedom, the natural rationality, or the natural equality of human beings, but rather a carefully crafted artifice framed with reference to a particular vision of society and the individuals who inhabit it. In this crafting, there is a strange timidity, for it does not vindicate itself in the conflict and dialogue between two rival freedoms, two rival rationalities-one mad, the other professing sanity. Instead, it is directed at an infant before he or she has "reason, reflection, or memory" with which to counterpose and perhaps resist the effects of this molding ... (Mehta 1992:117–118)

The modern self is intended to be more than a match for the other presences which can imbue it with ideas that the self might unwittingly think were its own. The self is purified of all that it is or has been except for its capacity to purify itself. Taylor sees this as "a new, unprecedentedly radical form of self-objectification" (1989:171). This form of continuous self-purification is a process which leads to being, as Dante might have put it, "Lord of oneself":

The disengagement both from the activities of thought and from our unreflecting desires and tastes allows us to see ourselves as objects of far-reaching reformation. Rational control can extend to the re-creation of our habits, and hence of ourselves ... (Taylor 1989:171)

Now, there are undoubtedly other streams of influence at work in this process of continuous self-reformation. As Taylor has noted, the increasing complexity, coordination, and control of European society exposed the individual to the oversight of superiors who exercised the functions of command and control in a variety of civil and military bureaucracies. The ideal of such a society is therefore a self that does not need such oversight: a self who can be counted on to engage in continuous self-monitoring in the absence of superiors. In modern societies it is precisely such a self that claims to be professionalized. The professional will continue to act in the best interests of a client when no one else is looking.

There is a paradox here. I have suggested that this modern, Lockean self is seeking a form of self-mastery as an antidote to subordination to the wills of myriad others, whose presence may or may not be visible and whose being may or may not be terrestrial. One engages in continuous self-scrutiny in order to purge the self from any thought or perception, feeling or experience that is not truly one's own. There is a fine line separating this sort of rational asceticism from a relentless form of self-torment. The self cannot let well enough alone. No form of the character is good enough to allow the self to relax its vigilance or to forgo further purgations of unwanted elements. Granted, the self is now presumably in control of this sort of self-inspection and must pass not the scrutiny of others but of the individual's own inwardly turned eye. Nonetheless, it is as if, in order to be "Lord of oneself," one had to remain in purgatory for ever.

Eternity now consists not in the after-life alone but in the head. For Locke, even the notion of time was an artifact of one's experience of a succession of thought. Succession comes first; the notion of time second: both existing, however, only in the brain. The self that has disengaged from this experience can thus knowingly – rather than, as before, unwittingly – turn time into something objective without giving it ontological status. Time for Locke is, like the rest of the universe, a deposit of the will. Man has thus deified himself.

There is still another paradox. The individual employs magical thinking in order to protect the self against the influence of others who, either in their presence or their absence, seem to determine the individual's fate. Magic is a form of self-protection: a way, as we have seen, of buying time. On the other hand, however, the individual who relies on magic inevitably will suffer from the most acute forms of self-doubt. Magic, while promising to help the individual, leaves the individual as helpless as before (O'Keefe 1983:328–329).

Indeed, magical thinking can turn on the self and torment it. I would therefore suggest that the continuous self-scrutiny that Locke prescribes for the self is just such a form not only of self-reformation but of self-torment. There is a masochistic element in the modern self that has internalized the oversight of authoritative and controlling presences and made that its own. Subordination to scrutiny thus becomes a way of life. This subordination to others' views and viewpoints is a secularized form, I would argue, of the continuous subjection of the soul to divine oversight. As Weber once remarked, "In the Occident the relationship of man to god became, in a distinctive fashion, a sort of legally definable relationship of subjection" (1964:179). The paradox of the reflexive self is that it becomes acutely aware of the pressure of other presences on the soul.

The effort to dispel the influence of invisible presences continued even in the new world, where the communion of the individual with the departed was as much an article of religious faith, even among Unitarians, as it was for Baxter himself. For instance, few were more dedicated to self-knowledge and reflexivity than the Unitarian minister William Ellery Channing, but, as I will point out in the next chapter, he lamented that the force of public opinion genuinely threatened to override the force of the soul. Writing in 1836 to a young clergyman who had gone west to Kentucky, Channing appeared to envy him the freedom from tradition, custom, and rules that, "warring with your individual," could otherwise stifle his soul. It was the ministers of the Boston area whose souls were being crushed:

A censorship, unfriendly to free exertion, is exercised over the pulpit as well as over other concerns. No city in the world is governed so little by a police, and so much by mutual inspection, and what is called public sentiment. We stand more in awe of one another, than most people. Opinion is less individual, or runs more into masses, and often rules with a rod of iron ... (Channing 1847: vol. II, p. 266)

It is no wonder, then, that Channing sought to marshal divine assistance in the battle to preserve his soul from the crushing weight whether of public opinion or of Calvinist theology.

What is most striking about Channing's solution to the problem of the soul, we will find, is that he made its continual progress a moral requirement of the highest order. It was a requirement that extended from this life well into the next, and a virtue that linked the spirits of the living with those of the dead. In this new American purgatory time became essential for the deliverance of the soul from its own limitations. The eternity of divine love was the yardstick by which to measure the time set aside for one's devotions. The infinite prospects of spiritual progress in this life and the next provided the timespan by which to measure one's own growth from moment to moment, day by day, year in and year out, until time runs out on this life and one begins the next. Even there, however, the soul must go from strength to strength forever. It takes a long time for the soul to become Lord of itself: a very long time indeed.

CHAPTER 5

The American purgatory and the state

The apprehension of some seems to be that Religion left entirely to itself may run into extravagances injurious both to Religion and to social order; but besides the question whether the interference of Government *in any form* would not be more likely to increase than control the tendency, it is a safe calculation that in this as in other cases of excessive excitement, Reason will gradually gain its ascendancy ... (Wilson and Drakeman 1987:81)

If one did not know that Madison had written these words, one might think that they came from the pen of John Locke. The republican spirit requires an electorate that knows its own mind. To know one's own mind, however, the citizen must be able to discriminate what is truly his or her own thought and experience from the subtle influence of alien suggestions. I have pointed out that Locke was no stranger to a world of apparitions and spirits; Locke also abhorred those aspects of Christianity and of the Bible that filled the youthful mind with unnecessary fears and anxieties. Such a fearful mind, and one so easily dominated by alien spiritual forces, would undermine the native common sense and good judgment of a populace that was now required as an electorate to make up its own mind without being subject to undue influences.

The Lockean solution required something of a conversion of the populace. Just as the individual becomes a Christian by swearing allegiance to Jesus, the Son of God, the individual becomes a citizen of the new order by undertaking to uphold the new civil constitution. Both the Christian and the citizen of the new order are freed from the burden of past debts and failings in order to take up the new discipline of liberty. Just as the Christian, however, maintains his or her *bona fides* by clearly adhering to the principles of the founder, so the new citizenry must maintain its liberty by observing the disciplines of freedom. Singleness of mind is as much the prerequisite of liberty as a divided allegiance is its enemy.

Primary among the new republican disciplines is the obligation to make up one's own mind. Remember, for instance, the efflorescence of coffee houses in late seventeenth-century England, where citizens would engage in discussing the news of the day, the better to form a public opinion. In the new United States, the news was also a quasi-sacred sacrament of public opinion that had to be received and digested by the body politic. There were two media, in fact, which were enshrined in the new constitution: the press and religion itself. Both were required to be free so that the individual could make up his or her own mind without being subjected to undue and alien influence. Paradoxically, both religion and the press came to be seen as a Trojan horse hiding the enemies of freedom in its belly.

Locke's faith in reason, it will be remembered, was in its capacity to offset irrational and alien authority or the pernicious influence of spirits and of burdensome, even frightening, religious stories, myths, and beliefs. Only by reason could an individual be sure of being in possession of his or her own soul. One's spirit was so open to influence and suggestion that one could not be sure, except by the exercise of reason, whether one was having one's own thoughts and experiences or those of another. The fear of coming under the control of alien spiritual influence is Lockean, therefore, and not merely American.

The paranoid tendency, as it has been called, thus belongs at least to British North America. It may have been intensified by the English fear of continental power, by the Scottish suspicion of English monarchy, and by the Protestant attack on the Catholic cosmos. In any event, the suspicion that reason could not be entirely trusted was also due to the enchantment of the social universe by unseen presences. In that universe the dead were in the same spiritual community as the living and inhabited the same time-zone. Even the Protestant Baxter, it will be remembered, called upon the living to remember that they would be joining with the saints in everlasting rest and to prepare their souls accordingly.

It is one thing to prohibit intercessions for the dead; it is quite another to get the dead out of the spiritual economy of the social system. Even in the land of the free, Channing was urging upon Americans the spiritual self-purification that fits the soul for heaven. Indeed, Channing's heaven continued to call for and reward the same sort of spiritual progress that was required of those living in this world. So long as the frontier between the living and the dead remains open, I am arguing, so will the fear that the life of the spirit will be open to outside influences. Individuals will understandably be afraid that their souls are not entirely their own. The fear of religious enthusiasm that haunted the framers of the constitution was due precisely to their recognition that individuals may not be lords of themselves but can act as if they are possessed or enthralled. So long as the frontier between this life and the next, or between the world of the visible and the invisible remains open, common sense and reason can still succumb to paranoia over outside spiritual influences and deceptive appearances.

As I will note in the next chapter, the fear that reason could be subverted by alien influences fueled popular suspicion not only of Catholics and the foreign born but also of certain "native Americans." Mormons were hated and feared by many otherwise rational and religious Americans, I would argue, precisely because they opened the frontier between the living and the dead, between antiquity and the present, and between the rational and the absurd. They baptized and ordained the living on behalf of the dead, and they viewed themselves as a continuation of a lost tribe of Israel that had lived without interruption in North America. Their social system is "coeval," in the sense that I have suggested in previous chapters: a society in which neither time nor space separates the living from the dead or the distant from those near at hand. Those who are absent are thus known as presences within the community.

It is not surprising, therefore, that Mormons came under

Protestant attack. Alexander Campbell, whose reasonable and common-sense Christianity clearly derived from Locke, finds in them the incarnation of every superstition that Locke would have feared or despised; Campbell called them "the most impudent delusion which has appeared in our time" (Campbell 1832; quoted in Faull 1969:7). Certainly Campbell's diatribe is an attempt to keep the mind – and politics itself – from going mad.[1]

Madness, for Locke, could come from two sources. On the one hand, the mind could become fevered by the possibility of associating one idea with another. What works in everyday life as imagination could lose its governing head; that is, the imagination could run riot without reason to keep its associations in check (Mehta 1992:114). Without reason nothing could stop the mind from generating a surplus of meaning on which the individual would eventually choke to death. On the other hand, of course, madness for Locke meant the unruly and often painful disturbance of the soul or the body politic by the outbreak of passion (Mehta 1992:115). Enthusiasm in all its forms, mental, emotional, physical, and political, could result in the loss of the individual's soul and could displace reason from its proper place in the governance of the body politic. To prevent free religious expression, however, could be equally damaging to the imagination. Freedom of religion and association, like the free associations of the imagination, could be permitted so long as reason, i.e. government, is in control. Otherwise free religious expression could lead to painful and disturbing outbursts in which both the nation and the soul could be displaced or disrupted by passion.

Only a state in which the executive can act the part of the firm parent, quite separately from the appeals of the legislative body to the citizenry; only, furthermore, a constitution which flatters the average citizen with his or her liberty in order to appeal to reason; only a state which could prevent religion from establishing itself, like the imagination, in the place of reason where it could overwhelm and crush the soul; only *such* a

---

[1] Throughout this paragraph I am particularly indebted to the discussion of Locke by Mehta (1992:111ff.).

state could keep the freedom of religious and political association from displacing reason.

The rule of reason in the soul does not immunize the individual from all outside influences. In Locke's pedagogy, the individual is concerned with the affection and approval first of parents, then of authorities, and finally of public opinion itself. The tyranny of the "generalized other," as sociologists have sometimes called it, ensures that imagination will be held in check by what passes for reason in a modern society. The alternative which Locke could not face was that of a shameless soul no longer incapacitated by reason or the fear of disapproval but capable of the "unfettered act."

What would one expect to be the fate of the soul in a new republic, therefore, like the United States? On the one hand, it was a secular republic in which no higher authority was owned by the individual than the conscience informed by the will of God. Tribal connections had been severed, and the individual was free to pursue a personal destiny for which there was no collective shrine or embodiment. However, our reading of Dickens will alert us to the possibility that the soul was not entirely free from such external constraints. Not only were American institutions often crushing to the soul, but American culture itself put heavy evangelical pressures on the soul to account for itself to the community through confession, conversion, and conformity. Although religion had been set free from establishmentarian and political inhibitions on its free exercise, the cultural center could still send religious emissaries to the periphery to exhort souls to sacrifice intellect and independence, to take up the duties of reproducing the nation from one generation to the next, and to give a full accounting of their citizenship.

Of course, there had been warnings about the effect of religion on public life even before the revolution. As Gaustad (1973:56) notes, Theodore Parker, years before the revolution, had warned of an authority, based on creed and revelation, that "cramps the intellect and palsies the soul of us ..."

Isaac Backus, speaking for the New England Baptists, warned that "we dare not render that homage to any earthly power which I and many of my brethren are convinced belongs only to God" (Gaustad 1973:12–13). In the same spirit Jefferson in 1808 had refused to recommend to Congress "a day of fasting and prayer" (Wilson and Drakeman 1987:79). However, the impulse to enlist the power and authority of the state to discipline the unruly soul was alive and well, and Jefferson therefore wished to contain that impulse by invoking a fictitious and unconstitutional "wall of separation" between church and state.

Individualism may have been a specter haunting Europe, but in the new United States, if Dickens was right, the dangers of a certain ruthlessness toward the soul – not of individualism – were clear and present. There were various forms of slavery, some of them in the South, some in American penitentiaries or in the Congress, where the soul was battered and only the hardiest could survive the attempt to crush the spirit. Now the dissenting clergy were hitching their wagons to the star of a secular state, thus adding to already excruciating pressures on the soul.

Indeed, the much misunderstood and wholly fictitious "wall of separation between church and State" was a formula used by Jefferson to buttress the individual soul against the intrusions of – and against thralldom to – the state. In a letter to the Baptist clergy of Danbury, Conn., in 1802, Jefferson said

Believing with you that religion is a matter which lies solely between man and his God, that he owes account to none other for his faith or his worship, that the legislative powers of government reach actions only, and not opinions, I contemplate with sovereign reverence that act of the whole American people which declared that their legislature should "make no law respecting an establishment of religion, or prohibiting the free exercise thereof," thus building a wall of separation between church and State ... (Wilson and Drakeman 1987:79)

As I have noted, however, Jefferson's "wall of separation between church and State" was imaginary, since it was not mentioned in – or intended by – the Bill of Rights. Indeed, the government was to allow politics to be infused with religion, and religion to enter into the political process, short of any infringement on particular rights or of governmental preference for some of the contenders over others. The market place of public opinion was to remain wide open. Under these conditions, Madison had hoped, true opinion might conceivably be sharpened and honed by the false; or, in a Durkheimian metaphor to which I will return at the end of this chapter, the "positive cult" would triumph over the "negative cult."

Vigilant in protecting the soul from alien influences, the cultural center brought to the periphery strong pressures to conform and even to sacrifice. The individual who bore the brunt of evangelical preaching was made to feel responsible for the survival of the new nation into the next generation and beyond. New societies were being formed to ensure a steady supply of citizens who were both temperate and Biblically literate. Their sacrifices of the soul and the intellect were to be received by the clergy who trafficked in the spiritual commerce between the cultural center and the periphery. The evangelists offered a cure for the soul shaken to its foundations not only by revolution and by aggressive politicians or brutal institutions, but by cruel losses, a harsh environment, and the movement westward away from home.

The evangelical cure for the soul, however, was to perpetuate the illness: a spirit that was perennially unsure of itself and which required a lifetime of certification and testing. It was a lifetime, as Emerson put it of the orthodox Calvinists who had taken up homesteads in Ohio, of "probation" ("John Brown," in Bode, ed. 1981:570).

Take the case of John Brown, who combined Calvinist upbringing, his own native strengths, experience of a rugged environment, and an extraordinary capacity to learn the virtues of a herdsman. From these Emerson created in John Brown himself a "romantic character, absolutely without any vulgar trait; living to ideal ends, without any mixture of self-indulgence or compromise . . ." ("John Brown," in Bode, ed. 1981:570). This is to be contrasted with the slavish spirit of politicians who could not believe that popular sentiment against slavery could arise from native soil, just as they were too servile in spirit themselves to oppose slavery ("John Brown," in Bode, ed. 1981:571). Compare Emerson's celebra-

tion of Brown's self-reliance with his condemnation of the
slavishness of spirit that was fostered in churches:

We are full of mechanical actions ... Love should make joy; but our
benevolence is unhappy. Our Sunday-schools and churches and
pauper-societies are yokes to the neck. *We pain ourselves to please nobody*
... And why drag this dead-weight of a Sunday-school over the
whole of Christendom ... Do not shut up the young people against
their will in a pew and force the children to ask them questions for an
hour against their will ... ("Spiritual Laws", in Bode, ed. 1981:190;
emphasis added)

It was in the churches, if Emerson is right, that individuals
were being put on probation: not in the forests and fields of a
wilderness where even Calvinism could not crush the soul.
With Calvinism, of course, there was always the danger that
individuals would become fascinated with their supposed
"call" or "election" and imagine themselves extraordinary,
chosen personally to accomplish what others could only
imagine. For Emerson, the antidote for this "fanaticism" was
to realize that, while one's "talent is the call," still it is "the
general soul [which] incarnates itself in him" ("Spiritual
Laws", in Bode, ed. 1981:193). Emerson clearly preferred his
own sources of enchantment to those of the Calvinists. The
Calvinist notion of a call put the individual on probation for a
lifetime of arduous spiritual labor. For this fall into self-defeat-
ing duty, Emerson prescribes a belief that:

a higher law than that of our will regulates events; that our painful
labors are unnecessary and fruitless; that only in our easy, simple,
spontaneous action are we strong, and by contenting ourselves with
obedience we become divine. Belief and love, – a believing love will
relieve us of a vast load of care. O my brothers, God exists. There is a
soul at the center of nature and over the will of man, so that none of us
can wrong the universe ... ("Spiritual Laws," in Bode, ed, 1981:192)

Here was a bold attempt to enable individuals to come to their
senses and to know their own minds. Subject neither to public
opinion or to ghostly authority, the soul could flourish best far
from those metropolitan centers where it could become
enthralled or lost altogether. Emerson's was a rhetorical flurry:
a trick by one whom Melville called a "confidence man."

Nonetheless, the new constitution enshrined the republic's doubt over how far it could trust individual citizens to make up their minds and to come to their senses without undue influences from invisible or alien sources. In its debates over the articles in the Bill of Rights affecting religion, the Congress was clearly divided over whether to adopt a phrase securing the rights of conscience to the people. The House's version of Article Three included the rights of conscience along with the free exercise of religion: neither of which were to be infringed upon by the Congress. In the Senate, however, there was less enthusiasm for enshrining the rights of conscience, although there was no major objection to securing the free exercise of religion. Even the States could infringe the rights of conscience, despite Madison's strong preference for an amendment that would secure them against actions of the States.

In retrospect, this is a most significant omission from the rights included in the articles that were adopted and became known as the "Bill of Rights." The life of the soul is thus guaranteed by the Congress if, and only if, the soul itself is somehow enshrined in religion. The soul, if it is rooted and grounded in a non-social relationship is beyond the social contract, is of no use or relevance to society, and deserves no recognition or protection.

The soul could now be put on trial: rights of conscience could not be guaranteed since they had to be given the protective coloring of religious belief and practice. Jefferson, who claimed to perceive in the Amendment securing religion against the Government a "wall of separation between church and state," also claimed to see in that amendment a victory for rights of conscience. That is why he refused to recommend, let alone to proclaim, a day of prayer and fasting. Madison continued to argue, despite the silence of the Bill of Rights on the subject, that the rights of conscience were "not included in the surrender implied by the social State, and more or less invaded by all religious Establishments" (Wilson and Drakeman 1987:80).

As I have noted, Madison was well aware that religion and its free exercise could pose dangers. How many churches would be above exploiting the piety, zeal, and remorse of individuals who wished to pay their debts to society at some altar? In some cases, of course, some religious group might trespass on the rights of others or seek to corrupt public officials. Nonetheless, a minimalist state was in order and would guarantee against the exploitation, as well as the excesses, of the soul. Because religious belief is rooted in the nature of man, diversity, competition, persuasion, and reason would in the long run prevail over ignorance, misguided opinion, intractable or erroneous belief, and perverse or unnatural religiosity. Speaking of Jefferson, Boorstin sums it up this way:

The ideas which a man professed were less important than whether these ideas were the characteristic expression of the mind which the Creator had given him . . . (Boorstin 1981:119–127; quoted in Wilson and Drakeman 1987:83)

Let nature take its course. In Jefferson's view, even the worst error will stimulate the search for truth. If nature is not allowed to take its course, the soul, the natural endowment of the creature by the creator, will be violated or squandered. The human core, so to speak, lies outside social life in the natural order; it is established by the cosmos, and its free exercise poses no ultimate threat to any society. For Jefferson the individual's soul is a given, a gift: not something to be acquired or achieved, but only an ultimate fact of life. To accept that endowment, to live in terms of that legacy, is the duty and the prerogative of the individual: not a privilege granted by the state or a social obligation to pursue the human "potential."

Consider, then, what happens as the terms of this original endowment are altered. To begin with, the soul achieves social recognition only to the extent that it is expressed in religious terms. The Congress until the Vietnam War had allowed for conscientious objection to military service only for those whose beliefs were expressed in religious terms. Noting the apparent effect of such a statute in establishing religion, the Supreme Court covered for Congress by interpreting the statute as enshrining any belief that had the same function as religion in giving a person's life order, orientation, and a set of priorities.

In practice the Court came to accept sincerity as a test of conscientiousness, if such could be demonstrated to the satisfaction of the state. "John Brown" would still have to pass muster before the Selective Service Board and could not yet be allowed to be lord of himself or to act on his own impulses, even if these were generous and aimed only at the making of peace. The soul is thus put on trial; rights of conscience are protected from state interference only to the extent that the state is satisfied that the individual is conscientious. The Bill of Rights did not prevent the Congress or the institutions of American society, like the pre-revolutionary church itself, from requiring that individuals give to the state a satisfactory account of themselves.

This account of the failure of the "revolution" departs from the usual celebratory discussions of the American Revolution. Take, for example, the argument of Clarke Garrett (1985), who compares the American experience favorably with the French (and also with the English Revolution). The French failed to establish a constitutional church in their revolution, he argues; it was overwhelmed by indifference among the more reformed Catholics and by the resistance of folk religion to a more rationalized and civic faith. Thus the split inevitably came that separated the religious from the secular orders. Not so in the United States, he argues:

Religion, revolution, democracy, and Millennium were conflated in popular culture into a sense of shared national purpose and common destiny that obscured, for a very long time, the tensions and incongruities that had in fact accompanied the revolution that created the United States ... (Garrett 1985:77)

By mixing religion with revolution, the millennium with democracy, I would argue, the new Republic found a way to put the fledgling soul of the new republican on perennial probation. While claiming to protect the individual from undue influence or alien authorities, the new nation was able to place the soul continually on trial and to render the individual accountable in all aspects of life either to the church or to the state. It would be difficult to find social conditions more conducive to turning everyday life into a this-worldly purgatory. The nation itself became a place midway between the European hell and a paradise that remained forever beyond a receding horizon. You could not be told that you were now "lord of yourself," your journey to the verge of paradise completed.

There were many calls to duty: many attempts to put the individual on probation. The specter of a secularized France was haunting Americans concerned with the spiritual foundations of the new order. Indeed, Gaustad (1973:43–49) argues that the Bible societies in America were an attempt to counter the secular virus at work in France. Although Thomas Paine, Gaustad notes, failed in America to put religion on the sidelines, he succeeded mightily in France. The American reaction was to inoculate the public with religious literacy, the Bible, and exhortations to sobriety.

Note, moreover, that the voluntary societies turning the new nation into a secular purgatory carried titles like the American Bible Society or the American Temperance Union. They were carrying on a full-scale mobilization of communities on the periphery to pay tribute to an emerging metropolitan center of politics and culture. Tribute and sacrifice, literacy and sobriety, authenticity and sincerity became civic and political duties: not the spiritual fruit of individuals who were lords of their own souls. In adamant opposition to the spirit of these times, Emerson wrote:

why should we be cowed by the name of Action? 'T is a trick of the senses, – no more. We know that the ancestor of every action is a thought. The poor mind does not seem to itself to be anything unless it have an outside badge, – some Gentoo diet, or Quaker coat, or Calvinistic prayer-meeting, or philanthropic society, or a great donation, or a high office, or, any how, some wild contrasting action to testify that it is somewhat. The rich mind lies in the sun and sleeps, and is Nature. To think is to act ... ("Spiritual Laws", in Bode, ed. 1981:206)

These voluntary societies sought to make the individual responsible for the continuity and survival of their own social system. Individuals could therefore be required to give a good account of the faith that was within them, especially if they were to be made responsible for the continuity not only of the Christian community but of the nation from one generation to the next. Instead of controversies over whether to baptize children, the preaching of the nineteenth century placed individuals squarely in the "nick of time": an imaginary fulcrum between past and present, on which the future of the nation teetered in a precarious balance that could be drastically altered by impiety and disbelief (Bercovitch 1978:148). As Bercovitch has noted, the spirit of the untrammeled soul was allowed to run free only within republican channels. Analyzing a typical "jeremiad," he finds that

We are new-born individuals ... only when we become one in the spirit of the "National birth day"; and we partake of the spirit only after we have shackled our impulses to the expanding cosmos of the American enterprise ... The promise forecloses all alternative avenues of reform and change, personal or collective. Process and essence merge in the symbols of the Revolution, teleology precludes dialectics, and progress and conformity stand revealed as the twin pillars of the American temple of freedom ... (Bercovitch 1978:149)

In this merging of "process and essence," progress is defined in terms that have already been agreed upon in the court of public opinion: a court controlled by the discourse of church and state. In that court it is the free-standing soul that is put on trial, with a guilty verdict practically a foregone conclusion.

At the risk of putting the thesis too baldly, I would say that, failing to establish religion, the United States did establish purgatory. Through evangelical preaching – after the revolution – the polity was able to place on the individual soul the spiritual requirements for conversion and citizenship that had previously been encapsulated within the religious community. By allowing religion to run free in the body politic, the nation could achieve what the state could not: a requirement that individuals bear within the soul the burden of responsibility for reproducing the society from generation to generation. If, as I am arguing, the independent and transcendent soul was a threat to the emerging religious and political order, the evangelical churches countered that threat by putting the soul on trial. It was precisely this fusion of civic and personal piety that Jefferson sought to prevent by his fictitious "wall."

Under these conditions the soul had less to fear from lifeless and indifferent sermonizing than it did from preaching that sought to imbue the soul with a zeal for public order. The soul's own self-doubt provided the opening into which the evangelist could instill the hope of a sure and certain redemption through self-improvement and public virtue; the American purgatory provided the soul with continuous opportunities for repentance, purgation, and refreshment. The guarantees of the soul's liberty could thus be found only in the same Constitution which had failed to enshrine the rights of conscience (Bercovitch 1978:150). Those who wished to save the soul from scholasticism, complexity, ecclesiastical embellishments and the overweening authority of church and state required of the soul that it make a civic contribution and get results. Those who were "working for souls with all our forces" (Gaustad 1973:18) made those souls responsible for developing a new order even on the fringes of the Republic. The center had found the periphery and made it into an image of itself.

There was indeed something positive in this wedding of the soul to the social order. Later we will see how Dickens was very much taken with the Boston area, where he found a serenity and social order that balanced the individual's security with ample social responsibilities. Even in institutions for the disabled or retarded, he found individuals being treated with dignity, while they were also expected to perform up to their abilities in weaving or sewing; industry was rewarded and the individual's dignity confirmed. It is this balance between individual strivings and a firm, secure institutional context that attracted Dickens. The demeanor and deference that individuals showed each other reflected a spirit that informed the whole society. This is what Durkheim (1915; 1965:350ff.) had in mind when he spoke of the "positive cult:" a sacred order that dignified both self and society and inspired both commitment and sacrifice.

The cult is "positive," in Durkheim's view, because the individual's own struggle to possess the soul is linked with the soul of the larger society. Time, as a medium that stretches between the individual's immediate self and the realization of individuality even after death is an environment in which the society as a whole lives, moves, and has its being. The society becomes like Winnicott's (1988) notion of the mother, a holding environment that constitutes time. This unification of personal and social time is more likely to happen, of course, when the shrines of the "positive cult" are found not only at the center of a society but also among the marginal. That is when society can begin to form a double for the individual soul, and the individual's own contests with death become significant to the larger society.

Think, for instance, of the peripheral small chapels that remind the faithful of their duties and give them hope of a larger world into which they may some day enter. In Weber's terms, this wedding of individual "spirit" with social "form" made the Protestant ethic a powerful force in shaping modern societies. David Martin (1990) has found strong Protestant and Catholic communities that have been opened up to allow their members mobility in work and a wider citizenship in politics, so that the center is open to the periphery, and vice versa. This is how Durkheim's "positive cult" performs; it is a virtual reservoir of moral masochism.

For Durkheim the "negative cult" consists of ascetic strivings for self realization; these would be "primitive," in his estimation, precisely because they are not "moral" in the sense of pertaining to the community or society as a whole. The rituals and prescriptions, the proscriptions and contests of the negative cult provide a testing ground for the individual's heroic strivings: a place for sacrifice, for initiation, and for struggles with elemental forces. Indeed, the American frontier was such a testing-ground for many who entered its empty spaces, and it remains so in American fantasy, in movies and paperback thrillers. By turning back from the Great Plains to St. Louis, for instance, Dickens was leaving the scene of the "negative cult" for the site of the "positive cult": returning to a city where the civil order was celebrated as the matrix of individual life and dignity, and where the individual, in turn, acknowledges the source and limits of personal freedom.

In this chapter, however, I am arguing that American society combined the negative with the positive cult. The nation enlarged on the trials of the individual soul with inner demons or external wilderness and literally enshrined spiritual combat in the pantheon of American virtues. Ascending to this civic pantheon was like ascending the Mount of purgatory. In this progress the pilgrim soul turned into a citizen of the nation of men and women who could be called lords of themselves because their impulses had been safely nationalized.

The negative and the positive cult therefore overlapped and mixed with each other in the experience of Americans who moved, as it were, between the village and the bush: between settlement and wilderness, between domestic order and unrestrained impulse, between life and death. The traveler, too, alternated between the shrines of the negative and the positive cults. For instance Dickens, on his way back to St. Louis from his chilling encounter with the Great Plains, found a pub where an Englishman, a doctor far removed from home, catered to Americans by declaring himself more than happy to live among the "free": a rhetorical strategy that did not convince Dickens for a moment. Among the Americans, he sensed a spirit all too willing to stand the test of the frontier, where it had not yet been yoked with the forms of civic order. Even the public carriages and houses had spittoons, and all the forms of address were far too abrupt or familiar.

The rigors of the American experience may well have contributed to a willingness to be put on trial or probation. As I have already noted, Durkheim criticized "a systematic asceticism ... which is consequently nothing more than a hypertrophy of the negative cult" (1915; 1965:350). This "hypertrophy" occurs when sufferings, trials, and prohibitions become so extensive that they fail to provide the satisfactions of citizenship. Clearly the negative cult has taken over when life becomes a continuous trial with no end in sight.

In many communities, of course, there were some who never did come beneath the tents of the positive cult; their masochism, if such it was, never became "moral." In a most telling and critical account of an American coal mining community in the ante-bellum United States, *St. Clair*, Anthony Wallace gives a Dickensian account of the hardships of the mines, where young men put themselves to tests that no seasoned miner would have dared to undertake, by crawling into gas-filled shafts with explosives to clear a blockage or to rescue a friend. In analyzing these heroics, Wallace openly wonders at the near-suicidal tendency to expose the self to certain risks. In fact, he asks the same question about the mining community as a whole, where generations went to their deaths for coal that was known from the first geological surveys to have been far too costly to extract and often quite inaccessible. By the same token, he asks why the operators failed to undergo the expense of routine maintenance that would have avoided many of the worst tragedies.

In the end, Wallace argues, there is no other explanation for the miners' and operators' recklessness than a desire to get away without paying the routine price of maintenance. I would suggest that the desire to beat the odds, to triumph over the routine and ordinary, was a desire to be put to the test. It may well have been accompanied by a wish, as though by magic, to escape a common fate in the mines that was all too predictable by any rational calculus.

In the final chapter I will argue that these conditions were conducive to the formation of a masochistic social character. Masochists do seek to take risks with pain that others would avoid, extend the limits of their endurance, and seek "unusually intense, novel experiences" (Baumeister 1989:207). Theirs is a "hypertrophy," as Durkheim put it, of the "negative cult."

There were, as I have suggested, many who tried but failed to climb the mountain to the pantheon of civic virtue in the United States. Such self-destructive trials were the option selected by many who could not enter into the public trials of the American purgatory. In Durkheimian terms, the failure of the "positive cult" to include and subsume the "negative cult" allowed a "hypertrophy" of asceticism: an exaggerated pursuit of trials of spiritual and physical strength to absurd and self-destructive lengths. In the mining community of St. Clair, requirements for entering the "positive cult" excluded the poor and the immigrant. Only those who could afford clean clothes and who were not terribly exhausted at the end of the day could go to the churches for evening prayer meeting or become members of various literary societies in the community. Progressively the town of St. Clair made the boundary between *bona fide* members and outsiders more explicit: not only in canons for propriety but in city ordinances after the Civil War that were intended to keep various forms of "trash" out of town (Wallace 1987).

In its attempt to keep death at a safe distance, the town put up barriers that allowed the negative cult to displace sane or healthful activities among those who could not afford to pay for church membership or for other tokens of respectability. Denied entrance into the "positive cult", the poor stayed outside the tent of salvation altogether, where they were labelled the Molly McGuires, Irish trash, vagrants, or other enemies of public safety. In turn, these groups developed their own tests and ordeals and submitted themselves to the worst rigors of the mines. Thus two kinds of masochism developed in these American communities as mirror-images of each other: the moral masochism of those who were full participants in the American purgatory, and the more dramatic and physical masochism of those who – left on the outside of the gate of purgatory – sought after the most painful and rigorous tests of prowess and endurance. Indeed the free-floating masochistic tendencies of marginal members of the society generally provide a perennial reservoir of potential new members for both church and state. They are most easily tapped for crusades, military service, and mass political movements.

CHAPTER 6

Protestants and Catholics in the American purgatory

In the first half of the nineteenth century it is still possible to sense the connection between purgatory and progress. Take, for example, the work of William E. Channing, a Unitarian divine whose lectures and sermons reached a wide audience in the East and, to a lesser extent, in England.[1] Among his heroes were Baxter and Locke, and Emerson was prominent among his devotees; Dickens he praised, with one small qualification, i.e. that Dickens had found entertainment in some of the most degraded forms of human nature.[2] This having been said, Channing's sympathies were broad and catholic, and he was convinced that, for all their corruption and spiritual failings, Americans were on the way toward unprecedented achievements in knowledge and science, in government and industry, and in the conduct of everyday life. It was religion that had crushed the souls of Americans and their forebears, and it was from that religion that Unitarian Christianity would set them free (Channing 1847: vol. III, pp. 224–225).

There is no doubt that Channing believed in a purgatorial life after death for the soul. Speaking of the individual whose life was still ruled by public opinion or by short-sighted interests, he wrote:

No ruin can be compared to this. This the impenitent man carries with him beyond the grave, and there meets its natural issue, and inevitable retribution, in remorse, self-torture, and woes unknown on earth. This we cannot too strongly fear ... ("The Great Purpose of Christianity. Discourse at the Installation of the Rev. M. I. Motte"; Channing 1847: vol. III, p. 222)

[1] See Robinson 1981:221.   [2] Channing 1847: vol. VI, pp. 210, 157.

Channing feared for the soul when the individual, in this life, reduces love to the pursuit of self-interest. Intellectual and moral vigor then become mere passive conformity to custom and others' opinions, and the soul forfeits both self-control and duty.

Note this paradox in Channing: his exhortation to fear eternal self-torture after death, and yet also his hatred of any ministers who use religion to terrorize their congregations. Channing insisted that heaven begins in this life and consists of the enlargement and purification of the human soul, and yet in the passage above he insists that remorse and untold agony await the (impenitent) soul in the life after death. It is to forestall that disaster that he seeks to impress souls with the need for their inner transformation now, while there is yet time; otherwise there will be time without end for self-recrimination in the future beyond the grave. That is why "there is, and can be, no greater work on earth, than to purify the soul from evil, and to kindle in it new light, life, energy, and love" (Channing 1847: vol. III, p. 210).

At the very least, life after death takes on the aspect of a continual self-improvement, with or without the agonies of self-accusation that he envisages for those whose penitence arrives too late in this life to forestall purgatorial torments in the next. The next life is a continuation of the spiritual improvements begun in this one: a continuous advance "in truth and virtue, in power and love, in union of mind with the Father and the Son" (Channing 1847: vol. III, p. 204). The task of making the human soul perfect is never ending, and there is no time to begin it like the present. Like the horizon beyond the Great Plains, which Dickens found to recede further from him with every step forward, the prospect of spiritual progress seems to enlarge with every advance toward perfection. While Dickens found the Western prospect disheartening and returned gladly to the comforts of the inn, longing for home, Channing thought that the frontier would offer a bracing tonic to the soul.

Channing enjoyed the prospect of endless spiritual growth just as fully as he deplored the prospect of endless self-reproach in the life after death. The mystic's delight in the presence of divine love and in the bursting of the bonds of the soul is matched in Channing by the ascetic's insistence on turning every step of the way into a test of spiritual power. It is the combination of these two in Channing, as in Baxter, that accounts for the persistence of a purgatorial after-life in their doctrine. With Catherine of Genoa, he spoke of great spiritual opportunities, none of which is to be wasted without remorse; on the other hand they both apprehended the possibility of spiritual agony not only in this life but the next and sought to forestall it by adopting a discipline of the soul.

One reason for this continuing obsession is that Channing, like Baxter, believed in the possibility of exchange and communion between the spirits of the living and the dead. In his brief "Discourse on the Church" (1841), he notes:

> This spiritual union with the holy who are departed and who yet live is the beginning of that perfect fellowship which constitutes heaven. It is to survive all ties. The bonds of husband and wife, parent and child, are severed at death; the union of the virtuous friends of God and man is as eternal as virtue, and this union is the essence of the true church ... (Channing 1847: vol. VI, p. 221)

The vestibule of heaven, as it were, extends to this earth, this life, in the spiritual commerce between the living and the dead. While that spiritual community is not limited to the church, it is, as Channing puts it, "the essence of the true church." That church, however, is no more likely to be found in the formal structures of the church than in the most dismal hovel. On the contrary, the latter surroundings often contain more of the spiritual virtue which Channing regards as eternal than does the church itself. Certainly it does not matter what earthly communion one belongs to, Roman, Presbyterian, Methodist, or whatever, so long as the minister can enable one "by wise and touching manifestations of God's truth, to become a holier, nobler man" ("Discourse on the Church"; Channing 1847: vol. VI, p. 198). If heaven begins with the spiritual communion of the living with the dead, the process of purifying the soul cannot begin too soon.

Indeed, the sense that time is running out provides a somber counterpoint to Channing's confidence that the "present age" is one of continuously expanding horizons. While he celebrates the progress of his nation, he grieves over the loss of soul-force among Americans who spend themselves in the pursuit of one material gain after another:

Undoubtedly eating and drinking, dressing, house-building, and caste-keeping are matters not to be despised; most of them are essential. But surely life has a higher use than to adorn this body which is so soon to be wrapped in grave-clothes, than to keep warm and flowing the blood which is so soon to be cold and stagnant in the tomb ... ("The Present Age" [1841]; Channing 1847: vol. vi, pp. 177–178)

Remember Baxter's insistence on cultivating an awareness that time is running out as death continues its approach. Only one thing really matters to Channing. It is "that which is alone ourselves ... our inward spiritual nature ... the thinking, immortal soul" ("The Present Age"; Channing 1847: vol. vi, p. 178). All of our activities fail if they do not tend to the purification of the soul. If progress does not bring greater spiritual purity, social life and the human spirit will become stagnant and corrupt.

What Channing feared in America was largely what Dickens found, as we shall see later in this chapter. Both agreed that there was much to be purified in the American soul, and Dickens could well have said of "The Present Age," with Channing, that "Life now has little music in it" (Channing 1847: vol. vi, p. 178). What both men saw were Americans at war with each other in every aspect of social life: religion, politics, business. For Channing, however, the westward expansion of America offered every prospect of spiritual growth, a secular purgatory on the way to heaven, but for Dickens the West offered only an empty horizon that chilled the soul. He could not wait to get home.

Indeed, for Channing the interior life of the self was like the American West: an unknown land that must be traversed if individuals were to come to a true knowledge of themselves. Here is Channing in perhaps the best known of his addresses, on "Self-Culture" (1838):

To most men their own spirits are shadowy, unreal, compared with what is outward. When they happen to cast a glance inward, they see there only a dark, vague chaos. They distinguish perhaps some violent passion, which has driven them to injurious excess; but their highest powers hardly attract a thought; and thus multitudes live and die as truly strangers to themselves, as to countries of which they have heard the name, but which human foot has never trodden" (Channing 1847: vol. II, p. 356)

There was no duty more solemn, he argued, than the task not only of discovering but of forming and developing the self. Indeed, he urged his readers to follow the example of clergy who had gone West in search of a spiritual challenge that would arouse and strengthen their souls: a point to which I shall shortly return.

The American West was not the only place for "self-culture"; Channing wanted the churches themselves to be leaders in that endeavor and to set an example for all social institutions by placing spiritual growth above every other goal. Because contemporary discourse tends to substitute the word "self" for the soul, it would be easy to miss Channing's point about progress. To progress is simply and primarily to prepare and purify the soul for its entrance into heaven. What Channing means by "self-culture" is really the development of the entire soul, whose force is also "the force of thought, moral principle, and love" ("Self-Culture" [1838]; Channing 1847: vol. II, p. 352). To engage the soul it is necessary to enter a spiritual world which is largely invisible, but which contains the highest reaches to which humans can – and should – aspire.

Channing's rhetoric recalls the imagery of purgatory, but is it fair to claim that the doctrine is also the inspiration behind Channing's thought? I think it is. Like Baxter, Channing was suspicious and critical of doctrinaire and exclusive Catholicism, while he recognized in the Catholic Church genuine impulses of spiritual life which make religion come alive and which also vivify the soul:

To him, who inclines to take heaven by violence, it [the Catholic Church – RKF] gives as much penance as he can ask; and to the mass of men, who wish to reconcile the two worlds, it promises a purgatory, so far softened down by the masses of the priest and the prayers of the faithful, that its fires can be anticipated without overwhelming dread ... (Channing 1847: vol. II, p. 274)

Channing was an enemy of religious doctrines that worked by inspiring terror and dread, and a friend to those doctrines which, like that of purgatory, had been softened to make them more useful and appealing. To withstand the increasing competition from Catholicism it would be necessary for Protestants to offer a spiritual challenge to those who could be induced to imagine that they could cross the horizon separating heaven from earth and have conversation with the invisible world of the spirit.

Other clergy in the first half of the nineteenth century were far more censorious of Catholicism than Channing himself. As we shall see later in this discussion, Alexander Campbell was taking on the Roman Catholic Church for a variety of sins, not the least of which was that it was an alien faith, subversive of the American spirit, and pernicious in its influence on the soul. The very practices which had built the Church of Rome, he argued, would undermine the freedom of spirit and the moral conscience that were the cornerstones for the American Republic. Like Channing, and like Locke before him, Campbell was concerned about the destructiveness of superstition and of a tormented conscience:

There are few persons who so observantly trace moral effects to their causes, as to be able duly to appreciate how much influence in the formation of human character may philosophically be ascribed to such idle, absurd, and irrational pretensions. We sometimes see with what little power reason, philosophy, and experience combat the belief in witches, ghosts, apparitions, and other legendary tales, the effect of the nursery and early impressions. When the imagination is once filled with such tales and delusions, it requires a power equal to the dispossession of demons to rectify it, and elevate it above such a tormenting infatuation ... (Campbell 1875:291)

Why would Channing be able to be so "soft" on Roman Catholicism and on the doctrine of purgatory, when a few years later, and on the very frontier that Channing thought would be so bracing for the soul and for spiritual growth,

Alexander Campbell would find purgatory to be part of "the anti-American, and anti-Republican theories of the Latin church"? It is a question to which I will return later in this chapter. Actually it is clear that Campbell was afraid of spiritual presences, of ghosts or apparitions, which could prevent individuals from developing the ability to think for themselves and from calling their souls their own. The paranoid style in American politics owes much not simply to anti-Catholicism but to the fear of ghosts and spirits: a fear that increases, moreover, when the intentions of one's fellow republicans become increasingly suspect, and one cannot take for granted that one is living with others in the same moral and spiritual economy. In Eastern cities increasingly populated by aliens, and on the frontier, an element of spiritual paranoia could resonate with one's actual experience of uncertainty about the intentions of one's fellow citizens. I will return to the subject of aliens and Catholics later in this chapter.

In Channing's Boston, however, one could make certain assumptions about the good faith, the *bona fides*, of others, and allow them a certain spiritual latitude. There the challenge was to cultivate the spirit to its highest potential: such cultivation being within reach of the average citizen in the form of a wide range of civilizing institutions. It is just such a challenge that Channing issued in his lecture on "Self-Culture," which was given to an audience that was intended to be filled with social isolates and workers: the constituency of Catholicism in urban America. He prefaced his remarks on Catholicism by insisting on the importance of knowing "the reality and nearness of your relations to God and the invisible world;" it was a consciousness of "something real, substantial, immortal, in Christian virtue" (Channing 1847:269). In opening up a challenge to the human soul and giving it the opportunity for conversation with the invisible world of the spirit, Protestantism could – and would – prevail. It was just that invisible world of the spirit that seemed to be so haunting on the frontier.

Other Protestant preachers were more censorious of Catholicism. For instance, in his dispute with Bishop Purcell, Campbell (in *The Battle of the Giants*) argued that Catholics rely too heavily on the intention of the priest for the validity of the sacrament and of its offices. Indeed, if the intention of the ordaining bishop were necessary for the validity of the priest's office, who could be regarded as truly ordained over the last centuries? Who indeed, considering the vast number of "hypocrites and imposters" that had held office in that Church (Campbell 1875:275).

Intensifying this controversy is the chronic doubt about the good intentions of vast numbers of citizens of foreign origin. As aliens, they were regarded as hypocrites and imposters who claimed to be American but who really regarded their old country as their home. My point, however, is simply that the suppression of the fear of alien influences in the world of the spirit fueled the suspicion that one was surrounded by alien spirits and was therefore vulnerable to what Scottish Campbell liked to call "This ghostly despotism" (Campbell 1875:280).

At the heart of that despotism, Campbell (1875:275–276) argued, had been the Roman Catholic Church's traffic in indulgences augmented by the fear of purgatory. Indeed, Campbell (1875:267) argued that purgatory and related doctrines were themselves alien in their origins:

we can trace supererogation, purgatory, penances, lustrations, the intercessions of angels and dead men, &c. to the philosophers and dreamers of the east – their divine Platos, Pythagorases and Aristotles.

Of all the pernicious and alien doctrines of the Roman Church, Campbell argued, the doctrine of purgatory supplied the Archimedean point; mixing his metaphors, Campbell (1875:267) goes on to say that:

That was the philosopher's stone – the lever which lifts the world – which has brought more gold to Rome, than the discovery of America itself.

Rather than worrying primarily about the greed and wealth of the Roman Church, however, Campbell appears to be following Locke in his concern about the dangerous effects of the doctrines of purgatory, transubstantiation, etc. Of transubstantiation he argues that it undermines faith in the individual's own senses and perceptions and places an undue reliance on the intentions of the priest rather than on the certainties of Scripture. Locke, too, was concerned about the cognitive foundations of a laicized social order, in which it would be absolutely necessary for the citizen to be able to distinguish his own perceptions and experience from that which originated from outside.

The fear of outside influence, in other words, is not only xenophobic but stems from the precarious spiritual authority of the autonomous individual. Some of the outside influences that Locke feared would undermine the individual's judgment, it will be remembered, were spiritual and ghostly. No wonder, then, that Campbell (1875:267) found Catholic doctrines, particularly that of purgatory, to be "immoral in their tendency, *and injurious to the well-being of society, religious and political*" (emphasis added). In a democratic society it was essential that individuals be able not only to trust their own perceptions but to commit themselves to a social order in which the intentions of others remain opaque. The foundations of the social order would have to be laid on a bedrock of trust that was far deeper than the uncertain layers of human intention, just as the authority of the individual's judgment would have to rest on a certainty of perception and experience that could not be undermined by invisible and alien sources of suggestion.

Quite paradoxically, there is no better example of such suspicion over anti-republican influences than the writings of Samuel F. B. Morse. In citing Morse I am getting ahead of the story, of course, but it may be useful to see just how rancid both religion and the press have become in his estimation. As a witness to nativist sentiments, Morse is a particularly interesting example, since he was of all Americans one of the most cosmopolitan. His own invention opened channels of communication that did much to integrate the American continent, just as transatlantic cables eventually enabled his code to transmit information across the ocean to England and Europe.

Despite his cosmopolitanism, Morse was profoundly afraid that foreign influence would soon undermine the independent judgment of the American people. Outside influences disguised as religion would fool a press that, for all its claims to fairness, was really a dupe of foreign governments when it was not actually biased in their favor. Not only were foreigners coming by the thousands to America; they were coming without the capacity of independent judgment, without Reason which alone could create the Republic. Their minds were not their own, but were under the control of absolutist governments, tyrannous emperors, and an authoritarian, because Roman Catholic, religion. In *Imminent Dangers to the Free Institutions of the United States through Foreign Immigration and the Present State of the Naturalization Laws*, Morse argues that the immigrant was merely a minion: an "abject and degraded slave of foreign superstition," governed in heart and soul by *"the foreign Jesuit, the Austrian stipendiary* with his intriguing myrmidons" (Morse 1835:18, 19).

Morse's anti-Catholicism was no doubt fed by many sources, not the least of which would be the status anxiety to which modern observers have attributed the "paranoid tendency" in Americans politics (cf. Hofstadter 1955). Such arguments do not indicate why Catholics should be such prime suspects of subversive tendencies. Their crime, after all, is not simply that they are alien; it is that they are allegedly alienated from their own reason; their souls are not their own but are in thrall to a "foreign superstition." The problem is not merely that their allegiance is foreign, but that a superstition so infects their reason that they are unable to be autonomous. One who serves instead the will and purposes of a master is indeed a slave and not a republican fit for the suffrage. Only those who, having passed through purgatory, are "lords of themselves" are fit for popular sovereignty.

In New England, however, at least during the time of Channing, the fear of the departed and of spiritual communion with the saints, and hatred of alien loyalties to an English king were not yet coalesced into a paranoid style. Sometimes, it is true, Channing seemed to speak of the soul as if it merely comprised the reason, the understanding, and the affections, yet the soul also was the aspect of the individual open to the invisible world of the spirit in this life and the next ("Self-Culture" [1838]; Channing 1847: vol. II, pp. 354, 352). Hence the road to the self was the way to a Protestant form of purgatory that was no further from heaven or closer to earth than the Catholic original. Indeed, I would argue, this form of self-culture, whether enacted in the streets of Boston or, most typically American, on the way West, was the Protestant's answer to the threat of Catholicism.

In his final exhortation to an audience assumed to be filled with an unusually high representation of the "obscure," the urban masses, Channing draws heavily on the imagery of death, guilt and penitence, of burdened souls and upright spirits, to make his plea for self-culture:

What a vast amount of ignorance, intemperance, coarseness, sensuality, may still be found in our community! What a vast amount of mind is palsied and lost! When we think, that every house might be cheered by intelligence, disinterestedness, and refinement, and then remember, in how many houses the higher powers and affections of human nature are buried as in tombs, what a darkness gathers over society! And how few of us are moved by this moral desolation? How few understand, that to raise the depressed, by a wise culture, to the dignity of men, is the highest end of the social state? Shame on us, that the worth of a fellow-creature is so little felt.

I would, that I could speak with an awakening voice to the people, of their wants, their privileges, their responsibilities. I would say to them, You cannot, without guilt and disgrace, stop where you are. The past and the present call on you to advance. Let what you have gained be an impulse to something higher. Your nature is too great to be crushed ... Awake! Resolve earnestly on Self-culture. Make yourselves worthy of your free institutions, and strengthen and perpetuate them by your intelligence and your virtues ... (Channing 1847: vol. II, pp. 410–411)

In the letter to a young clergyman in the West cited earlier in this chapter, Channing depicted the West as a place in which the soul could grow and be tested. Indeed, a pilgrimage westward was a drama of the soul. It is as if space – not time – marked the soul's progress. The West could easily be compared then with a secular purgatory in which the soul could be purified of its extraneous burdens and trappings and rise to its own height. Here is Channing (1847: vol. II, p. 268) writing to the young clergyman:

Of all men, the minister should be first to inquire, where shall I find the circumstances most fitted to wake up my whole soul, to task all my faculties, to inspire a profound interest, to carry me out of myself? I believe *you* have asked yourself this question, and I think you have answered it wisely. You have thrown yourself into a new country, where there are admirable materials, but where a congregation is to be created by your own faithfulness and zeal. Not even a foundation is laid, on which you can build … That under such circumstances, the man who starts with the true spirit will make progress, can hardly be doubted. You have peculiar trials, but in these you find impulses, which, I trust, are to carry you forward to greater usefulness, and to a higher action of the whole soul.

Note that while he is employing the rhetoric of progress, Channing still sees the field of human endeavor as a drama of the soul. It is also worth noting, however, that at this point in his argument there is only a faint residue of mysticism in the ascetic impulse toward perfection of the soul through earthly trials. There is still a promise of ecstasy in Channing's suggestion that the man whose soul is fully engaged in some project will be carried out of himself. His thoughts on women assign them a significant role in the spiritual awakening of Americans, but that is not quite *à propos* here, where I am concerned with what still appears to be a male impulse toward ascetic trials and proofs of the soul. Women are thought by Channing to domesticate and civilize the public sphere, as they did the home. It is primarily men who are on probation and who must prove themselves in spiritual struggle.

In fact, it would be necessary to go far from home to test the soul's true capacities, if Channing's comments about Boston are to be believed. In his Letter "On Catholicism [1838]," Channing (1847: vol. II, pp. 265–266) describes Boston as a city in which public opinion weighs heavily on the individual, and ministers are especially fearful of criticism. Far from being endangered by too much individualism, Bostonians in Channing's view are quintessentially American in their caution and in their fear of public criticism: ministers being particularly frightened of their parishioners' judgments. Congregations "must hear a voice which . . . still comes from the soul" which manifests "Life":

it [Life] consists much more in the clear perception, the deep conviction of the Reality of religion, the *reality* of virtue, of man's spiritual nature, of God, of Immortality, of Heaven. The tone which most proves a minister to be alive, is that of calm, entire confidence in the *truth* of what he says, the tone of a man who speaks of what he has seen and handled, the peculiar tone which belongs to one who has come fresh from what he describes, to whom the future world is as substantial as the present, who does not echo what others say of the human soul, but feels his own spiritual nature as others feel their bodies, and to whom God is as truly present as the nearest fellow creature . . . (Channing 1847: vol. ii, p. 268)

Baxter could not have said it better.

What is missing, says Channing, is not only the conversation of the minister's own soul with God; the world of the immortals, so to speak, has disappeared beyond the minister's spiritual horizon. For heaven to be palpable and immortality so real to the believer that the individual's soul is quickened at the prospect is still, for Channing as it was for Baxter, the single most important act of faith. It is clear, however, that the prospect of the soul's heavenly rest has become far less enticing for many clergy than the prospect of a comfortable living in a Boston congregation.

It is therefore one of the ironies of American history that Protestants and Catholics should have sought to define themselves in symbolic opposition to each other when both communities place the individual on a lifetime of spiritual probation. Within both communities there is a profound seriousness about time that spills over into devotion both to those who have gone before and to the saints who have entered into their heavenly rest. Indeed, in the piety of Catherine of Genoa one can find an orientation toward the future as devotedly passionate as any Protestant's longings for heaven. As I have suggested, she is a figure that bridges both communities with her view of life as an introduction to purgatory. In this life, and not only in the next, the soul can seek to be purified of all affections except the heavenward. That purification takes more than the lifetime of the believer, however; it consumes the next life as well as this one. Nonetheless, the time to begin such purification is always in the present, and that beginning requires a new baptism of the spirit for which any evangelical Protestant may yearn with the devotion of the Catholic mystic (Groeschel 1977:39–40).

I will suggest that these apologetics have led American historians and sociologists to agree that the conflict between the two religious communities is based on two quite different types of civility.[3] One was the social order into which the Protestant enters through conversion. It is through conversion that the Christian pilgrim leaves behind the security and bondage that come with family and neighborhood, the local village and the landowner. Only those who are flexible, sustained by inner resolve, and oriented toward a future that is unlike the past, have a hope of entering the new city, although they may be tempted at times to return to the false securities and the confinement of the City of Destruction. The other was a civility that fits the individual for continued membership in a community that is based on traditional ties to family and place.

In the conflict between the two religious communities, Protestant apologetics place their own virtues in symbolic opposition to those of the Catholics, who remain within the old city and forfeit the prize that can only be won by pilgrims who leave the old world behind. As Paul Creelan and Robert Granfield (1986:162–179) have observed, Bunyan's *Pilgrim's Progress* was a model for at least one Protestant-inspired critique of immigrant communities in the United States, viz. W. I. Thomas's celebrated *The Polish Peasant in Europe and America.*

---

[3] Their two types of civility are associated with two types of social order conventionally designated as *Gemeinschaft* and *Gesellschaft*. The *gemeinschaftlich* order is one in which one's chances in life, like one's name, are largely given at birth. There one's pathway through the family and education is likely to be a "given," determined by one's family and gender, one's place and one's time or birth order. In the more highly differentiated *gesellschaftlich* order, on the other hand, one's pathway through the family and education is only partially "given" but more largely "achieved." One's statuses, even in the family, are more negotiable. In education, for instance, one advances primarily on the basis of one's interests and merits. This form of "individuation" extends to other chances in life: one's choice of occupation and domicile, and one's engagement in politics and religion.

We will return to such apologetics shortly. The key to the Protestant apologetic, it is clear, is in the supposed effect of conversion on the individual's affections and loyalties toward the people and places, the times and practices of traditional and stable communities. To be a Christian one must have, as it were, a spiritual circumcision that cuts the tie linking one's ideas and imagination to old memories and emotions. Only then can one be fully open to spiritual suggestion and to the opportunities and demands of the new and unexpected.

It is not surprising, then, that Bunyan's *Pilgrim's Progress* would have served to sharpen the Protestants' critique of immigrants in their cities who preserved their ties. Along the way Protestants no doubt encountered hardships that made them yearn for the securities and confinements of the communities that they had left behind. Even British Americans may have had unacknowledged longings and affection for the old country, even though two wars had made England an apparent foe. The move westward, the frequent uprootings, and the sojourn in unfamiliar and inhospitable land made for an uncertain soul. Perhaps as a reaction against such backward looking, and perhaps as a way of defining themselves more sharply against the immigrants who brought their traditions with them from homelands in Ireland and Europe, Protestant Americans kept their public and spiritual faces resolutely turned forward.

Their differences with Catholics were therefore partly polemic, partly rhetorical, and partly, of course, a product of their different ways of leaving the past behind. Sociologists who, like Andrew Greeley, can document that American Catholics have outdone Protestants in achievements of various kinds, nonetheless also can show that the two religious communities have distinctive, however overlapping, approaches to the social virtues.

The *gesellschaftlich* type of social order is no respecter of persons but is associated with the impersonal and rationalized conduct of business and administration. There one's private life, personal background, religious beliefs, and to an increasing extent one's hereditary characteristics are far less relevant to one's chances in life and to one's performance. Of course, background factors do come into play, either formally or informally, either legitimately or behind the scenes, from politics to administration, in science and industry, even in a society whose formal organization is rationalized along the lines of the *Gesellschaft*. The two forms of social order overlap and interpenetrate; it is only a question of which is predominant in any given situation. Certainly it is clear that to stereotype Catholics as being predominantly *gemeinschaftlich* and Protestants as *gesellschaftlich* is to miss the complexity and variety within both religious communities.

THE AMERICAN PURGATORY

American society in the nineteenth century was profoundly influenced, both directly and indirectly, by the doctrine of purgatory. Here I am referring not only to the impact of Locke on the republic's organization and self-understanding or to the preoccupation of the churches with preparing souls for heaven through a lifetime of penitence, purification, and self-culture, whether in the urban areas of the East or, more strenuously perhaps, on the expanding Western frontier. There is a more direct connection between the American experience and purgatory, of course, and it comes, as one might expect, through the Catholic churches. It is not simply the immigrant population of Catholics from Europe that came to focus their devotions on purgatory. As I will point out later, liberal and evangelical Christians found inspiration in Catherine of Genoa and other saints' single-minded surrender of the soul to the hope of being granted entrance to purgatory on the way to final beatitude. Nonetheless, the Catholic population was evangelized by their own clergy with unprecedented intensity throughout the nineteenth century, and purgatory was at the heart of the campaign to save lost souls not only in the next life but in this.

Perhaps the best example can be found in the evangelizing efforts of the Irish clergy. As Finke and Stark (1992:136–138) have pointed out, it is hard to imagine the success of the

Catholic church in the United States without the vast numbers of well-trained and disciplined Irish Catholic clergy who responded to calls for help from American bishops. More to the point, after 1850 the Irish clergy and laity came to the United States with high levels of devotion and commitment as a result of what Finke and Stark (1992:138), citing an essay by Larkin on the subject, call the "Irish devotional revolution."[4]

Prior to 1859, indeed, the level of discipline and commitment among Irish clergy, not to mention the laity, was very low indeed. Larkin notes that at mid-century Archbishop Cullen inherited an Ireland where the clergy were often drunken, avaricious, adulterous, and litigious, with the laity lax in devotion and lacking in instruction in their faith and worship. Soon, however, Archbishop Cullen saw to it that:

missions were held in nearly every parish in Ireland in the decade of the fifties. Pastoral gains thus made were consolidated by the introduction of a whole series of devotional exercises designed not only to encourage more frequent participation in the sacraments but to instill veneration by an appreciation of their ritual beauty and intrinsic mystery. *The spiritual rewards, of course, for these devotional exercises were the various indulgences, which shortened either the sinner's or the sinner's loved one's time of torment in purgatory* . . . (Larkin 1972:644; emphasis added)

There were many exercises that one could perform for the sake of one's own soul or for the souls of others still suffering in purgatory. The church imported from Rome to Ireland, and then exported to the United States, a vast array of exercises ranging from processions, pilgrimages, and retreats to saying the rosary or novenas or attending services in honor of the blessed sacrament, the Sacred Heart, or the Immaculate Conception (Larkin 1972:645). The process of salvation was thus more highly rationalized and the performance of duties more consistent and continuous than the purchase of indulgences that had incensed the reformers of the fifteenth and sixteenth centuries. The rescue of souls was thus contingent not on fees but on the regular and wholehearted performance of spiritual duties. Time could not be bought or sold, just as it must not be

[4] Larkin 1972:625–652.

wasted, but spent wisely and soberly in the single-minded pursuit of salvation.

It is not merely incidental, of course, that the Irish reform movement started in the wake (quite literally) of the famine and plague that had devastated Irish society from 1846 to 1850. It was more than incidental that the doctrine of purgatory itself in the thirteenth century was introduced following the plagues that still grieved so much of Europe. The responsibility of those who have survived for those who have not perished brings with it a spiritual burden that often cries out for relief in the form of doing something for the departed, whether it is laying flowers at a graveside or engaging in activities designed to minimize their suffering (and, no doubt, that of the mourners). It is not entirely clear whose soul it is that is lost or needs to be saved: that of the dead or of the living.

What is clear is that the affections and duties of the living cannot be understood without examining their continued connections and conversations with the dead, who plead with the living to remember their suffering. The web of obligation that ties people to one another in the family extends through the guild, the confraternity of the friends, neighbors, eventually to one's fellow citizens in the city. Debts must be paid, if there is to be any hope for the future. Conversely, there is an intimate connection between one's hopes for salvation in the next life and one's fulfillment of obligations in this life.

On this point there was little disagreement between the Protestants and the Catholics who evangelized the masses of immigrants and frontier people. Religious polemics, as I have noted, have long obscured the fact that Catholics and Protestants were imbued with very much the same evangelical fervor in the nineteenth and most of the twentieth centuries. Both religious communities were bent on saving souls from hell and in preparing them for heaven. As Roger Finke and Rodney Stark put it:

In the final analysis, the Catholic Church succeeded in America because it too was an upstart sect. It offered an intense faith with a vivid sense of otherworldliness – Catholic evangelists could depict the fires of hell as graphically as any Baptist or Methodist. Like the

Protestant upstart sects, moreover, the Catholic Church made serious emotional, material, and social demands on its adherents – to be a Catholic was a far more serious undertaking than to be a Congregationalist or an Episcopalian. And the American Catholic Church was served by ardent clergy and nuns, recruited from the common people and prepared to make great sacrifices to serve their faith. The Catholics too could staff the frontiers and wilderness areas because they were prepared for hardship and for little or no pay ... (1992:143)

The similarities between the Catholics and Protestants were greatest precisely at the point where they sought to save souls. Both these religious communities found it necessary to mobilize a people who were not yet a laity. Just as many Protestants were unchurched, so were many of the Protestant and Catholic immigrants from Ireland and Europe. To reach them required the near-heroic efforts of circuit riders and itinerant Catholic evangelists. To be mobilized the people had first to be brought to an emotional peak or crisis. As Finke and Stark (1992) point out, the Catholic evangelists were no less indefatigable or adept than their Methodist competition. Sights familiar from the tents of Protestant revivalism could also be seen in Catholic parishes during a "mission": people sobbing in contrition for their sins, going by the thousands to confessionals and undertaking the prescribed penances, all out of fear of hell and hope of heaven (Finke and Stark 1992:119–122). After these parish missions, moreover, the Catholic laity were turned over to the local clergy and involved in parish organizations where their faith could be sustained and their adherence to the Church maintained: Catholic priests being no less alert to the need for building large congregations by turning the masses of the newly devout into the persistently faithful.

In their competition with the Protestants, however, the Catholics had a major asset in the strong webs of affiliation and obligation that tied their constituents together:

The Catholic clergy also understood that sermons were for saving souls and energizing the faithful. They exhorted sinners to confess and be saved, and they did so in the most direct and forceful language they could summon. But they did something more. Typically they preached to their immigrant parishioners in their native tongue and did so within the security of a familiar ethnic as well as religious community-a community that helped both to gain and to retain the active participation of the immigrants and their children ... (Finke and Stark 1992:126)

The Catholics who came to this country were like their fellow Catholics in Europe and the British isles. They brought with them the same webs of obligation and the same sober hope for the future of the soul in this life and the next. Indeed, as Greeley reminds us, Catholics were adept "at coalition building, community development, and reconciliation ..." (1977:224). Not only did they support each others' businesses, vote for each others' candidates, and teach each others' children; they remembered the widows and the orphans and developed a web of institutions for health, education, and welfare that extended from the cradle to the grave.

These webs of obligation, however, were hardly seamless. The Catholic communities were often pitted against each other along ethnic lines, and these lines were often reinforced by intractable class differences that even today give Irish Catholics a disproportionate hold on wealth and power. Within Catholic neighborhoods, ethnic and national churches often divided the community as much as they united it. Nonetheless, the bonds of affiliation were strengthened by corporate memories of origin long after the first wave of immigration from each of the contributing countries came to American shores. To these original bonds, of course, should be added the new obligations that confronted them through the Catholic church's fight for survival in a Protestant milieu. Indifferent to their religion though the Catholics may have been in their countries of origin, in their new land they were confronted with strenuous demands on their souls and their purses, their time and their energy, their loyalty and their commitment. Social life became profoundly serious in America.

This is not to say, however, that Protestants were less subject to emissaries that reminded them of their social obligations. Even on the frontier, Protestants found themselves in tiny clearings talking to Methodist circuit riders who literally would not leave them alone (Finke and Stark 1992:80). The webs of obligation were drawn tighter during revivals and camp meetings, where also one could observe controls over drinking, sex, and aggression being released. The effect was to impress society's norms, with the fear of hell and hope of heaven, upon the soul.

More than social pressures on the soul relate Catholics to Protestants in the nineteenth century. Evangelical and liberal Protestants drew unashamedly from Catholic devotional literature to demonstrate what they meant by Christian perfection and the baptism of the Holy Spirit.[5] Catherine of Genoa was used as a model of the perfection of the Christian soul by Thomas Upham, who compared her favorably with John Wesley, while the evangelical John Morgan saw Catherine of Genoa as an example of the second conversion (the baptism of the Holy Spirit) which was necessary for all Christians if their souls are to be saved from hellfire.

APOLOGETICS

When religious groups or communities are becoming more like each other and fighting for the same territory, they are likely to exaggerate their differences. This exaggeration is a necessary exercise in maintaining cultural boundaries when social differences are beginning to erode. It was not only the inevitable competition between Protestants and Catholics that intensified the strong anti-Catholic reaction in the United States during the nineteenth century. It was their evangelical similarities that created a demand for formal distinctions and made each seem like a clear and present danger to the spiritual life of the other. The more cosmopolitan Protestants, therefore, were most likely to be excited by the "dangers" of Catholicism. Channing, who counseled a life of purification of the soul and the seeking of perfection, was persuaded by the danger of contamination from Europe. Samuel Morse, as I have noted, while seeking contracts in Europe for his new invention and

---

[5] In this paragraph I am drawing entirely on Groeschel 1977:39–40.

while laying the foundations of continental and inter-continental communication, was adamant about the dangers of a Catholic infusion in the American body politic.

For instance, during several decades of the century, Samuel Morse had been warning of a Catholic conspiracy against the Republican institutions of the United States: a conviction that he found widely shared in his European travels and confirmed by his association with Lafayette (Morse 1914: vol. II, p. 35). Catholics, he argued, were not really Americans but foreigners in disguise: heart and soul tied to an alien allegiance that could only make them subversive of American morals and institutions:

Every year, indeed every day, is demonstrating the necessity of our being wide awake to the insidious sapping of our institutions by foreign emissaries in the guise of friends, who, taking advantage of the very liberality and unparalleled national generosity which we have extended to them, are undermining the foundations of our political fabric, substituting (as far as they are able to effect their purpose) on the one hand a dark, cold, and heartless atheism, or, on the other, a disgusting, puerile, degrading superstition in place of the God of our fathers and the glorious elevating religion of love preached by his Son (Morse 1914: vol. II, p. 337)

What Morse took to be a "degrading superstition" was the piety of the Catholic immigrants: a piety, I have noted, that resembled the Protestants' fear of hell and sought the perfection of the Christian soul on the way to heaven. No doubt the same piety sanctified the memory of the living and the dead to whom Catholics were bound by ties of affection and blood, place and time.

Given the sectarian enthusiasm of both Catholics and Protestants, it is understandable that Protestants have sought to emphasize their differences with Catholics. This desire is reflected not only in the populist's aversion to foreigners or in the Know Nothing's hostility to a papist fifth column; it can be found in the best American historiography. Take, for example, Hofstadter's argument that between Catholics and Protestants there is a clash of political cultures that is endemic to the American experience. I quote him at length here, because the same argument, and almost the same phraseology, appears in more recent sociological appraisals of the perennial difference between Catholics and Protestants with regard to both memory and obligation:

Out of the clash between the needs of the immigrants and the sentiments of the natives there emerged two thoroughly different systems of political ethics, the nature and interactions of which I have tried briefly to define. One, founded upon the indigenous Yankee-Protestant political traditions, and upon middle-class life, assumed and demanded the constant, disinterested activity of the citizen in public affairs, argued that political life ought to be run, to a greater degree than it was, in accordance with general principles and abstract laws apart from the (sic) superior to personal needs, and expressed a common feeling that government should be in good part an effort to moralize the lives of individuals while economic life should be related to the stimulation and development of individual character. The other system, founded upon the European back-grounds of the immigrants, upon their unfamiliarity with indepen-dent political action, their familiarity with hierarchy and authority, and upon the urgent needs that so often grew out of their migration, took for granted that the political life of the individual would arise out of family needs, interpreted political and civic relations chiefly in terms of personal obligations, and placed strong personal loyalties above allegiance to abstract codes of law or morals ... (Hofstadter 1955:9)

In the language of Parsonian sociological theory, this insight has developed into a rather simple-minded view of the differ-ences in value-orientation that affect the institutions of any society, and not only those of the United States. According to this view some individuals place a higher value than do others on their old associations; these "valued associations" are less easily transferred to other people and places, to other institu-tions and activities. Such cherished associations result in an orientation to the "particular" and to certain "qualities" rather than toward certain more general features of individuals or toward universal standards. The same dichotomy has been used by Mannheim to describe what distinguishes the con-servative from the liberal: the conservative also being more tied to certain people and places than the liberal, who is correspondingly more able to function in a wider variety of persons and contexts. This latter ability depends, of course on the willingness to generalize: to feel affection and loyalty not only toward the people and places that one has already known but toward others that may have similar qualities but lack the specific attributes of what one remembers as the familiar. One's duties, then, are not prescribed by the past but inferred from universal laws. One pays one's debts not only out of gratitude or loyalty but out of a sense of what is right. One seeks progress and improvement not only for the members of one's own ethnic community but through laws designed to lift the general condition of the citizenry. It is the old conflict between the *Gemeinschaft* and the *Gesellschaft*, played out not only between Catholics and Protestants but also within every institution regardless of ethnic or religious differences. The conflict is fundamental to social life, since Protestants also develop specific loyalties and bend the law to suit both themselves and those to whom they feel quite specific ties of obligation.

Is there any truth to the academic apologetics that emphasize the cultural differences between Protestants and Catholics? If Andrew Greeley (1977:232ff.) is right, some differences still separate Catholics from Protestants even in the second half of the nineteenth century. The differences, he argues, are not major, since the majority of both groups subscribe to the same notions about telling lies, respecting property, and paying one's bills. Nonetheless, he has located data which suggest that there have been continuing and systematic differences between Catholics and Protestants in their willingness to bend the rules especially when extenuating circumstances come into play. Many of these circumstances involve a situation in which one has to do the wrong thing in order to protect the feelings or interests of a member of one's own family or a friend. For instance, respondents were asked to consider a situation in which a father could cheat a bus company by sending his twelve-year-old son at half-fare, a price reserved only for children under twelve. One of the extenuating circumstances was that the father could only afford to send his child on the bus to visit his grandparents if he could get away with paying the lower fare. Many of these extenuating circumstances involved making things work for the interests of friends and families rather than lesser justifications for opportunism. For instance, Catholics were more likely than Jews or Protestants to argue that a man could falsely claim a tax exemption for his mother only if that meant that he could continue to give his mother the limited financial aid he currently could afford. In most cases, Catholics were somewhat less flexible than Jews in these regards but more flexible than Protestants.

As I mentioned in the introduction, it is clear that Catholics are just as serious about time as their Protestant co-religionists, and that the differences among Protestants and among Catholics are probably far more significant than the differences between them. The longer Catholics have been in the United States, the more likely they are to value work for its intrinsic significance and not primarily for the income it brings, and one can hardly distinguish Catholic from Protestant Germans or Irish in this regard. Those Catholics who tend to value work for its external rewards, and primarily income, are not less successful than Protestants; indeed collectively they are more so (Greeley 1977:248–249). It is partly that they have not been able to settle for more prestige and less income. The same groups, largely the southern and eastern Catholics, are according to Greeley (1977:249) far less sanguine about the future than the Irish Catholics and the Protestants. The memories of home, of sad departures, and of suffering in the new world not only linger; they color the future. The Catholics are not the only ones, I will argue, to transfer a sense of loss from the past into a chronic sense of dread toward the future.

The "taint of time" lingers in the soul, whether one is Protestant or Catholic. Old flames continue to flicker in the memory. Like Dante one can be consumed with old passion and reminded of awe in the presence of those who, like Beatrice, are long absent. Whether that presence is renewed in memory, in present experience, or in anticipation of heaven matters greatly, as we have seen. An orientation toward the past can burden the soul with debts that must be paid. A lively experience of the presence of spirits that are no longer visible

makes it difficult for the individual to trust his or her own perceptions and experience. Unfinished emotional business with
the past, once projected on to the future, can fill the soul
either with longing for a beatific rest or with dread of a final
accounting. To attribute one set of longings, experiences, or
anticipations to the Protestant and another to the Catholic is
to falsify both the historical record and to ignore current data
on the similarities and differences between the two religious
communities.

The passion for saving not only the souls of the living but of
the dead was certainly not confined to Catholics. The Latter-
Day Saints, who have grown from six members in 1830 to the
fifth largest denomination in the United States by at least one
current estimate (Finke and Stark 1992:237, 242), are perhaps
the best case in point, in view of their well-known practice of
baptizing the living for the sake of the dead. In the eighteenth
century the Mormons had their own disasters: persecution and
massacre, ostracism and forced mobility. It is not surprising
that they felt the heavy emotional obligation of the living to
the dead that accompanies disaster, but even had their way
been smooth they would have been exposed to the same
evangelical currents as the rest of the country. These currents,
I have argued, forced the living to contemplate the fate of the
soul after death. One elder of the Latter-Day Saints, John
Morgan (1904:16), writing in 1904 complained that "The
fearful horrors of the never-ending punishment of the guilty
are portrayed in the liveliest colors from the Christian pulpits
of the land." While not minimizing the punishment deserved
by those who, hearing the gospel, reject it, Morgan was far
more concerned to spell out the love and justice of a merciful
God. That God, he avowed, had conferred on his people
through Elijah the power to baptize on behalf of the dead;
thus

the Latter-Day Saints are assiduously engaged in erecting temples
wherein this ordinance may be performed. The object of Elijah's
visit having been partially accomplished, in causing the hearts of the
fathers, dead and gone, to turn to the children here on earth, the
children are feeling after the fathers and seeking to open their prison

doors, and bring them through the door of baptism into the sheepfold.

Not only are the elders of Israel traveling, preaching the gospel and baptizing the people by the thousands, but the Saints are flocking to the temples of the Lord and redeeming their dead from the grasp of Satan. They are performing a great and mighty work for the human family who have lived upon the earth in the different ages of the world's history, and who, in some instances, by revelation, make manifest to their children or friends the fact that they have accepted the gospel in the spirit world ... (Morgan 1904:28)

Of course, it is not only for the souls of the dead but for their own salvation that the Latter-Day Saints perform their duties. As Morgan (1904:9) pointed out,

man has a work to do to prepare himself for a future exaltation in the eternities to come. He is called upon to "work out his salvation in fear and trembling" for the work done in this life will have its influence in that to come.

ON TIME

Those who are preparing their souls for future beatitude do indeed have "work to do," as Morgan put it. The future is a clear extension of the past and the present, without sudden interruptions from beyond. Purification is a serious business that requires discipline, self-control, and willingness to make plans for the future. Note that Morgan entitled his description of the Mormon faith as a "Plan of Salvation." There are no apocalyptic visions to sustain the believer in the process of self-purification: only a lot of hard work, from one day to the next.

If the souls of the dead were not part of the same time-zone as the souls of the living, there would be nothing that one could do in this life that would save a day or a minute of time in purgatory for the souls of the departed. It is the continuity of the dead with the living in the same spiritual community that makes it possible for the living to be baptized for the dead. It is possible to make up for lost time because that time is not really beyond retrieval or redemption. The continuity of time from this world to the next also makes it possible, as Morgan put it for the Mormons, to "influence" the future, even when that is the future of one's soul in the next life rather than this. For those who believe, time does not offer the chilling or terrifying prospect of sudden ruptures. Its passage is beyond the control of believers, but believers do retain control over their own passage into the night ahead. There is work for them to do.

This relative confidence in the passage of time, or of one's passage through time, does not lead to quiescence. On the contrary, it is crucial for the believer to make the most of the time available. Every day that passes without compassionate regard for the dead or some spiritual action on their behalf perpetuates their suffering. Conversely, every day counts in the preparation of the soul in this world for a tolerable fate in the next. There may still be work for one to do in the next life; progress goes on as the believer goes "from strength to strength in the life of perfect service." Nonetheless, every step taken now brings one closer to the goal of spiritual beatitude or the gates of heaven. There is no time to be wasted. I will return to the subject of this seriousness of time in connection with the introduction of time pieces in American society during the nineteenth century. Here it is enough to point out that the complex of beliefs regarding the next life that I would call "purgatorial" helps to explain how the watch became an emblem of one's good faith and moral direction. The "punctual self," to use Taylor's apt phrase for the social character outlined by John Locke, was being formed in large numbers in the revivals and meetings hosted by Catholic and Protestant evangelists alike.

CHAPTER 7

Charles Dickens in the American purgatory: the eternal foreground

Yet as the Church shall thither westward flie,
So Sinne shall trace and dog her instantly:
They have their period also and set times
Both for their vertuous actions and their crimes.

Thus also Sinne and Darknesse follow still
The Church and Sunne with all their power and skill.

(George Herbert, "The Church Militant," 70–73, 235–236,
259–263; *Works*, ed. F. E. Hutchinson [Oxford, 1941],
pp. 216–218; quoted in Bercovitch 1975:105)

Where, then, could the ascetic and hardy minister find a prospect where the future could be engaged if not in the West, where the future was indeed coming into view? It is the West that gave a spatial location to the soul's spiritual encounter with the future; it was time incarnate. There Dickens found what he called "the eternal foreground": and it was a chilling prospect indeed. Like Herbert, he thought that sin would follow the soul westward. The westward trek, then, was to a place where the soul would meet its highest test as it confronted it own darkness. Not only was Dickens less sanguine than Channing about the spiritual progress of the soul traveling westward; he was also far more excited about the soul's prospects in Boston, as we shall now see.

DICKENS ON AMERICAN INDIVIDUALISM: FROM NEW ENGLAND PARADISE TO URBAN AND RURAL DECAY

Foreign observers often get it very wrong when they comment on America. One of the most often and deferentially cited is

Tocqueville, whose warnings against American "individualism" have framed several generations of criticism. However, another Frenchman, not Tocqueville but Crevecoeur, was far closer to the American reality and less inclined to project his own European fears of "individualism" on the new American republic. For Crevecoeur American individualism was the moral and spiritual core of the new country; the American individualist would fulfill his or her vocation by building communities and the new nation's institutions (Arieli 1964).

Dickens (1985:105) found this individualism incarnated in the social life of Boston, which he held up as a "model." There he visited homes and asylums for the poor and wretched, for the blind and the insane. In an asylum for the blind, for instance, he found that one young woman, who was tragically at a loss for the usual avenues of contact and communication between human beings, was nevertheless fully in possession of her "immortal soul," despite the fact that she could not hear or speak, let alone see or even use her sense of smell. That an institution could be so committed to allowing an individual to discover her "immortal spirit" was precisely the model for which he was looking; by it he judged everything else that he saw. If he was harsh on other institutions and communities, other people and places, it was only because he had found the possession of one's own soul to be possible in these New England institutions for the halt, the lame, and the blind, whereas elsewhere in America the soul was often lost, wandering, or crushed.

Among the blind he found a community marked by "cheerfulness, industry, and good order"; although the blind could be compared with bees in a hive, their "individuality" was nonetheless "unimpaired" (Dickens 1985:79–81). It is as if Dickens had found there the remedy for heartbreaking industrial conditions, for a coldhearted utilitarian arrangement of industry and social life, and for the indifference of the rich and the potential bestiality of the desperate. As if to test his theory he went into stinking basements and attics in New York, into the most cruel of prisons in Philadelphia, and talked with those whose own souls were lost in chaos and poverty or slowly crushed by solitary confinement designed to make them "resigned." His is a chilling account, since he goes behind the scenes of institutions to talk to their victims, just as he moves from the very polite company of his American friends into the places where filth and wretchedness make one sick at heart.

Thus, if Dickens had a moral, it was simply that individuality and institutions need each other. A good institution is known by its fruits in building strong individual character; individual character is known by its fruits in a thriving community. If individuality is taken out of context, it becomes an individualistic striving for life, liberty, and happiness that quite literally destroys the lives of others and erodes both the community and nation. If the nation enshrines any value higher than the individual, the souls of the people are therefore crushed. A fancier term for the relationship, which Dickens fortunately ignores, is dialectical.

It is as if Dickens is saying that Bostonians (not to be confused with most Americans) have learned some of the lessons of antiquity. On the one hand, the individual is enshrined in the household of the asylum: a benign institution that is composed of persons, not merely positions, and yet offers everyone a secure place. On the other hand, this household is part of a city, to which it contributes disciplined citizens and from which it derives strength, guidance, resources, and talent. Like Emerson, Dickens found these Americans to be self-reliant and industrious, autonomous and capable of following the dictates of their own souls without becoming anti-social or destructive. Capable of hard work, of close friendships, of building communities and forging industries, all kept the public good well in mind. They were remarkably free, Dickens felt, of moral hypocrisy, fancy arguments, and pretentious intellectual gamesmanship, and they were "true, manly, honest, bold," and with a "hearty disgust of Cant" (Dickens 1985:107). If Dickens found these virtues in America, Emerson found them in England. No doubt America served as a double for England fully as much as England served as a double for America.

Remember that Dickens found his own convictions being

echoed on this side of the Atlantic in Emerson's Transcenden-
talism and in the ethic of heroic – but civic-minded – individualism. While Dickens was a bit vague and ironic about just
what it is that is being transcended, Emerson makes it clear
that it is the soul-crushing burden of tradition and public
opinion that is being overcome by the self-reliant individual.
As a shaman, furthermore, Emerson exhorts individuals to
seize the moment, to make the times their own, to engage in
creative and community-building activity as if their souls
depended on such exertion. The cure for soul-loss and despair
over running out of time is to rise to the occasion. It was a
capacity for timely action that Emerson (Bode, ed. 1981:399ff.)
in "English Traits" found preeminent among the English. The
irony of that discovery was not lost on Emerson, who had
expected there to find empty souls drained of spirit. What he
found was "bottom" and "mettle": the very qualities he was
exhorting his American audiences to develop in themselves.

Outside the context of community, Dickens found individualism ugly and destructive. Whereas the Bostonian institutions created the conditions in which individuals could come
into the possession of their own souls, in New York, Dickens
found, Americans were in danger of losing their souls. Outside
New York City he discovered a tomb marked "The Stranger's
Grave" (Dickens 1985:143), dedicated to the hotels of the city.
As if that note were not sufficiently chilling, Dickens found
caricatures of utilitarians and self-reliant individuals in the
animals that inhabited the streets of New York. The utilitarian
monkey and the self-reliant pig were contrasted with the happy
bees working in the Bostonian hives. Whereas even the mad of
Boston were accorded dignity, the sane but self-serving con-
sumers of New York seemed merely to become what they were
eating (Dickens 1985:134–136).

If Boston represented an improvement in the human condition, New York City embodied the worst of both antiquity
and modernity. On the one hand, New York was a city of
opportunity: a sea of options, to avail oneself of which one
became like the swine of the street. On the other hand,
America's prisons recapitulated the institution of slavery in

antiquity; perhaps the most destructive was New York's Tombs. There a wall separated the prisoners from the execution-ground: a barrier beyond which no prisoner could see until his time to die. Once that time had arrived, however, prisoners were deprived of the witnesses, the very eyes, that could have enabled the condemned to be "true" and "manly," "honest" and "bold" in the face of death. If the purgatorial complex was foreshadowed in the cities of antiquity, which tantalized the soul of the slave with the possibilities of redemption and of citizenship in an earthly kingdom, it was realized in New York, where the free citizen enjoyed an animal-like form of consumption, while the prisoners were isolated and enslaved in conditions designed to crush the soul before the body expired.

Earlier Dickens had surmised that the blind were better off than those with sight, because the eyes make one unduly aware of others' appraisals of the self and get in the way of individual self-reliance. Here in the god-forsaken execution yard of the Tombs, however, the only witnesses were the judge, the jury, and a few carefully chosen witnesses, none of whom were on the side of the condemned or could encourage them to be strong and endow them with respect at the end. Without that human recognition, those who have been doing time finally resign their spirits and accept their sentence. Theirs is an anticlimactic end following the destruction of their souls.

There is no doubt that Dickens, like Durkheim, shared a distaste for the utilitarian. In a Philadelphia prison devoted entirely to solitary confinement, he noted the "superior efficiency" of that legalized process for killing the soul. The prisoners whom he interviewed seemed – on the whole – to be crushed: "resigned," in the words of their warders, and thus on the way to a penitential state that was officially designed to be the beginning of their putative salvation. That system of institutionalized soul-murder seemed to Dickens the coldest and most rational, heartless, and potent form of destructive asceticism. A spiritual discipline, which at its Bostonian best could make individuals take to heart the honesty and respect with which they were being treated by their guardians, could

also take the heart and soul out of the individual when turned
to sadistic purpose. What Dickens (1985:106) wrote of the New
England pulpit still dominated by the Puritan ethos could as
well have been directed at the piety that constructed and
designed this brutal penitentiary:

They who strew the eternal path with the greatest amount of brim-
stone, and who most ruthlessly tread down the flowers and leaves that
grow by the wayside, will be voted the most righteous; and they who
enlarge with the greatest pertinacity on the difficulty of getting into
heaven, will be considered by all true believers certain of going there:
though it would be hard to say by what process of reasoning this
conclusion is arrived at.

Penitentiaries, like purgatory, offered a time for purification
of the soul based on repentance. A secularized "process of
reasoning" lead to the formation of a prison based on solitary
confinement, which broke the soul and buried a prisoner alive
for a time that seemed to have no end and no redeeming
moment. The prisoner endured the slow and progressive dissolution of the soul into something incapable of enjoying life
outside the prison. Dead to the world and incapable of imagining themselves whole and restored to their former lives, the
prisoners were shattered beyond repair and recall:

The cell-door has been closed too long on all its hopes and cares.
Better to have hanged him in the beginning than bring him to this
pass, and send him forth to mingle with his kind, who are his kind no
more ... (Dickens 1985:156)

It is possible that these words were also beginning to describe
Dickens's own state of mind on being too long in America and
too far removed from the familiar sights and faces of his own
former world beyond the Atlantic, to which he was longing to
return. Had he expected to mingle with his own kind on
American soil, only to find that they were "his kind no more"?
Certainly time was increasingly on his mind. Earlier he had felt
that the times were urgent, and that time itself was always
running out. For these solitary prisoners time was empty, the
years wasted and dragging by. For the soul in purgatory, even
for one who, like Dickens on this journey, is bravely self-reliant

and bold at undertaking new ventures, there can indeed be a "tyranny of time" that threatens to destroy the soul.

In a trip to Lowell to inspect the mills, he had been impressed by the very good use of leisure time, through the piano in the library and their own writing, achieved by the women employees. Far from their own homes, and hard at work for ten hours a day, they nonetheless were capable of cultural accomplishments and compared favorably with their English peers. He contrasted these fortunate mill-workers with those in England who were confined to the most wretched conditions at their "dark, satanic" mills. It is on their account, whose lives were surrounded with evil and blight, that Dickens urged his readers to experience the urgency of their need, because "*the precious time is rushing by*," (Dickens 1985:119; emphasis added).

Although Dickens's view of America became more jaundiced the further he traveled from Boston, he nevertheless found times and places where the republic seemed to thrive on the full expression of individual responsibility. Here, for instance, is his description of a gathering at the White House one evening, a "Levee":

The great drawing-room ... and the other chambers on the ground floor, were crowded to excess. The company was not, in our sense of the term, select, for it comprehended persons of very many grades and classes; nor was there any great display of costly attire: indeed, some of the costumes may have been, for aught I know, grotesque enough. But the decorum and propriety of behavior which prevailed, were unbroken by any rude or disagreeable incident; and every man, even among the miscellaneous crowd in the hall who were admitted without any orders or tickets to look on, appeared to feel that he was part of the Institution, and was responsible for its preserving a becoming character, and appearing to the best advantage ...
(Dickens 1985:173)

Now, the moral that was just sounded in these lines extends to other cases in which individuals clearly did not feel this sense of civic responsibility for the welfare of the whole community. Dickens is frequently quite acid about the individuals who would regard it as infringing their personal liberty and independence to be true to their own word. Steamboat captains leave when they feel like it but never at the time they have announced. Not only travelers but guests in one's own house send out streams of chewing tobacco wherever they choose to spit, even on one's own floor and carpet. There is little in the literature on slavery more scathing than Dickens's comments about individuals whose pursuit of liberty requires them to buy and sell women and children and to separate them from their husbands and fathers. As for the personal liberties of Congressmen, Dickens (1985:168) found some using their powers of speech and the press itself to distort the truth and to vilify their opponents:

It is the game of these men, and of their profligate organs, to make the strife of politics so fierce and brutal, and destructive of self-respect in all worthy men, that sensitive and delicate-minded persons shall be kept aloof, and they, and such as they, be left to battle out their selfish views unchecked.

For Dickens it is the unforgivable sin of any society to crush the spirit of the individual; just as it is the purpose of social life to inspire the soul: to breathe, as it were, the breath of spiritual life into the individual.

Now, Dickens found an extraordinary lack of spirit among many Americans, an apathy that in some approached a state of melancholy. Apathy may well be one of the first signs of a soul under the tyranny of time: the deadness of one who feels that one's innermost self is mortgaged, as it were, either to the past or to the future and will not come alive in the present. No doubt such a sense of being mortgaged – hopelessly indebted – to time was what Dickens observed among the prisoners and what so saddened him in these institutions.

It is clear that in his American journey Dickens was something of a lost soul himself and became progressively more depressed and disenchanted the further West he went. The landscape became full of trees that were half destroyed by rot and by careless woodsmen, with soil eroding and swamps taking over the fields. The Ohio river was hemmed in by banks of endless green without a trace of human life: "the same, eternal foreground" (Dickens 1985:205). The houses, or huts and log cabins, are uniformly bleak. It is as if Dickens himself felt that he was in solitary confinement, hemmed in by prison walls, beyond which was an execution ground: an unbearable prospect that could destroy a man's soul. In fact, when he reached the edge of the great plains, he did find that endless prospect unbearable and turned backward and inward in evident pain and anxiety about the fragility and shortness of life and of the soul itself. It may well be that he despaired of returning home alive, especially since steamboat passengers had recently been killed by explosions. Finally, on the plains, he encountered the ruins of a convent: the sign of a spiritual life desolated by the openness to a horizon that was forever receding. America was a purgatory for crushed, lost, wandering, and departed souls: an "eternal foreground" and bleak prospect all in one.

While we must therefore take into account the depression that gave his own perspectives such a negative coloring, it is possible still to find his pictures of individuals very illumining, especially when they focus on the difficulties of sustaining the self outside the protective surroundings of benign communities and institutions. Clearly the asylums of Boston were "holding environments" that gave the individuals time to sort themselves out and to achieve a high level of self-definition. Even the factories of Lowell turned out to be similarly benign matrices, where individuality could flourish without premature demands being placed on the soul. In the distance, however, are the forester and plainsman, who are solitary figures, utterly alone, and consigned to the fate of doing things the hard way in an environment that was anything but benign. Indeed, in the vignettes of life along the Ohio river or bordering on the great plains, time is already running out, and the earth itself is either decaying or parched.

In between these two extremes we find a purgatorial way of life that is entrenched both in the pulpit and in the prison system. Both church and state place an individual's soul on trial for life, with little hope of redemption. Only strenuous exhortations from the pulpit and conversion itself can enable the sinner to make up for lost time or at least to postpone the evil day of a final accounting.

As I have noted, the services of shamans in defending the soul against the prospect of running out of time are necessary in "modern" as well as in "primitive" societies, but there was something about America that kept their magical services in demand. The evangelical and sacramental cures they dispensed, furthermore, perpetuated indefinitely the disease of the soul. There was no rescue, despite all the earlier rhetoric of a new heaven and a new earth: no new creation.

Along the streets of New York, and in the legislative chambers of Washington, Dickens found that the public enjoyed unrestrained license to consume and to destroy the individual's self-respect. To live under these conditions is to consign the self to a continuing and demeaning struggle, in which one's own soul is endangered by the greed and license of others who, far from being like oneself, behave in ways that are quasi-bestial. Finally, in the prisons and on the loneliest frontier individuals face their fate in solitude. Their souls slowly died within them, as they lost hope of being restored to the company of their own kind. It is not too difficult to imagine that a masochistic social character could be formed under these conditions.

Central to Dickens's view of America is that it makes the self quite marginal, even though the republic is centered upon the individual's rights to life, liberty, and the pursuit of happiness. Speaking of the poverty and erosion ("the withered ground") of farms based on slavery, Dickens (1985:180) had said that "there is an air of ruin and decay abroad, which is inseparable from the system." That same air of ruin and decay pervades his vignettes of life along the Ohio river, where formally free settlers are living in circumstances as bleak as those of poor slaves in the South: half-finished huts, eroded soil, fields filled with stumps, windows protected by rags, children playing in the same mud with pigs, and the solitary individual left standing without social support. This description of a family of settlers left on the Ohio river bank is typical:

They all stand where they landed, as if stricken into stone; and look after the boat. So they remain, quite still and silent ... There they stand yet [as the steamboat departs – RKF], without the motion of a hand. I can see them, through my glass, when, in the distance and

increasing darkness, they are mere specks to the eye: lingering there
still: the old woman in the old chair, and all the rest about her: not
stirring in the least degree. And thus I slowly lose them ... (Dickens
1985:206)

The point is that this is how the system works. Individuals
are left stranded; they become marginal and immobilized. It is
as if they could only see one another through a glass darkly, but
not face to face. Dickens's sense of loss is palpable, but the
immobility of the settlers who remain motionless on the bank,
like stone, suggests that the sense of loss was not his alone.

This is not merely a poignant vignette but a story told by
Dickens to tell us how the system works. The story echoes his
observations of slavery and prisons: that these institutions
slowly crush the spirits of their inhabitants; and it is consistent
with his criticisms of legislatures and communities that destroy
the individuality and self-respect of their members. Here I
would simply add that his many descriptions of settlers left
stranded in a wilderness typify Americans as wishing to do
things alone, the hard way. Perhaps some felt themselves
required to suffer for some unnamed sin, while others wished to
dramatize a feeling of loss and separation from which they had
not yet recovered. All were nevertheless in a secular purgatory.

After staring the wilderness in the face, Dickens immediately
turned back to the familiar comforts of a transplanted European civilization in the New World. He found St. Louis vastly
reassuring after staring into the "Looking Glass Prairie," and
who would not? The bare, brown patches of earth in front of
him on the prairie had reminded him of the difficulty of
realizing the self and its projects in time as well as in space; the
patches of earth, like the remains of the old convent, were a
monument to the futility of any attempt to realize one's self in
the absence of a secure and continuous social context.
Although he was fascinated by the ruined convent and the bare
patches of the plains, he also was preoccupied with spittoons,
the precarious hold on civility, and the crudeness of the
American public places. Like a sociologist he was concerned
with the intrusions of the impure or the unworthy: the forces
that sneak in through the gates or the cracks in the wall of the

holy city, as it were. If there were no such place as heaven, there would be no Purgatory, and it is the wish for such a safe haven for the soul that turns the world into a place of trial and purification, torment and testing, that go on forever.

QUESTIONS ABOUT AMERICAN SOCIAL CHARACTER

Did Dickens project his own tendency to self-torment and long-suffering on the American people? Dickens fits the psychoanalytic picture of adults who, abused as children, have turned suffering into a way of life (Shengold 1989). There is a masochistic social character that develops from such abusive families, and beneath that masochism there is a cruelty which, turned on the self, perpetuates painful attachments into adult life. The refusal to sever those attachments and to resolve the pain characterizes the masochistic character. The question is whether Dickens is painting the American scene with the dark hues of his own masochism, or whether he may have discerned what it is like to live in a secularized form of Purgatory. To many it may seem strange to argue that so energetic and hard-working a country as the America of the early 1800s should be considered purgatorial.

What does the American social character, with its willingness to persevere in the hardships of the wilderness or of the city, with its toleration of incivility in public life, have to do with masochism? Theodor Reik (1941) argued years ago that masochists are often quite energetic, persevering, determined and therefore also successful. As a people they may endure and survive what other peoples would find daunting. Contemporary psychoanalysts would appear to agree. In the grim determination of the masochist, writes Cecilia Jones (1989:22), can be

seen, in however distorted and destructive a form ... the powerful stirrings of our patient's will, which in normal development would have so adaptively subserved individuation and the unfolding autonomy of the self. In masochism, however, it becomes diverted in its aim in order to subserve clinging and the disavowal of loss-what might be called a "perversion of the will" in masochistic phenomena.

Jones (1989:22) goes on to say that, among masochists, asceticism becomes "a lethal end in itself," and the course of a therapeutic analysis depends on turning such asceticism into a means to the end of confronting the deeper pains and more poignant losses that the patient has been so far unwilling to experience directly and thus to resolve.

Dante would have concurred with Dr. Jones's diagnosis. It is indeed a perversion of the will that one finds in Purgatory: a will to endure pain and a reluctance to abandon "clinging and the disavowal of loss": hence the need for a Purgatory in which to act out separation and loss over and over again.

There is more to the perversion of the will than simply a denial of old losses and a desire to cling to a maternal figure, however damaging or unreliable that figure may have been. What accounts for the peculiar persistence, the grim determination, of the masochist? Remember at this point Reik's (1941) argument that the masochist is engaged in a "flight forward" toward a day of battle and vindication. This day may indeed represent old losses, abrupt departures, and early wounds projected from the past, where they have not been resolved, into the future. In the future, however, the masochist enjoys – if only in fantasy – the prospect of revenge: a final triumph over every enemy. It is that underlying sadistic resolve that makes the masochist hungry for love, according to Reik, and all too willing to cling to the security and comfort of the womb: there to be protected from, but also to enact, the continuing struggle for domination.

Dickens indeed found in Americans a chronic desire to put others to the test. As Dickens (1985:285) points out in his *American Notes*:

One great blemish in the popular mind of America, and the prolific parent of an innumerable brood of evils, is Universal Distrust. Yet the American citizen plumes himself upon this spirit, even when he is sufficiently dispassionate to perceive the ruin it works; and he will often adduce it, in spite of his own reason, as an instance of the great sagacity and acuteness of the people, and their superior shrewdness and independence.

Granted that Dickens (1985:285) is talking about the doubts

that individuals have of others rather than of themselves, he is also speaking of the tendency of "every national character to pique itself mightily upon its faults." For Dickens these national flaws are a point of national pride; translated into psychoanalytic idiom they are merely narcissistic ways of fending off and disguising hurtful and cruel impulses. In the case of each individual, moreover, these flaws are projected on to the world of "others," who are then imagined to harbor one's own tendency to cheat others in their business and public affairs. Note also the attributions of "superior shrewdness and independence:" Dickens has caught the narcissistic overtones of a master-mind at work in each sharp-dealing individual or self-reliant citizen.

To live with such sadistic fantasies about others does indeed take the joy out of life and lay the groundwork for masochistic self-deprivations. Dickens (1985:289) goes on to observe:

I was quite oppressed by the prevailing seriousness and melancholy air of business: which was so general and unvarying ["out of the large cities" – RKF],that at every new town I came to, I seemed to meet the very same people I had left behind me, at the last. Such defects as are perceptible in the national manners, seem, to me, to be referable, in a great degree, to this cause: which has generated a dull, sullen persistence in coarse usages, and rejected the graces of life as undeserving of attention.

Earlier I noted that, if you scratch a masochist, you will find a rebel: someone with secret fantasies of triumph over enemies. These are the fantasies that underlie the Americans' pride in their own shrewdness and cleverness in business and politics. As Reik (1941) noted, however, the masochist must pay in advance for these fantasies: an eye for an eye, as it were, but in the form of a down payment. It is a subtle, no doubt unconscious, advance payment for the enjoyment, if only in fantasy, of triumph and retribution over enemies that Dickens may have observed in the Americans' melancholy and in the ugliness of public places.

It is seldom that one can find a more bald statement of these triumphant fantasies than did Dickens when he was visiting Sandusky, Ohio. There Dickens (1985:241) noted that a

Cleveland newspaper was trumpeting the arrival in Washington of an English statesman, Lord Ashburton, "To adjust the points in dispute between the United States Government and Great Britain." On this occasion, however, the editor of the local newspaper saw far more at stake than the careful business of negotiation; underlying such transactions, he found, was the promise of triumph for America over Britain:

informing its readers that as America had "whipped" England in her infancy, and whipped her again in her youth, so it was clearly necessary that she must whip her once again in her maturity, and pledging its credit to all True Americans, that ... they should, within two years, "sing Yankee Doodle in Hyde Park, and Hail Columbia in the scarlet courts of Westminster." (Dickens 1985:241)

Note that the newspaper itself is now fantasizing, in the way that psychiatrists refer to the part of the self that feels omnipotent and wishes to own and control the world for itself. In the same process, however, the newspaper is promising a return to the mother country: a chance to triumph in the most sacred shrine of the mother country itself, Westminster, and there to sing the song of national self-congratulation. It is this combination of a desire to triumph over the mother, who is both "damaging" and "damaged," with a desire to return to her in some sort of union, that typifies, according to Rosenfeld (1988:172–173), the masochistic patient:

It is very important for the analyst to know about the highly suggestive, almost hypnotic, panic-spreading propaganda of the destructive narcissistic organization. The patient is very easily paralyzed by it, and there is a real danger that the patient, weakened by the panic, will fall back on the false, seductive "help" that is often offered by the destructive organization in disguise ... I have also come across patients whose narcissism was characterized by feelings of omnipotence and intense desire to be looked after by a powerful person with whom they could experience a sense of symbiotic union.

These reflections on Americans' desire for retribution and triumph are not meant to minimize the terrible pains and losses in the lives of many of the individuals with whom Dickens spoke. He has many accounts of settlers who have had to bury their children in a lonely place and now must move on: accounts, also, of individuals who have left their homeland in England or in New England, and who have recently moved westward to live in what are, for Dickens, clearly pitiable and sometimes hideous surroundings. The sum total of human hardship, combined with the emotional injuries of leaving one's home to settle westward, would certainly have caused sufficient pain to test the endurance of many, even most, of these settlers. Nonetheless, there may have been an additional source of emotional loss in the separation of the country as a whole from England: an awareness of which Dickens's own presence on this trip would heighten and sharpen.

Dickens may indeed have stimulated, simply by being in this country, some of the yearning for the attachment to the old country that psychoanalysts have found to inhere in the masochistic character. Certainly Dickens's trip produced an immense popular response. He writes of people coming from the West to see him in the East, and he was literally exhausted from the hours spent with visitors, day and night, even when he was staying in some hotel. His attempts at privacy were sometimes misunderstood and resented, and yet it seems difficult to imagine how he could have made more time available to the thousands of Americans who wished to see and to talk with him. In addition, he reports many encounters in which he is approached, as an Englishman, by individuals who still had a quarrel with England; of these encounters perhaps the most hostile were with Southerners irate with England's stand against slavery. On the whole, however, he was nearly adored by thousands and thousands of Americans. The editors of *American Notes*, in explaining why Dickens should not have been surprised at the crush of people to see him and his consequent lack of privacy, reveal how deep was the attachment to Dickens and, I would argue, through Dickens to England itself:

He *was* the most famous novelist in the world and his books were read to tatters in the most remote parts of America. Early in 1841 Dickens received a letter from a backwoodsman, John Tomlin, stressing how much the Englishman's novels had meant to him. In his answering letter Dickens referred to this as "a source of the purest delight and pride to me," (23 February 1841). Bret Harte describes rough prospectors sitting round a camp fire enthralled and moved by the pitiable plight of Little Nell and all Dickensians revel in the fact that, as the ship carrying the final numbers of *The Old Curiosity Shop* sailed into New York, a vast crowd waited on the quay shouting "Is little Nell dead?" In the words of J. B. Simons, "they stood, haggard with anxiety, a dense mass of five or six thousand people" (Whitley and Goldman 1985:301–302)

Time was indeed running out for the people gathered, "haggard with anxiety," on the dock in New York. They are being kept waiting; like Joseph K. in *The Trial* what seems like fate is keeping them waiting for news of the end. As Reik (1941) pointed out of the masochistic character, the masochist is often engaged in a "flight forward"; suspense over the end, and a desire for a final accounting and a chance to turn the tables on the enemy drive the masochist headlong into the future. Similarly the crowd on the dock, eager for news of Little Nell, cannot wait to see how the end will turn out. Now masochists project the memory of an old loss or injury from the past into the future where it can be anticipated with dread. Thus the full force of the earlier loss can be avoided by seeking to cope with a secondary loss (for example, the death of Little Nell). Such suffering is rendered all the more enjoyable by imagining oneself again in the company of the person who has died or gone away; like Dante, who cannot resist reunion with his old flame. That is how the will is perverted, by denying old grief and holding on to persons long gone. For many Americans, it would appear, this perversion of the will had become a purgatorial way of life.

Indeed, Jill Montgomery (1989:84) speaks of the "sadomasochism of purgatory" as typifying patients who have perpetuated their suffering in order to postpone the full separation of themselves from their parents:

My patient told the following story about his birth: His mother was pregnant on the ship taking them to the new military base. He was expected to be delivered on the ship during the journey, but mother wanted first to settle in her new home. Although ready to be born he had to wait two weeks until she was ready to deliver him. He blamed what he felt to be his humiliating lack of will on this event.

This patient, like many Americans, was caught between the desire to cling to the mother – or mother-country – and the desire to become a separate person. One of his dreams, as Jill Montgomery (1989) goes on to report, begins with the main character, a soldier, outside the prison camp; he is alone, facing an alien and hostile world. When he returns to the prison camp, he finds himself recaptured, engulfed in a net against which he struggles and pushes to assert what is left of his independence. The patient typically did regress, going back to infancy in his imagination, where he could be surrounded by maternal space and still fight against the overwhelming authority of his parents. In that way the patient could achieve a very limited sense of selfhood and assert his boundaries, although through very regressive means. For instance in the dream he endured punishment by a father-figure in the prison camp (perhaps a disguise for his threatening mother) and suffered confinement by nets that surrounded him, like a womb, so that he could at least in his imagination fight against them and achieve a sense of identity. As Greif (1989:95) put it, masochistic patients "fear once again being enslaved within the context of a non-gratifying attachment that leads nowhere and satisfies few if any needs, except perhaps the most basic one of all, which is simply to be related to another human being no matter how painful this relatedness may be."

Jill Montgomery points out that the desire for merger with the mother is experienced as a great danger, as though one would lose one's own soul. That is precisely the case: such a reunion is paid for by self-loss. The fear of losing one's own soul through such a dissolution of boundaries leads to a surrender of the soul to the instructions of a shaman: a commitment to act on the shaman's instructions as though one's own being depended on such timely response. Not only the shaman but any grandiose and destructive figure disguised as a helper, once internalized, can become a source of torment, of continuous and painful testing.

Of course, there is no way in retrospect of assessing the mind of an urban crowd; even being contemporaneous with the visit of Dickens to this country or in observing the crowd longing for news of Little Nell would not have yielded the information on the psyche that would answer our questions about masochism in the American social character and its purgatorial roots. We will never know whether the crowd's anxiety for the fate of Little Nell was a disguise for their anxiety about partial emotional separation from the distant but still threatening mother-country of England. Were Americans so tempted by dreams of restoration and return to the mother country or to "home" that they were in a state of chronic purgatory? Was the sense of trial and tribulation that afflicted the characters in Dickens's novels a purgatorial drama of redemption in which large numbers of Americans expressed their own sense of being on trial for their lives: facing terrible dangers, yearning over irretrievable losses, and wondering if there will be anything to show for the time, the lifetime, that they have spent in the new wilderness?

As Bercovitch (1975) points out, the colonists felt that they were living in a time of trial; no wonder that the history of the colonies reads like an "epic of the soul." In this spiritual trial, furthermore, Satan's wrath "would intensify as the time to exert it grew short" (Bercovitch 1975:106). In that time, furthermore, the life of the saint would be unified with the congregation, the congregation with the community, the community with the nation, and the nation with the history of God's elect.

As you will remember, the prospect of losing one's soul can seem all too immediate in the face of death. There is no doubt that the colonists found themselves in a world that was alien, superior, and both frightening and prepossessing. Speaking of seventeenth-century New Englanders, Bercovitch finds them caught between an old world of suffering, calamity, and failure, on the one hand, and a New World that was sheer "wilderness" and "desert." His description of these early colonists could well apply to the Americans that Dickens found, two hundred years later, on his trip from New England westward to the frontier:

The terms speak for themselves of his [the New Englander's – RKF] fear; the adjectives with which he formulaicly surrounded them are more explicit still: *howling, hideous, boundless, unknown, Satanic, wild, forlorn* ... (Bercovitch 1975:102)

The later generation, like the early New Englander, had to distinguish their visible circumstances from what was revealed to the eyes of the consecrated soul who alone could discern light in darkness, grace in torment, national glory in what otherwise might seem to be merely local tribulation:

Early New England rhetoric is a titanic effort to secularize traditional images without abandoning the claims of exegesis. The clergy compensated for their extreme subjectivism in substance by an extreme orthodoxy in approach. The perceiver, they insisted, had to identify with the divine meaning of the New World if he was to understand his environment correctly ... (Bercovitch 1975:114)

That meaning, I have suggested, was that America was somewhere between hell and heaven: a new purgatory.

Epilogue

Modern societies generate fresh supplies of masochistic tendencies that enable individuals to make those very compromises with potent persons and objects that offer temporary, partial, and unsatisfying protections from soul-loss. Individuals will see large corporations or institutions as powerful and self-contained, albeit potentially damaging and destructive; and at the same time, individuals will regard these large-scale social formations as sources of power and comfort without which they cannot survive. Like the primitive, some – perhaps most – individuals will make a compromise with these organizations, taking them, as it were, into their souls, and by incorporating them into their own beings recover a sense of their own presence in the world. It is only when corporations default on their parental obligations, abandon their children, divest themselves of property in local communities, and join forces with people in other countries that the individual will realize the risks of such a premature identification with the world, not as it is but as one imagines it to be. The recovery of the soul will become of paramount importance, lest the individual lose his or her soul to the disappearing or indifferent organization.

Under these conditions, a masochistic social character develops: unsure of itself, running out of time, arrested in development, relying on identifications with a world endowed with imaginary powers, while denying that world's very real powers. This is a character in which the danger of soul-loss becomes chronic rather than acute; purgatory, as I have suggested, has become a way of life. Masochistic individuals may long to be "lords of themselves," and to be able to act on impulse from a purified will, but they are a long way from the verge of paradise, and they know it.

One example of such rebellious passivity is Jean Jacques Rousseau, whose advocacy of the "spirit of revolt" fed much of the revolutionary enthusiasm of the French in the late eighteenth century, just as it had reinforced similar impulses on this side of the Atlantic. According to Blanchard (1984:15ff.), on whose account I am relying in this discussion, Rousseau clearly needed and wanted to be cared for, felt entitled to endless love and care from his (mostly aristocratic) benefactors, and maintained a child-like naivety well into adulthood. It was precisely because of this passivity that he was so fierce an advocate of independence, just as his dependence on the aristocracy for a safe haven in which to think revolutionary thoughts required him to be adamantly egalitarian. These reactions against his own passivity reflect a deeply held wish to turn the tables on the adult world, a world that had left him, since early childhood, feeling not only abandoned and misunderstood but grievously wronged and shamed for crimes that he did not commit. It would seem obvious that Rousseau himself fits Reik's picture of the moral masochist as someone with strong fantasies of triumph and revenge: so strong, in fact, that only a lifetime of humiliation on his part could atone for the punishments that he intended to visit upon his enemies, of which he imagined himself to have many. Blanchard (1984:157) compared the careful and defensive approach of Rousseau toward revolutionary action with the dilemmas of the masochist who first must suffer before succeeding:

Reik has insisted that the basic aim in masochism is one of revenge and destruction. The masochistic fantasy is really a cover for basic sadistic desires Thus, the desire to suffer while working for revolution would seem a perfect blend of both the overt masochistic fantasy, with the sadistic aim also conscious, but delayed. One *submits* to self-imposed suffering, to the discipline of a revolutionary movement with the thought that 'someday' one will gain full power and be able to punish and dominate the enemy.

However, in order to sustain this fantasy, delay is essential. The basic sadistic impulse, which was probably directed toward the father or possibly both parents, is restrained by guilt. Therefore, one can not merely rush out to make a physical attack on some government figure. One must have the *feeling* of conducting an attack without actually incurring the responsibility for such an act, [note the element of passivity – RKF]. The building of a theoretical structure for revolution and the gradual organization of activist groups serves this purpose.

Thus the rebel is consigned to living in a this-worldly purgatory precisely because delay is so essential to combining a revolutionary posture and a rebellious spirit with outward compliance with the demands of one's society and its authorities. To be "in" the world but not "of" it is therefore typical of the soul in purgatory and is conducive to the emergence of a masochistic social character. This holding back of a part of the self, along with the protracted and delayed triumph, makes the individual believe that time – always of the essence for the revolution – is running short. So great a tyrant does time now become – as the surrogate of the tyrants whose overthrow is the masochist's true aim – that some, like Rousseau, make a show of throwing away their watches, as though to proclaim their liberation from the tyranny of time. To recover the soul from its subjection to the tyranny of time is tantamount to getting the soul out of its particular purgatory.

There is thus a peculiar combination of rebelliousness and conformity in the American character. Too often celebrations of the American spirit of voluntarism and pragmatism, of our republican and civic virtues, and even of the responsible quest for life, liberty, and happiness have ignored the purgatorial aspects of American social character. Often suffused with a desire to remedy a deficit in the self, to atone for a crime, or to authenticate the self in the eyes of a powerful ideal, Americans have had something to prove to themselves and the world. Rebellious against all forms of tyranny and particularly of the British, they have practiced conformity and admired the English. Indeed, while Emerson found in the English strong souls that could withstand the test of time, Dickens found in Americans a chronic desire to put themselves – and others – to the test. The narcissistic spirit, the false self, thus displaces the true self, the soul. That is, after all, the disease for which purgatory is both symptom and cure.

"TEMPORAL PANIC": THE NEW FACES OF MORAL MASOCHISM

The legacy of purgatory is thus a mixture of both hope and torment. On the one hand, the prospect of reunion with those who have gone before and of an "everlasting rest" holds out the hope of a final sanctification. On the way, individuals can perfect themselves, indeed must seek to purify themselves, so that they will not forfeit this heavenly prospect. There is, however, as Luther discovered, no way to do enough in the way of purifying the self (Bainton 1985:26ff.). There was no sure way of realizing, as one might now say, one's spiritual potential. The way to one's everlasting rest becomes increasingly arduous the further one travels along the road to perfection. Purgatory held out what might be called the myth of the possibility of the infinite. In effect, however, the myth becomes one among infinite possibilities which, by definition, because they are infinite, can never be realized.

Neither was there any way to be so penitent as to be sure beyond the shadow of a doubt of one's forgiveness. Luther was not the first, and was far from the last, to experience the exquisite suffering of the soul seeking confirmation that its contrition had been sufficient and its confession complete (cf. Bainton 1985:131). Generations, now centuries, of evangelicals have perfected the art of tormenting the soul with doubts of its own capacity to confess and to receive pardon. The possibilities of the infinite have been translated into an infinite set of possibilities for improving on one's contrition and confession. That torment has sometimes driven souls into religious melancholia and suicidal despair (Rubin 1994). In its secularized form, soul-searching for hidden sins has turned into endemic self-doubt and into a chronic hunger for spiritual validation by a secular priesthood of experts on human development.

For instance, Tom Lutz's recent (1991) study of *American Nervousness* (published by George M. Beard in 1881) finds public figures from politicians to writers, from conservatives to progressives expressing their sense of what troubles them as an illness or malady of the body and the soul. These public figures lived in what Lutz (1991:168) calls an "economy of pain." It was an "economy" since they shared that pain with others, and they took turns in lamenting the loss of time and energy in their own lives or in the lives of other Americans; it was "pain" because they appear to have been afflicted with what moderns might call depression and its many symptoms. Had Lutz cast his story as an investigation into the masochistic aspects of the American character, none of his descriptions would have had to change: only his interpretations and perhaps some of his explanations.

The "myth of infinite possibilities" has several aspects: the chronic anxiety over lost opportunities or over dreadful events in the future; the sense of binding attachments that come with heavy duty and obligation; the angry demand to wipe the slate clean, to rid the field of rivals and enemies, and – of course – to pay in advance for such retribution. For instance, one way to justify and to deny the pain inflicted by Anglo-Saxons on their immigrant laborers was to claim that only Anglo-Saxons could suffer (Lutz 1991:7); Lutz's accounts suggest that there were many scores being settled and payments being made in the melancholy self-doubt that afflicted the neurasthenic. American men for the time being recovered their manhood by vigorous, even violent expeditions into the wilderness, by colonizing other nations, and by returning women – tempted by the rewards of professional or public life – to their domestic duties, where women then suffered attacks of conscience or new losses of nerve. Women and blacks temporarily regained their vigor by leaving the confines of the home and their restricted ethnic communities, only to suffer the burden of new responsibilities and questions about the substance and solidity of their inner selves. For some, like Teddy Roosevelt, time was running out on the Anglo-Saxon race and the upper class; for Charlotte Perkins Gilman, time was being wasted in the home and was running out for women whose lives were therefore also being wasted. Time was of the essence, and some, like William Dean

Howells, feared that it was perhaps too late for them to come to grips with their souls. It would be hard to find a more telling set of illustrations for the masochistic social character, except for the fact that the cases Lutz has chosen come from a cultural elite. Nonetheless, they set the tone for a painful self-awareness that was willing to transform the individual from a chronic sinner into a perennial patient (Lutz 1991:42). Purgatory has become secularized into a perennial drama of the soul.

Earlier studies of what ailed Americans put the blame squarely on the intensification of time. Another study of *American Nervousness* "partly blamed 'clocks and watches' and the 'necessity of punctuality' for the American middle class's generally strained nerves" (O'Malley 1990:150). O'Malley's discussion of Beard's study makes it clear that the problem with time extended deep into the psyche. There were psychosomatic consequences to the preoccupation with time; the new timepieces "laid claims on both body and spirit" (O'Malley 1990:150). As Beard pointed out, anyone inclined to be nervous would be further disturbed by contemplating a watch; even the pulse would go faster with the awareness of time. O'Malley underlines the point by referring to "the peculiar – and fascinating – relationship between the watch and its owner" (1990:151).

There is no doubt that the relationship between individuals and their watches was spiritual; there was indeed a danger that the increasing emphasis on time, efficiency, and punctuality would threaten the individual's own sense of being in the world. The soul was at stake, and the time piece was seen as an arbiter of one's spiritual destiny. In example after example, O'Malley (1990:145ff.) points out how the watch and the clock not only became a talisman of the individual's inner self but also threatened the soul. On the one hand, advertisements for clocks claimed that one could read anyone's character from the sort of watch he or she carried; those who were going places were punctual, their watches accurate, and their daily lives efficient; the contrary could be said of those who, by wasting time and being late, appeared to have wasted their lives and would never reach their destinations. Being late was itself a sign of spiritual weakness and a guarantor of eventual failure.

On the other hand, editorials and essays remarked on the tyranny of standard time and longed for the restoration of a world of natural harmonies, in which time was told by the sun rather than a mechanical timepiece. This ambivalence toward time is well illustrated in O'Malley's choice of two passages from *McGuffey's Readers*:

McGuffey's Readers from the antebellum decades had always stressed conserving time, but later revisions began emphasizing the urgent necessity of punctuality in meeting debts and following orders. "A railroad train was rushing along at almost lightning speed," one 1881 fifth-grade lesson began. "The conductor was late ... but he hoped to pass the curve safely ... in an instant there was a collision: a shriek, a shock, and fifty souls were in eternity, and all because an engineer was behind time." A commercial firm failed, the lesson continued, because its agent had been late in remitting payment, and an innocent man died because the watch of a messenger, who bore pardon, was five minutes late ... (O'Malley 1990:148)

It would be hard to miss the residues of a sense that spiritual fates hang in the balance of time, and that souls are at stake where debts have not been paid and penances completed. These are residues of purgatory, however, rather than clearly articulated pieces of a drama of redemption. The break-up of what might be called "the purgatorial complex" is fairly far advanced, since the pressures of time itself have taken on a life of their own. It is no wonder, then, that, as O'Malley goes on to point out, there were repercussions and resistance to the hegemony of secularized time:

But resistance to clock authority continued – a third-grade *McGuffey's Reader* of the same year, for example, persisted in locating time in nature and the sun. One often reprinted story, "The Clock and the Sundial," related the humiliation of a boasting steeple clock, who had laughed at the humble and primitive sundial in the church yard below. The clock praised itself for telling time on cloudy days, and at night, but fell into embarrassed silence when the sun "broke forth from behind a cloud, and showed, by the sundial, that the clock was half an hour behind the right time" ... While daily life and business seemed to demand ever more attention to clocks and watches, tradition – and nostalgia – insisted on the wisdom and the virtue of nature's example ... (O'Malley 1990:149)

The tyranny of secularized time was exercised by a wide range of institutions, from the nineteenth-century Sunday School to the modern factory, and the tyranny continues: from contemporary Christian schools to the bureaucracy that assigns a time-value to each minute action, including that of reading a letter. The nineteenth-century Sunday School provided a work discipline that insisted on regularity, punctuality, and prompt obedience (cf. Thrift 1990:115–116). At first, times for recreation became scarce, but as they returned, along with space provided for games and leisure activities, Thrift goes on to note,

the almost empty stage enabled the rise of such organized and commercialized recreations as railway outings ... new spectator variants of old sports (such as cricket or football), as well as activities like Bible Study groups. The new recreations were based on paying consumption rather than participating production and could be more easily confined to particular locations and precise time slots ... (1990:116–117)

Even to take "time out" in sports and to be able to enjoy the "spell of time" cast by religious or athletic events, one had to pay: to pay not only in coin but in the loss of one's own right to choose the time and place of one's actions. One could no longer be a producer of these events but merely a consumer. The degradation of the self that was imposed in the work-place continued on the playing field and in the religious institutions that provided the time-frameworks for a supervised and sponsored self-realization.

It would be a mistake to underestimate the psychological costs of living under the tyranny of time-constraints in a complex society. The more one's activities are governed by an organization, the less they are governed by one's needs or moods, by the times suitable for personal relationships with others, by the natural seasons, by anniversaries of public and private events, and by aspirations for a future that could ennoble the present and transform one's existence. J. David Lewis and Andrew J. Weigert reviewed the literature on the personal costs of living in organizations that demand that one synchronize one's activities to fit the actions of others in the same organization. They found that the more such demands for "synchronization" increase, the more individuals experience time as scarce. More importantly, the more that individuals find time to be scarce, the less control they feel that they have over their lives. After reviewing the literature on the personal costs of such loss of control, these authors conclude that time-constraints and the scarcity of time thus produce:

anxiety, depression, feelings of role incompetence, and similar psychological symptoms of temporal panic ... (Lewis and Weigert 1990:97)

Now, you will remember that the world of the thirteenth century as Le Goff described it, was also a time of increasing synchronization of individual activities. The urban world was becoming increasingly complex and diverse, with a division of labor and a commerce that required intensive coordination and control. Time became of the essence of such highly interdependent activities, and the churches were the primary agencies of social control.

It is under these conditions that individuals seek to save their souls by doing something in – and on – time. They turn to priests and shamans to give them a sense of the right time in which to act: the time for planting or sowing, for instance, or for work and play. As I have noted, the monastery bells became transformed into the bells of the city and the workplace, and they were slowly replaced in the next century by clocks that spelled out the hours of work and leisure, of civic meetings and social obligation. De Martino (1988:77) speaks of natives whose own sense of presence, of being-in-the-world, was threatened by the presence of missionaries in long robes and by the sound of church bells. It may well have been so for the citizen of the late medieval city. Certainly time becomes increasingly scarce, and the institutional control over time can displace the individual's sense of his or her own being. As temporal pressures on the individual intensify, the possibilities of soul-loss inevitably increase. It is not surprising that individuals have sought to cure themselves of "temporal panic" by taking symbolic control over time and by stipulating the times at which significant and life-saving activities will occur.

Certainly the notion of purgatory has given the individual a place in which to imagine the loss and recovery of the soul; preparing for purgatory has enabled the individual to engage in preparations to ensure that loss, temptation, and death will not deprive the soul of its real presence. Firth (1955:13) notes that the doctrine of purgatory and the literature of Dante have long enabled Westerners to speak about the displaced soul. It is only with the loss of a vivid cultural imagination regarding heaven and hell that it has become difficult to conceive of souls who have lost their place.

The feeling of running out of time does induce such anxiety that individuals will seek new ways to capture – and to live under the spell of – time. For some it is in socially prescribed activities of an agonistic nature, such as sports or the theater, where one can take some vicarious satisfaction in the sufferings of others while enjoying a temporal remission of one's own problems, pains, and duties. For others relief from temporal panic may take the form of a flight into the future, where one can face old pains cast in the light of new crises. The point is that there is a dynamic relationship between the tyranny of time, temporal panic, and demands for places where one can live again under the spell of time. Thus the weekend becomes a form of time out where one can engage in family dramas, celebrate anniversaries, contemplate the future, become immersed in theater or sports, or anticipate the comforts of timelessness and eternity.

What is striking is the dynamic interplay between the tyranny of time in work, civic organizations, supervised play and recreation, or other structured activities and the demand for time out, for a chance to enter into trance-like states of mind, and to feel again the spell of time. The more tyrannous the time-constraints of everyday life become, the more intense the demands for a transformation of one's experience of time. As the selections quoted above from *McGuffey's Readers* made clear, the pressure of clock-time led to nostalgia for time governed by nature itself.

Thus, O'Malley (1990) argues, modernity came to terms with time as an alien, superior, and prepossessing force, as individuals wore watches, submitted to the constraints of industrial schedules and demands for punctuality in the payment of all social obligations, and as entire communities and regions altered their schedules to fit the requirements of daylight-saving time. That was the meaning, as O'Malley (1990:295ff.) points out, of the Scopes trial; the victor in that trial was secular time over the sacred. These events, however, solidified the contingency of time as a social construction. Time thus construed replaces the notion of time as a prelude to an eternity to be entered into beyond the verge of paradise.

In his study of the meaning and measurement of time in American society, for instance, O'Malley (1990:1ff.) notes that time has been of the essence of both individual and social life. It was a loan from God, and to waste it was a sin, while to save it and use it for productive purposes was a sign of one's spiritual and civic virtue. Indeed there were Puritan residues in this secularized devotion to time, but, as we have seen, the sense of wasting time as sinful can be traced to the thirteenth and fourteenth centuries and to the notion of purgatory itself.

Not that time was an unambiguous symbol; on the contrary, the clock stood for both linear and cyclical time, and so it could be used for conservative arguments about preserving a society based on natural rhythms, just as it could be used to support arguments for innovation and progress. The dial was circular, but time was linear. Time, then, was double-coded. So-called digital clocks are more straightforward, presence yielding to absence with the disappearance of successive numbers one after another; there is no sign on the face of these time-pieces of any recurrence of the hours or days. On the face of it, time was secularized, but, as I have argued, the mechanical face of time concealed an underlying seriousness of time that derived from the long secularization of purgatory and from the formation of a social contract that gives the individual the *bona fides* of citizenship in return for chronic self-doubt about the state of the individual's soul.

Time was thus a double of the soul and a sign of its mortality:

scarce and a herald of the soul's own departure. Here is O'Malley's account of the folklore of antebellum America on the subject of time and the time piece:

a substantial body of American folklore linked clocks with mortality and the linear brevity of life. Their striking, coming unexpectedly, was said to denote death. A mysterious ticking, heard where no clock stood, was commonly referred to as the "wall clock" or "death watch." Recalling "the ticking of an old-fashioned clock, reckoning time towards eternity," this superstition appears as a portent of death in the folklore of at least thirteen states. A suddenly silent clock indicated death or at least very bad luck. "A clock stops when someone dies ... when there is a death in the family ... If a clock suddenly stops, it's a sure sign of death." The clock, in these examples, embodies God's time – a silent clock showed that death had brought someone's time to a halt.

Altering the time, or allowing a clock to run down, was therefore dangerous: "never turn a clock counterclockwise ... a run-down clock is a sure sign of death." Other proverbs held that broken clocks should be buried or stored well out of sight, and that one should "never keep a clock that does not run ... it is bad luck to keep a clock that is not running".... (O'Malley 1990:33–34)

Although O'Malley rightly attributes the sense of awe in the presence of a time-piece to religious residues of belief in a God who owns and controls time, it needs to be said also that there may have been some elements of magical thinking in this reverence for clocks. Certainly clocks were being seen as emblems and extensions, embodiments and tokens of the individual's own vitality and soul, so that when clocks stopped they brought life and the soul into eternity: timelessness being the secular token of eternity itself. So to keep clocks running, to mark time, to be timely, in rural and urban America could help to prevent the soul from running out of time. To stand the test of time, to do things in a timely fashion and in time: the shaman's function was now taken over by the timepiece and worn with pride as an emblem of the individual's own spiritual life. The life of the soul has simply become a matter of time. If sociological or anthropological analyses of religion are to be trusted, we would have to conclude that the notion of purgatory has lost its power over the religious and secular imagination. In his study of English Catholics, for instance, Hornsby-Smith (1991) documents the general decline of strong beliefs in heaven and hell. Many think of these as states of mind or as qualities of life in this world; others still hold on to some residues of these notions as applying to life after death, although few still subscribe to a belief in hell as a place of eternal torment. As for belief in purgatory, Hornsby-Smith reports very little indeed. Many English Catholics remember the doctrine as part of the arsenal of pre-Vatican pressures on the individual to conform; others still hold on to a belief in life after death which involves a place for recompense: as one respondent put it, "a place of punishment, perhaps more purgatory than hell" (Hornsby-Smith 1991:100). For some, then, purgatory fills the imaginary place left by the eclipse of hell; for others, purgatory becomes a metaphor for this life or simply a residual sense that life is serious business indeed.

Priests and shamans, by taking time into their hands, by announcing the right time to undertake significant departures like planting or taking a journey, can give the individual an illusory sense of control over time, whether or not with some immediate and short-lived practical benefit. That is why, for instance, the time pressures on individuals in the thirteenth century were conducive to later intensification of time by the church and by city governments, as monastery bells became adapted to the usages of work, the market-place and public affairs. As time became of the essence of social life, popular seriousness about time reflected the existential awareness that time was running out on the souls both of the living and of the dead. Purgatory, I have argued, was not merely a doctrine but, for complex social and psychological reasons, became a way of life.

In this epilogue, therefore, I will argue that there has been a merger of the Catholic and the Protestant in a sensitivity to the passage of time itself. That merger, however, may be easier to perceive in the United States than in England. Even there, however, the merger of consciousness is not at the level of doctrine or popular religious belief but in the sense of the seriousness of time. To tap into such a consciousness, furthermore, may well be beyond the capacities of the social sciences, even when conducted with the sensitivity brought to bear by Hornsby-Smith on his English respondents in probing interviews. Instead, I would turn to popular literature for a range of metaphor suggestive of the residues of purgatory in the secular imagination.

In his study of Catholic arts and letters in the United States, for instance, Giles (1992) has found ample evidence that this life has become a surrogate for purgatory. It is life, to borrow a title from F. Scott Fitzgerald, on *This Side of Paradise*:

Fitzgerald is locked in by what he called "the dead hand of the past:" not by any otherworldly conception of religion, but by its detached, gloating signifiers that transfer themselves into more amorphous forms of psychoanalytic resonance ... (Giles 1992:174)

These "detached ... signifiers" may show up in strange places, where they are not easily recognized as Catholic. In the work of Jack Kerouac, for instance, San Francisco becomes a this-worldly purgatory. There you will find souls struggling to rid themselves of the dead hand of the past: souls who are running out of time in the quest for the fulfillment of their own desires. Kerouac compares many of the "beat" characters in *The Subterraneans* to saints or to ascetics. Even in the midst of the pursuit of the object of his desire, the protagonist is weighed down by a sense of a crushing past: of long migrations, displaced peoples, and of hopeless labor in desolate environments: "ah – time." It is not only the Catholic novelist who makes time into a burden or a fetish. As I noted in the introduction, the preoccupation with time is widespread over a wide range of literature that attests to immigration, the loss of old comforts and constraints, and the opening to a future that is as uncertain or empty as it is promising.

For the Catholic immigrant, the future may seem to be Protestant, attractive for the promise of selfhood or success, but unattractive because it is still seen from the viewpoint of the perennial outsider as a set of games, heartless skills, and empty pretensions. The past, however, is attractive because it was a source of identity and certainty, but stifling because of violence and abuse, because of shallow and flat emotional expression between parent and child, encapsulated in an ethnic or class ghetto, with an impoverished imagination. Hence the need to make up for lost time. That is why Proust was the major influence on James T. Farrell (Giles 1992:165). Hence as a secularized form of purgatory, this life represents an indefinite and unbearable interim period, a purgatory between ethnic hell and heaven. Farrell's novels, writes Giles (1992:166):

> very often feature a long drawn-out death both as an ontological memento mori and as a sacrificial offering to the gods of the historical clock.

That long drawn-out death was the experience of life after leaving the confines of the family and of the ethnic community.

> The feeling of irretrievable loss, of impoverishment itself, which underlies the emotional world of these stories expresses his own exile as much as it does the actual worlds of the real-life counterparts for his characters ... Farrell's later stories involve a world where nothing can be taken for granted because no experience is securely possessed (O'Connell, "The Lost World of James T. Farrell's Short Stories," in Casey and Rhodes 1979:68)

That is what a secularized world is all about: getting on with social tasks as time unfolds, while doubting the fundamental basis of one's own perceptions. Long-term goals, values, and purposes are soon lost to view as procedures and planning, options and contingencies, occupy the forefront of a public attention focused on what Dickens might still call "the eternal foreground." Time-perspectives also are foreshortened to the present, in terms of which both the past and the future acquire their temporary meanings. The sense of time is further shrunk to the proportions of fiscal, electoral, or academic calendars, and public time becomes further out of joint with the time-sense of the individual.

The world in which time is reduced to a set of contingencies, however, does not decrease the pressure of time-constraints, others' expectations, and the increasingly tight regulation of personal and social life by public and private bureaucracies. These make the soul feel even more beleaguered and unsure of its own being. No wonder that self-awareness may become "unpleasant" and that individuals seek relief from such self-awareness through a variety of masochistic pursuits, including risky forms of exercise, recreation, and consumption (Baumeister 1989:207).

Like Dickens before him, as we shall see, Bryan Wilson turns away in some revulsion at the emptiness of the secular prospect. Wilson (1982:46ff.) argues that modern societies have success-fully contained or eliminated the major sources of irrational disturbance, e.g. charismatic leaders or millennial religious groups, but he fears that, in doing so, these societies have lost the sources of their own inspiration:

Even the facilities, arrangements, procedures, and disposition which constitute the humane and aesthetic culture of a people are increas-ingly readily sacrificed in the name of efficiency and progress, although this must lead to the ultimate impoverishment of all social life. Unless the basic virtues are serviced, unless men are given a sense of psychic reassurance that transcends the confines of the social system, we may see a time when, for one reason or another, the system itself fails to work, because men lack the basic dispositions to "give themselves" for the benefit of each other ... Contemporary society operates as if affective-neutrality were a sufficient value-orientation for things to work; it may yet discover that there are other necessities, the virtues nurtured essentially in local communities, in religious contexts, which in the long run will be shown to be as indispensable to the society of the future as they were to the communities of the past ... (Wilson 1982:52)

The sense of loss – and the sense of waste – are unmistakable in this sociological lament. In such a world, the virtues of the small community are left behind, and the promise of the future remains to be seen. No wonder that the Catholic sensitivity to death and to the long passage of the soul into beatitude or beyond merges with the Protestant intensification of time. Far more is at issue here than a Puritan strain in Catholic literature (Giles 1992:170). Here I am focusing on the pathos of time, on time not only as the burden of the soul but as a taint within the soul. That inner sadness over things coming to an end, over opportunities not taken, clearly characterizes what F. Scott Fitzgerald, in speaking of one of his characters, calls a "sense of waste" (Giles 1992:172). Not only does the past weigh heavily on the soul in this life and produce a "guilt-ridden, masochistic streak" in some of Fitzgerald's characters (Giles 1992:172). There is a sadness about time itself: "the necessarily melancholic operation of time sub specie aeternitatis" (Giles 1992:173). In this merging of Catholic and Protestant anxiety and regret over the passage of time there develops an image of America as a perpetual purgatory.[1]

This secularized form of purgatory shows up in the Catholic novelists' sense that the world they are entering is both attractive and yet unreal: that there is less to success than meets the eye. There is a real presence – the presence of something ultimately real – on the mind of Gatsby, but it is known only in its absence. The true sources of his wealth are not apparent, but their manifestations are suggestive. Another character, Nick Carraway, disclaims that he fits the illusions of those who love him (Giles 1992:184). No ideal can be realized in practice, and attempts to do so lead to disillusionment, whether in love or in business; on the other hand, it is necessary to see this life under the aspect of eternity, even though that brings a certain sadness about the passage of time itself. One is reminded of Dickens's bleak landscape, with the ruins of a convent on the great plains. It is the viewpoint, too, of Henry Adams, whose "native Protestant soul is overwhelmed and not a little perturbed by this landscape of failed empires and the melancholy grandeur of ruined civilizations" (Giles 1992:106). The point here is the merging of the Catholic and the Protestant subconscious in a tragic view of life as ending in the loss of individuality, in unfulfilled promise, in a tragic awareness of the limits of human freedom, and in the hopeless pursuit of transcendence over time.

---

[1] There is even a strong similarity between Richard Baxter and F. Scott Fitzgerald on the crucial issue of the literal or metaphoric use of language. Giles (1992:185) points out that Baxter was loath to use any metaphor for life everlasting without entering a disclaimer to the effect that our own ideas of something are a far cry from the real thing.

RELIGIOUS MASOCHISM AND THE SECULARIZATION OF PURGATORY

Lynn Chancer (1992:107) recently has argued that the Protestant ethic is particularly conducive to masochism because it subordinates the self to a distant, inaccessible, and demanding Other who requires sacrifice and expects love, and for whom no sacrifice is sufficient. Furthermore, Chancer (1992:35) cites the work of F. Scott Fitzgerald and Theodor Dreiser as evidence of masochistic tendencies in their main characters: sources that are certainly clearly Catholic in provenance. Chancer has clearly moved beyond the stereotypy of Henry James, who paints one of his female Catholic figures as "Impregnated with the idea of submission, which was due to anyone who took the tone of authority" (Giles 1992:92; quoting Henry James, *The Portrait of a Lady*, 1881). To be sure, Giles (1992:141) acknowledges the masochistic tendencies of Dorothy Day and *The Catholic Worker*, who "were in fact still attached to those idylls of worldly failure and deferred, otherworldly gratification that had characterized the American Catholic mentality during the nineteenth century" (Giles (1992:141). But later Catholic writers like James T. Farrell, Scott Fitzgerald, or dramatists like Martin Scorsese and Eugene O'Neill were more detached and reflective about the masochist aspects of their tradition.

A recent study of melancholy in American society places responsibility for the crushing of the soul squarely at the door of evangelical Protestant piety. Rubin (1994) makes it very clear that many converts, in various revivals and awakenings, suffered terrible anxiety about the state of their souls and about their chances of heaven. So great was their anxiety that many of them sought reassurance through drastic rituals of purging the self of every form of pollution in what Rubin (1994:86) calls "the continued obsessive-compulsive use of ritualized fasting, or ... evangelical anorexia nervosa." Jonathan Edwards had described the experience of conversion, leading to salvation, as including:

(1) the legal conviction of the sinner prostrated before the tribunal of justice of an angry and absolute sovereign; (2) the selfless agony of the believer who humbly awaits for divine mercy; and (3) the joyful, rapturous infusion of grace and forgiveness of sin that marks conversion ... (Rubin 1994:75)

Many never reached the third stage of spiritual confidence, and some took their lives in despair while others merely longed for death. As this exercise in purification developed in evangelical rhetoric, the soul was subject to fresh humiliations in order to make new and intense identifications with God and Christ. These new identifications may well have been less tormenting and sadistic than the old, but they nonetheless required something approaching the death of the soul in order to save it. For some, Rubin (1994:74) notes, the pressures on the soul were too great, and these either languished in despair or committed suicide.

It is crucial to understand the masochistic aspects of the Western religiosity in the light of this perennial quest for spiritual certainty. The more dramatic flagellations of the soul occur in a search for a purified conscience. The figures described by Rubin, poor souls desperately seeking the confidence of a soul that knows its divine acceptance, are clearly purgatorial: weighed down by the burdens of the past and struggling to rid themselves of that excruciating burden.

What are we to say, however, of the more pallid and chronic forms of spiritual uncertainty that fail to take such a histrionic form? It is just such a usage that Giles employs in contrasting early Puritanism with contemporary Catholicism:

The Puritan conflicts of the light and the dark, the elect and the damned ... in Melvile, Twain, and Faulkner bear little relevance to the Catholic worlds of Dreiser, Farrell, and Fitzgerald, where all morality is a more mixed, purgatorial affair ... Within this human world, neither ultimate regeneration nor any kind of "certain knowledge" of heavenly preferment appears possible. In these circumstances, the only viable option becomes to wait patiently for the advent of "divine" grace ... (Giles 1992:136)

What we have witnessed in this progression from Melville to more recent novelists is simply the secularizing of purgatory:

the loss of overt dramas of the soul set before a divine tribunal and the substitution of chronic spiritual irresolution which can neither forego the past, embrace the present, or let the future begin.

In using what has been "Catholic" symbolism to describe the alienating aspects of social life, it is therefore important not to fall back into a usage which implies some difference in this regard between Catholics and Protestants. The Catholic Church – even for Catholic writers – has been a symbol of the impersonal, inexorable and tragic forces that crush the individual, like the great plains themselves. Theodor Dreiser's heroine Jennie Gerhardt finds in the church's funeral rites a reminder that life begins and ends in loss and mystery: an insight that has clearly masochistic implications for Jennie herself (Giles 1992:150). Giles goes on, however, to talk about this as a "displacement of individuality" which could also be found in the works of Henry James and Henry Adams, noted above, for whom Catholicism was a metaphor or screen on which to project a sense of the tragic and unintended consequences of the human pursuit of individuality and freedom. What we are witnessing, as Giles has pointed out, is a flowing together of Protestant and Catholic imagery for the plight of the displaced soul. In the end, the focus is simply on the tyranny and power of social life over the soul, a tyranny expressed in the form of time:

Hawthorne's characters are impelled toward a recognition of the universal thralldom of the human condition. As Miriam notes in Chapter 13: "As these busts in the block of marble ... so does our individual fate exist in the limestone of Time"... (Giles 1992:88)

Giles (1992:108) notes the loss of innocence in the discovery that Protestant Americans could be as mechanical or corrupt or duplicitous as Catholics. Non-Catholics like Henry Adams saw in Catholicism a metaphor for "man as an object interpellated within a world he can no longer fully control" (Giles 1992:107).

Disturbed at a world where behavior seemed increasingly determined by factors external to individual choice, American writers sublimated this general sense of anxiety by resurrecting the oldest symbol of oppressive impersonality in the national consciousness, the Catholic Church ... (Giles 1992:99)

That is, Protestantism is inconceivable without Catholicism because Catholicism has been that which it abhorred and sought to leave behind – sensuality, impersonality, duplicity, tyranny – only to find that Protestant America had all of these qualities. The irony of this is that not only was America becoming "incorporated," but that Americans were imbued with the intensification of time that stems, as I have argued, from the secularization of purgatory from an other-worldly doctrine to a this-worldly doctrine.

Bibliography

Altman, Leon. 1957. "The Waiting Syndrome," *The Psychoanalytic Quarterly*, 20/4:508–518.

Arieli, Yehoshua. 1964 *Individualism and Nationalism in American Ideology*. Cambridge, Mass.: Harvard University Press.

Arlow, Jacob A. 1969. "Unconscious Fantasy and Disturbances of Conscious Experience," *The Psychoanalytic Quarterly*, 38/1:1–27.

    1984. "Disturbances of the Sense of Time, with Special Reference to the Sense of Timelessness," *The Psychoanalytic Quarterly*, 53/1:13–37.

    1986. "Psychoanalysis and Time," *Journal of the American Psychoanalytic Association*, 34/3: 507–528.

Asch, Stuart S. 1988. "The Analytic Concepts of Masochism: A Reevaluation," in Robert A. Glick and Donald I. Meyers, *Masochism: Current Psychoanalytic Perspectives*, pp. 93–115. Hillsdale, N.J., London: The Analytic Press.

Auerbach, Carl. 1991. "Development of the True Self: A Semiotic Analysis," *Psychoanalysis and Contemporary Thought*, 14/1:109–141.

Axtell, James, ed. 1968. *Some Thoughts Concerning Education*, by John Locke. Cambridge University Press.

Bainton, Roland. 1985. *The Reformation of the Sixteenth Century*. Enlarged edition, with an introduction and supplementary bibliography by Jaroslav Pelikan. Boston: Beacon Press.

Banfield, Edward C. 1967. *The Moral Basis of a Backward Society*. With the assistance of Laura Fasano Banfield. New York: The Free Press.

Baumeister, Roy F. 1959. *Masochism*. Hillsdale, N.J.: L. Erlbaum Associates.

Baxter, Richard. 1854. *A Christian Directory*, in *The Practical Works of Richard Baxter*. London

    1868. *What We Must Do To Be Saved*. Edited by Rev. Alexander B. Grosart, Liverpool. Printed for private circulation.

    1909. *The Saints' Everlasting Rest* or A Treatise of the Blessed State of the Saints in Their Enjoyment of God's Glory. A new edition, edited by William Young, B.A. Philadelphia: J. B. Lippincott Company, and London: Grant Richards.

Bercovitch, Sacvan. 1975. *The Puritan Origins of the American Self.* New Haven and London: Yale University Press.

1978. *The American Jeremiad.* Madison, Wis.: University of Wisconsin Press.

Bergler, Edmund. 1949. *The Basic Neurosis: Oral Regression and Psychic Masochism.* New York: Grune and Stratton.

Bergmann, Werner. 1992. "The Problem of Time in Sociology: An Overview of the Literature on the State of Theory and Research on the 'Sociology of Time.' 1900–82," *Time & Society,* 1/1:81–134.

Blanchard, William H. 1984. *Revolutionary Morality: A Psychosexual Analysis of Twelve Revolutionists.* Santa Barbara, California and Oxford, England: ABC-Clio Information Services.

Blos, Peter Jr. 1991. "Sadomasochism and the Defense Against Recall of Painful Affect," *Journal of the American Psychoanalytic Association,* 39/2:417–430

Bode, Carl, ed. 1981. *The Portable Emerson.* In collaboration with Malcolm Cowley. Harmondsworth: Penguin Books.

Boorstin, Daniel J. 1981. *The Lost World of Thomas Jefferson.* With a new preface. University of Chicago Press.

Boyer, Paul. 1992. *When Time Shall Be No More: Prophecy Belief in American Culture.* Cambridge, Mass. and London: The Belknap Press of Harvard University Press.

Bradley, K. R. 1987. *Slaves and Masters in the Roman Empire: A Study in Social Control.* New York and Oxford: Oxford University Press.

Bradshaw, John. 1990. *Homecoming: Reclaiming and Championing Your Inner Child.* New York et al: Bantam Books.

Brown, Peter. 1988. *The Body and Society: Men, Women, and Sexual Renunciation in Early Christianity.* New York: Columbia University Press.

Bunyan, John [1884]; 1939. *Pilgrim's Progress.* Retold and shortened for modern readers, by Mary Godolphin [1884]. Philadelphia: J. B. Lippincott Company.

Burkert, Walter. 1983. *Homo Necans: The Anthropology of Ancient Greek Sacrificial Ritual and Myth.* Peter Bing, translator. Berkeley: University of California Press.

Campbell, Alexander. 1832; 1969. *Delusions: An Analysis of the Book of Mormon; with an examination of its internal and external evidences, and a refutation of its pretenses to divine authority, with prefatory remarks by Joshua V. Himes.* Boston: Benjamin H. Greene; reprinted in *Inside Mormonism,* compiled by George L. Faull. Joplin, Missouri: College Press.

1875. *The Battle of the Giants: A Debate on the Roman Catholic Religion, held in Cincinnati, between the Late Alexander Campbell and the Rt. Rev. John B. Purcell, together with The Vatican Decrees in their bearing on Civil Allegiance, by the Right Hon. W. E. Gladstone, M.P., with the replies of Dr. Newman, Archbishop Manning, the Right Rev. Monsignor Capel, Lord Acton, and Lord Camoys, and a full abstract of Gladstone's rejoinder.* Cincinnati: C. F. Vent, Chicago: J. S. Goodman, 1875.

Casey, Daniel J. and Rhodes, Robert E., eds. 1979. *Irish-American Fiction: Essays in Criticism.* New York: AMS.

Catherine of Genoa. 1847. *Catherine of Genoa, Purgation and Purgatory.* New York: Paulist Press.

Chancer, Lynn. 1992. *Sadomasochism in Everyday Life: The Dynamics of Power and Powerlessness.* New Brunswick, N.J.: Rutgers University Press.

Channing, William. 1847. *The Works of William E. Channing, D.D.* Seventh complete edition, with an introduction. Vols. II, III, VI. Boston: James Munroe and Company.

Charlesworth, James H. 1985. *The Old Testament Pseudepigrapha and the New Testament.* Society for New Testament Studies, Monograph Series 54. Cambridge University Press.

Chasseguet-Smirgel, Janine. 1985. *Creativity and Persuasion:* Foreword by Otto Kernberg. New York and London: Norton and Co.

1991. "Sadomasochism in the Perversions: Some Thoughts on the Destruction of Reality," *Journal of the American Psychoanalytic Association,* 39/2:399–416.

Cohn, Franz S. 1957. "Time and the Ego," *The Psychoanalytic Quarterly,* 26/2:168–189.

Cohn, Norman. 1970. *The Pursuit of the Millennium.* Revised and expanded edition. New York: Oxford University Press.

Cook, Harold J. 1986. *The Decline of the Old Medical Regime in Stuart England.* Ithaca: Cornell University Press.

Cooper, Arnold M. 1988. "The Narcissistic-Masochistic Character", in Robert A. Glick and Donald I. Meyers, *Masochism: Current Psychoanalytic Perspectives,* pp. 117–138. Hillsdale, N.J., London: The Analytic Press.

Creelan, Paul and Granfield, Robert. 1986. "The Polish Peasant and the Pilgrim's Progress," in *Journal for the Scientific Study of Religion,* 25/2:162–179.

Dante Alighieri. 1955. *The Comedy of Dante Alighieri, The Florentine, Cantica II (Il Purgatorio).* Translated by Dorothy Sayers, Baltimore: Penguin Books.

1961. *The Purgatorio: Dante's Timeless Drama of an Ascent through Purgatory. A New Translation by John Ciardi.* New York: New American Library, Mentor Books.

Deikman, Arthur J. 1990. *The Wrong Way Home: Uncovering the Patterns of Cult Behavior in American Society*. Boston: Beacon Press.

Dickens, Charles. 1985. *American Notes for General Circulation*. Edited and with an introduction by John S. Whitley and Arnold Goldman. Harmondsworth: Penguin Books.

Dillenberger, John and Welch, Claude. 1954. *Protestant Christianity Interpreted Through Its Development*. New York: Charles Scribner's Sons.

Durkheim, Emile. 1915; 1965. *The Elementary Forms of the Religious Life*. New York: The Free Press.

Elias, Norbert. 1992. *Time: An Essay*. Oxford and Cambridge: Basil Blackwell, Publishers.

Eliot, T. S. 1929. *Dante*. London: Faber and Faber.

Faull, George L. 1969. *Inside Mormonism*. Joplin, Missouri: College Press.

Fenn, Richard. 1991. *The Secularization of Sin*. Louisville, Ky.: Westminster Press.

1992. *The Death of Herod*. Cambridge University Press.

Finke, Roger and Stark, Rodney. 1992. *The Churching of America 1776–1990: Winners and Losers in Our Religious Society*. New Brunswick, N.J.: Rutgers University Press.

Finley, M. I. 1983. *Ancient Slavery and Modern Ideology*. New York: Penguin Books.

Firth, Raymond. 1955. *The Fate of the Soul: An Interpretation of Some Primitive Concepts*. The Frazer Lecture for 1955. Cambridge University Press.

Forman, Frieda Johles, ed. 1989. *Taking Our Time: Feminist Perspectives on Temporality*. Oxford and New York: Pergamon Press.

Forrester, John. 1992. "'In the Beginning was Repetition': On Inversions and Reversals in Psychoanalytic Time," *Time and Society*, 1/2:287–300.

Freud, Sigmund, 1961; 1989. *Beyond the Pleasure Principle*. The Standard Edition, edited by James Strachey, with a biographical introduction by Peter Gay. New York, London: W. W. Norton & Company.

Garrett, Clarke. 1985. "Popular Religion in the American and French Revolutions,' in *Religion, Rebellion, Revolution: An Interdisciplinary and Cross-Cultural Collection of Essays*. Edited by Bruce Lincoln. New York: St. Martin's Press.

Gaustad, Edwin Scott. 1973. *Dissent in American Religion*. Chicago History of American Religion, edited by Martin Marty. University of Chicago Press.

Giddens, Anthony. 1990. *The Consequences of Modernity*. Stanford, California: Stanford University Press.

Giles, Paul. 1992. *American Catholic Arts and Fictions: Culture, Ideology, Aesthetics*. Cambridge University Press.

Godolphin, Mary, ed. [1884]; 1939. *Pilgrim's Progress*, by John Bunyan [1884]. Philadelphia: J. B. Lippincott.

Greeley, Andrew. 1977. *The American Catholic: A Social Portrait*. New York: Basic Books.

——— 1990. *The Catholic Myth: The Behavior and Beliefs of American Catholics*. New York: Scribner.

Greif, Ann C. 1989. "Failed Efforts at Identification: The Masochistic Patient's Response to the Analyst's Pregnancy," in *Masochism: The Treatment of Self-Inflicted Suffering*, edited by Jill D. Montgomery and Ann C. Greif, pp. 95–104. Madison, Conn.: International Universities Press.

Groeschel, Benedict. 1977. "Introduction" to *Catherine of Genoa, Purgation and Purgatory*. New York: Paulist Press.

Grosart, Alexander B. 1868. *The Annotated List of Baxter's Writings*. Printed for Private Circulation. Liverpool.

Hart, Laurie. 1992. *Time, Religion, and Social Experience in Greece*. Lanham, Md.: Rowman and Littlefield, Publishers.

Hartocollis, Peter. 1975. "Time as a Dimension of Affects," *Journal of the American Psychoanalytic Association*, 20/1:92–108.

Hofstadter, Richard. 1955. *The Age of Reform*, New York: Vintage Books.

Hopkins, Keith. 1983. *Death and Renewal: Sociological Studies in Roman History*, vol. II. Cambridge University Press.

Hornsby-Smith, Michael. 1991. *Roman Catholic Beliefs in England: Customary Catholicism and Transformations of Religious Authority*. Cambridge University Press.

Hunter, James Davison. 1991. *Culture Wars: The Struggle to Define America*. New York: Basic Books.

Johnson, Edgar. 1986. *Charles Dickens: His Tragedy and Triumph*. Revised and abridged. Harmondsworth: Penguin Books.

Johnson, Frank. 1985. "The Western Concept of Self," in *Culture and Self*, edited by Anthony J. Marsella, George Devos, and Francis L. K. Hsu. New York and London: Tavistock.

Jones, Cecilia. 1989. "Problems of Separation and Clinging in Masochism," in *Masochism: The Treatment of Self-Inflicted Suffering*, edited by Jill D. Montgomery and Ann C. Greif, pp. 19–28. Madison, Conn.: International Universities Press.

Kafka, Ernest. 1979. "On Examination Dreams," *The Psychoanalytic Quarterly*, 48/3:426–447

Kernberg, Otto F. 1991. "Sadomasochism, Sexual Excitement, and Perversion," *Journal of the American Psychoanalytic Association*, 39/2:333–362.

Larkin, Emmet. 1972. "The Devotional Revolution in Ireland, 1850–1875, *American Historical Review*. 77:625–652.

Lasch, Christopher. 1978. *The Culture of Narcissism*. New York: Norton.

Le Goff, Jacques. 1984. *The Birth of Purgatory*. Translated by Arthur Goldhammer. The University of Chicago Press.

1988. *The Medieval Imagination*. Translated by Arthur Goldhammer. The University of Chicago Press.

Levy-Bruhl, Lucien. 1966. *The "Soul" of the Primitive*. Translated by Lilian A. Clarke. New York/Washington: Frederick A. Praeger.

Lewis, J. David and Weigert, Andrew J. 1990. "The Structures and Meanings of Social-Time," *The Sociology of Time*, edited by John Hassard. London: Macmillan Press.

Locke, John. 1823; 1963. *The Works of John Locke, in Ten Volumes*. London; reprinted Aalen: Scientia Verlag.

Lutz, Tom. 1991. *American Nervousness: 1903: An Anecdotal History*. Ithaca and London: Cornell University Press.

McDannell, Colleen and Lang, Bernhard. 1988. *Heaven: A History*. New Haven and London: Yale University Press.

McEntire, Sandra J. 1990. *The Doctrine of Compunction in Medieval England: Holy Tears*. Studies in Medieval Literature, vol. VIII. Lewiston, Queenston, Lampeter; The Edwin Mellen Press.

McGrath, Joseph E. and Kelly, Janice R. 1992. "Temporal Context and Temporal Patterning: Toward a Time-Centered Perspective for Social Psychology," *Time & Society*, 1/3:399–420.

MacMullen, Ramsey. 1974. *Roman Social Relations 50 B.C. to A.D. 284*. New Haven and London: Yale University Press.

Maleson, Franklin G. 1984. "The Multiple Meanings of Masochism in Psychoanalytic Discourse," *Journal of the American Psychoanalytic Association*, 32:325–366

Martin, David. 1978a. *The Dilemmas of Contemporary Religion*. New York: St. Martin's Press.

1978b. *A General Theory of Secularization*, Oxford: Basil Blackwell.

1980. *The Breaking of the Image: A Sociology of Christian Theory and Practice*. Oxford: Basil Blackwell.

1990. *Tongues of Fire: The Explosion of Protestantism in Latin America*. Oxford [U.K.] and Cambridge, Mass.: Basil Blackwell.

De Martino, Ernesto. 1988. *Primitive Magic: The Psychic Powers of Shamans and Sorcerers*. Dorset: Prism Press.

Meeks, Wayne. 1983. *The First Urban Christians*. New Haven: Yale University Press.

Mehta, Uday Singh. 1992. *The Anxiety of Freedom: Imagination and Individuality in Locke's Political Thought*. Ithaca and London: Cornell University Press.

Melghes, Frederick Towne. 1982. *Time and the Inner Future: A Temporal Approach to Psychiatric Disorders*. New York: John Wiley and Sons.

Montgomery, Jill D. 1989. "The Hero as Victim: The Development of a Masochistic Life," in *Masochism: The Treatment of Self-Inflicted Suffering*, edited by Jill D. Montgomery and Ann C. Greif, pp. 75–93. Madison, Conn.: International Universities Press.

Morgan, Elder John. 1904. *The Plan of Salvation*.

Morse, Edward Lind. 1914. *Samuel F. B. Morse, His Letters and Journals*, edited and supplemented by his son, Edward Lind Morse, vol. II. Boston and New York: Houghton Mifflin Co.

Morse, Samuel F. B. 1835; 1969. *Imminent Dangers to the Free Institutions of the United States through Foreign Immigration, and the Present State of the Immigration Laws. A Series of Numbers originally published in the New-York Journal of Commerce. By An American*; reprinted in *Imminent Dangers to the Free Institutions of the United States through Foreign Immigration*. 2 vols. New York: Arno Press and the New York Times.

Neustadter, Roger. 1992. "Beat the Clock: The Mid-20th-Century Protest against the Reification of Time," *Time & Society*, 1/3:379–398.

Norman, E. R. 1968. *The Conscience of the State in North America*. Cambridge University Press.

Novick, Jack and Novick, Kerry Kelly. 1991. "Some Comments on Masochism and the Delusion of Omnipotence from a Developmental Perspective," *Journal of the American Psychoanalytic Association*, 39/2:307–331.

Nyland, Chris. 1990. "Capitalism and the History of Work-Time Thought," in *The Sociology of Time*, London: Macmillan, Ltd.

O'Connell, Barry. 1979. "The Lost World of James T. Farrell's Short Stories," in *Irish-American Fiction. Essays in Criticism*, edited by Daniel J. Casey and Robert E. Rhodes, pp. 53–72. New York: AMS.

O'Keefe, Daniel. 1983. *Stolen Lightning: The Social Theory of Magic*. New York: Vintage Books.

O'Malley, Michael. 1990. *Keeping Watch: A History of American Time*. New York, London, etc.: Penguin/Viking.

——— 1992. "Time, Work, and Task Orientation: A Critique of American Historiography," *Time & Society*, 1/3:341–358.

Orgel, Shelley. 1965. "On Time and Timelessness," *Journal of the American Psychoanalytic Association*, 13/1:102–121.

Ornstein, Anna. 1991. "The Dread to Repeat: Comments on the Working-through Process in Psychoanalysis," *Journal of the American Psychoanalytic Association*, 39/2:377–398.

Paterson, Orlando. 1982. *Slavery and Social Death: A Comparative Study*. Cambridge, Mass. and London: Harvard University Press.

Rahner, Karl. 1978. *Foundations of Christian Faith: An Introduction to the Idea of Christianity*. Translated by William V. Dych. New York: The Seabury Press.

Rank, Otto. *The Psychology of the Soul*. Philadelphia: University of Pennsylvania Press.

1971. *The Double: A Psychoanalytic Study*. Chapel Hill, N.C.: University of North Carolina Press.

Reik, Theodor. 1941. *Masochism and Modern Man*. Translated by Margaret H. Beigel and Gertrud M. Kurth. New York: Farrar Straus and Co.

1970. *Myth and Guilt: The Crime and Punishment of Mankind*. New York: Grosset and Dunlap, Universal Library Edition.

Robinson, David. 1981. "The Legacy of Channing: Culture as a Religious Category in New England Thought," *Harvard Theological Review*, 74/2:221–239.

Rose, Susan. 1988. *Keeping Them Out of the Hands of Satan: Evangelical Schooling in America*. London: Routledge.

Rosenfeld, Herbert A. 1988. "On Masochism: A Theoretical and Clinical Approach," in Robert A. Glick and Donald I. Meyers, *Masochism: Current Psychoanalytic Perspectives*, pp. 151–174. Hillsdale, N.J., London: The Analytic Press.

Rothstein, Arnold. 1991. "Sadomasochism in the Neuroses Conceived of as a Pathological Compromise Formation," *Journal of the American Psychoanalytic Association*, 39/2:363–376.

Rubin, Julius. 1994. *Religious Melancholy and Protestant Experience in America*. New York: Oxford University Press.

Sayers, Dorothy L., trans. 1955. *The Comedy of Dante Alighieri, The Florentine, Cantica II (Il Purgatorio)*. Baltimore: Penguin Books.

Schilder, Paul. 1936. "Psychopathology of Time," *The Journal of Nervous and Mental Disease*, 83/5:530–546.

Schor, Judith. 1991. *the Overworked American: The Unexpected Decline of Leisure*. Basic Books.

Shengold, Leonard. 1989. *Soul Murder: The Effects of Childhood Abuse and Deprivation*, New Haven and London: Yale University Press.

Shepherd, Massey. 1950. *The Oxford American Prayer Book Commentary*, New York: Oxford University Press.

Sommerville, C. John. 1992. *The Secularization of Early Modern England: From Religious Culture to Religious Faith*. New York, Oxford: Oxford University Press.

Stekel, Wilhelm. 1939. *Sadism and Masochism: The Psychology of Hatred and Cruelty*. Authorized English Version by Louise Brink, volumes I and II. New York: Liveright Publishing Company.

Tarcov, Nathan. 1989. *Locke's Education for Liberty*. Chicago and London: University of Chicago Press.

Taylor, Charles. 1989. *Sources of the Self: The Making of the Modern Identity*. Cambridge, Mass.: Harvard University Press.

Thrift, Nigel. 1990. "The Making of a Capitalist Time Consciousness," in *The Sociology of Time*, edited by John Hassard. London: Macmillan, Ltd.

Trilling, L. 1963. *Beyond Culture*. New York: Viking Press.

Vernant, Jean-Pierre. 1991. *Mortals and Immortals: Collected Essays*. Edited by Froma I. Zeitlin. Princeton University Press.

Wagner, Roy. 1981. *The Invention of Culture*. Revised and expanded edition. Chicago and London: The University of Chicago Press.

Wallace, Anthony F. C. 1987. *St. Clair: A Nineteenth-Century Coaltown's Experience with a Disaster-Prone Industry*. New York: Knopf.

Weber, Max. 1964. *The Sociology of Religion*. Fourth, revised edition. Boston: Beacon Press.

Whitley, John S. and Goldman, Arnold. 1985. "Introduction," in *American Notes*, by Charles Dickens [1842]. Harmondsworth: Penguin Books.

Wilson, Bryan. 1982. Religion in Sociological Perspective. Oxford and New York: Oxford University Press.

Wilson, John F. and Drakeman, Donald L., eds. *Church and State in American History*. Second edition. Boston: Beacon Press.

Winnicott, David W. 1988. *Human Nature*. New York: Schocken Books.

Wolters, Clifton, ed. 1980. *The Cloud of Unknowing and Other Works*, translated and edited by Clifton Wolters. Harmondsworth: Penguin Books.

Wuthnow, Robert. 1992. *Rediscovering the Sacred: Perspectives on Religion in Contemporary Society*. Grand Rapids, Mich.: Eerdmans.

Yolton, John W. 1993. *A Locke Dictionary*. The Blackwell Philosopher Dictionaries. Oxford: Blackwell Publishers.

Young, William, ed. 1909. *The Saints' Everlasting Rest*, by Richard Baxter. Philadelphia: J. B. Lippincott Company, and London: Grant Richards.

Index